# XANDY'S CHOICE

## A "ONE-OF-ITS-KIND" RELATIONSHIP WORKBOOK

*Belinda Johnson-Mitchell*

ISBN: 978-0-692-80552-7

# Dedication

To:

The late, Edna B. Williams, my grandmother & guardian angel

And

Bettye J. Guy, my mother
I dedicate this, my FIRST book to the two of you!

My grandmother was my first and most profound example of sacrificial and unconditional love. It is an epic love that has managed to transcend death and the boundaries of heaven. She is at the foundation of who I am today.

My mother, it is you and your never-ending belief in me and my abilities, that have pushed me to this walk of faith. In your eyes and heart, "*Lin can do ANYTHING*" (you re-confirmed that for me while sitting around our cousin's table on July 13, 2016).

In the past, when I have been convinced that some "*fly-by-night, get-rich-quick*" schemes were going to be the BIG THING for me, you were right there with an open mind, heart, and POCKETBOOK! Most importantly, when I failed repeatedly, your belief in me has never wavered to this day!

Thank you, and I LOVE YOU!!

# Acknowledgements

My sincerest appreciation goes to Authors, Stacy Juba and Dr. Lana Mowdy for your editing, proofing, patience, and insightful guidance. You allowed my vision and story to remain MINE! Thank you! Debbie Geiger and Yolanda Wooten, my die-hard volunteer "*guinea pigs*"; your very generous time, support, feedback and most of all <u>consistent</u> encouragement will never be forgotten.

And last but certainly not least, Glenn Bontrager, Sarco Press... I could not and would not have done it without YOU! You have gone above and beyond to help me. Your kindness, patience and support has truly made THE DIFFERENCE!

Thank you!!!

# Contents

# ◆ INTRODUCTION ◆

This book is the product of many years of my turning to what I referred to as my "*it*," referring to "*it*" as "*just something*" that I'm writing with no real purpose in my mind, other than I enjoyed doing it (just like a hobby).

As the characters continued to develop and the number of chapters grew, I started to realize that "*just maybe – my imagination is being guided, orchestrated, and structured for a purpose beyond my scope of expectation or understanding!*"

When I was able to redirect my thinking and focus, the outcome and story developments made me ask myself... "**Where did THAT come from?**"

Although, my professional experience in the helping field spans 30 years, it has been in the past 10 years that I have been involved professionally in relationship assessments, education, and partnerships (I don't like the word counseling). My focus did not become "*purpose-driven*" until the year 2006. My place of employment chose me to travel to Atlanta, GA to participate in the National Smart Marriages Conference to receive a relationship education certification. It was during this trip and at the threshold of this first certification that I questioned and attacked myself and my qualifications, capabilities, and intentions.

Apparently, I have earned several Ph.Ds. from the **University of Hard Knocks** in the field of relationships. I have the emotional scars, insecurities, as well as tangible and intangible baggage (as lifetime souvenirs). While standing at the threshold of my first certification, I had an emotional meltdown and had basically decided that I was not qualified or suitable to function as a helping professional in this area. I give thanks to God for giving me the foresight to call my pastor and his wife who quickly corrected me by saying to me; "*Who, better to help those that are failing, struggling, and in relationship despair than someone who knows first-hand how they got there, how it actually feels to be there and most importantly - how to get out?*" In essence, I was told and in some biblical instances, reminded that God uses broken people for his service and qualifies those he calls for his glory! My failures and setbacks do not define me. God uses them to help others!

WOW!!! I received THAT!!!

The rest is history! Here I am, 2 ½ degrees and 8 certifications later - walking in faith in my purpose. Since that time, I have devoted my life to helping others; in some shape, form, or fashion to have happy, healthy, and successful relationships. (Conclusively, I am a die-hard romantic person that truly believes in LOVE and that some degree of ***fairy-tale romance can exist IF two healthy people are willing to WORK AT IT***).

The fact that I have 3 degrees and working on a 4th (a REAL Ph.D. this time ☺) has nothing to do with this path that I'm on which I refer to as my "*trial-by-fire divine assignment.*"

I believe that at the very core of WHO we are and HOW we are… are our relationships. From our family of origin to our intimate relationships, the condition and dynamics of our relationship past and present can and will shape our personal world. When it comes to striving for a lifelong healthy relationship, it is necessary to take a long and HONEST look at yourself. This must also include an analytical inventory of the history of your relationships. Are there certain qualities, both good and bad, that you repeatedly fall for, therefore establishing a pattern? If so, in the words of Dr. Phil McGraw, "*How's that been working for you?*"

It is very helpful to take the time to get to know "**YOU FIRST**" and to learn what's going on inside of you that is motivating the choices you are and have been making when it comes to relationships. Regardless of what you may feel or think, it is never too late for self-exploration. If you are currently married or in a committed relationship, there is ALWAYS room for improvement. As the quote goes; "*Let the change begin with ME*" Taking an introspective look at YOU is a magnificent place to start.

"**Xandy's Choice**" is a one-of-its-kind "self-help" WORKbook, being that it hinges on the reader becoming actively involved in the personal life of a fictional character that's drowning in a sea of relationships.

Some of us, if not most, have been at a relationship crossroads where we have felt that we, for various reasons either; we're ready to settle down, should settle down, or needed to settle down, but was clueless when it came to the question "**Who? Or Which one?**"

Yeah, yeah, yeah, I know that all of us have a list of traits and things that anyone who is serious about being with us **MUST** have. However, truth be told, at the end of the day, when we take an HONEST look at our choices, are there things on that proverbial list that he/she <u>does not have</u>?

If the answer is "**Yes**," please allow me to ask the following rhetorical questions pertaining to **WHY**?

Did you choose to "just settle" instead of wait?

Did you choose to compromise your principles?

Did you choose to lower your professed standards?

Did you choose to ignore the "red flags?"

Did you choose to ignore the wisdom and warnings of others?

If you answered "yes" to either of these questions, WHY?


**NOTE:** Don't expect scientific/therapeutic explanations for your present or past choices in this book. It is designed to be a tool to cause you to think and possibly look "within."


NOW …Enter the world of Alexandria Morgan, "Xandy," and see where she takes you mentally and emotionally when it comes to relationship choices.

Hopefully, at the end of this journey, WORKbook and discussions (I hope you have discussions), you will learn a little something about YOU, and...

HOW & WHY **you** make YOUR relationship choices!

# ◆ MEET XANDY ◆

Hello, my name is Alexandria Rae Morgan. I have had many relationships in the past, both good and bad. There were some that I feel as though I should have given a better chance of working, and then there are those I never should have gotten into...PERIOD. I feel as though I have come to the place in my life, where I am really ready for a serious committal relationship that can lead to a healthy and successful marriage. Now that I am here, I feel somewhat confused. If the truth be told, I'm not really sure what I want. The choices in men that I have made in the past show me that I really don't have a concrete set of eligibility criteria. I tend to decide by using my eyes, head, heart, and hormones at different times. "And those eye and hormone choices were some doozies." Then there were those that something inside of me was repeatedly saying... "This is a good one...give him a chance" BUT...I didn't listen!

Ever since I was about twelve years old, it's as if I have had two little women standing on my shoulders. There's a little woman in a red suit and red pumps sporting an amazing hairdo on my left shoulder and a little woman in a white robe with a bedazzled halo and Jesus sandals standing on my right shoulder. Needless to say, my track record indicates that I tend to listen more to Miss Red pumps than I do to Miss Jesus Sandals. There has been once or twice that Miss Jesus Sandals and I were in sync about someone. The outcome was still the same...they didn't work.

I love the feeling of being in a good relationship, as long as I am able to still be an individual. Men, who desire to become your Siamese twin, are the most challenging to me. And let's not leave out those who insist on acting as if they have just been hired as the CEO of your life. The ones where it would appear to a stranger that you were nothing, had nothing, and could do nothing, until they came along and took charge! No SIR! I have far too much going for me (because of me) to become someone's doormat or extension. I want a man who complements me and accepts me for who I am —without trying to change me in any way. I guess that means he has got to have a great sense of self-confidence.

My girlfriends say I don't give guys a fair chance before deciding to delete them from my iPhone and my life. Maybe they are right. Maybe I do have some kind of mental block, inhibiting me from making sound relationship choices. I know what my heart wants, but it seems I allow my head to get in the way. I have had my share (and someone else's share) of men to choose from. I have an active social and dating life. It's just that my dating life seems always to be short-lived. My mother tells me I throw away men that most women would give their right arm and a Chanel bag to have. I simply dismiss my mom's ranting, because I think she's overly anxious for me to have a husband, so she can reap some grandchildren out of the deal. She tells me that one of her greatest fears is that she will be too old to enjoy her grandchild the way a grandmother should-at the rate I'm going. I'll admit; there have been a couple of times that I have allowed myself to daydream about being a mother, but I dismiss it quickly. My average "serious" relationship seems to last about nine months to a year, with one exception...

And then there was...

# CHAPTER 1
## ◆ RALPH ◆

**Age**: Thirty-eight

**Occupation**: Financial consultant /Stock Broker

**Marital status**: Single (married during our relationship)

**Children**: none

**Family Background**: Youngest of three children. He has two sisters. He was raised by both parents. Ralph is from an affluent family and has lived a life of privilege that's obvious at first sight. His parents are still living and are very involved in his life.

**The Details**:

Ralph was different from all the others. I chose Ralph, using all five of my senses, with my hormones being the common denominator. We met in my freshman year in college. He had finished college and had been working for a brokerage firm for about two years. If you looked up the definition of handsome in the dictionary ...You would find Ralph's picture. He had a smile that could melt steel, a mind by Microsoft, and a body by Bally. As you can see, Ralph was the total masterpiece with one exception-his attitude.

Ralph was one of the sweetest men I've ever known....as long as everything was exactly to his liking. It was like/lust-at-first sight. We were drawn together like a magnet and metal. He was my older man, and I was his "schoolgirl crush" (I should have paid more attention to being referred to as a 'crush'). We were inseparable. He had a really nice apartment, and that's where I spent most of my time. I had little to no time for the guys or girls on campus. I was a part of the socialite club. Ralph was very generous with me. He lavished me with beautiful outfits, trips, and the finer things in life (that were affordable to someone his age and income. He never wanted to participate or attend any of my collegiate activities, such as parties, concerts, and sorority and/or fraternity events. His response to me would always be… "Honey, major leaguers don't run with the minors!" Occasionally, we would attend a university football or basketball game, and in hindsight, I believe that was solely due to his colleagues being big sports fanatics.

We dated for two and a half years. We met and spent time with each other's families (more with his than mine). We did everything together, except attend church. I was raised in a Christian home, where church attendance was not optional. I may have veered off course from my Christian upbringing in a lot of ways, but completely staying away from church was out of the question. While I was with Ralph, I usually averaged one to two Sundays a month (while lying to my mother- telling her differently). Ralph was usually successful in talking me into lazy Sunday mornings, lounging around and getting dressed in time for Sunday brunch with his buddies and their girls.

In my senior year in college, things began to change between Ralph and me. I would always tell him I loved him, and his response had always been "me too." He never initiated love confessions. Heaven forbid I bring up the big "M" word-marriage. He would always say marriage is for people past their prime, who are looking for someone to take care of them in their old age. Do you think that should have been a red flag for me? Well…it wasn't. If I talked marriage or pressured him to be more verbally affirming with me… he would turn cold and, all of a sudden, get really busy with his work. During those times, I'd find myself in my dorm room for days without contact. After ignoring my phone calls at work and at home for a while, I would receive some flowers with a card, saying something to the effect "stop trying so hard to mess up a good thing!"

Or I'd get a phone message that was left during a time when he knew I was unavailable that said, "Schoolgirl, have you learned your lesson yet?" Still no red flag for me!

The times we spent with his family should have been an eye-opening experience for me. His family consisted of his parents and two younger sisters. His father was a handsome man with a commanding presence. He was the owner of his own nationally franchised real estate company. He was the kind of man who never took "no" for an answer. He was intent on being right by any means necessary. Ralph's mother was an attractive, impeccably dressed woman, with a beautiful smile and exemplary social graces. She was sweet and always accommodating, but there was something missing…there was no light in her eyes. There was a hint of sadness in her face whenever she was not "socially engaged." Although she did not have to work, I believe she chose to work as an escape. She was a noted finance officer on the state level. Ralph's paternal grandparents were simply a joy to be around. They were what one would call just "plain old down home folks." However, Ralph's father always seemed to be uneasy when all of us were in social settings and appeared to try to control how much they interacted and actually spoke during these gatherings. Ralph's sisters were spoiled brats! Enough said. Although, on one occasion, I do believe his oldest sister was trying to warn me. While we were all having dinner one evening, she became agitated with Ralph and blurted out, "Ralph, you and yourself will live happily ever after, because you aren't capable of loving and thinking about anybody, but yourself." After she announced this, she glared at me and laughed.

My family interacted with Ralph when they came up to visit me on campus. Each time, after their four-hour drive, Ralph greeted my mom with flowers and took all of us out to dinner. He said all the right things and impressed them… especially my aunt. My mother, the perpetual scrutinizer, never was as taken with Ralph as I wanted her to be. I believe my sixteen-year-old brother, William Taylor Morgan, felt he had met his role model. Ralph allowed him to do the unfathomable …drive his car-the Benz! After that, Taylor would have voted to kick me out of the family tree and replace me with Ralph. He always chided Taylor about his interest in basketball. "If you are not going to be 7 ft. tall or faster than the family car, Taylor…why bother with sports?" "Why run the risk of hurting or disfiguring yourself?" You guessed it. Taylor wanted to quit the high school sports team. My mother refused to allow him to do it and warned him about the dangers of living someone else's life.

◆

Getting an MBA had suddenly become Taylor's goal, so he could play in the best playgrounds and compete in the best arenas. Oh my Goodness! Ralph was in the process of creating a "mini me" of himself. My aunt, mind you, has never been married and would have swooped down on Ralph like an eagle if he had not belonged to me. She said, "Xandy, you have got yourself a serious piece of eye candy with good breeding, brains, and money." She ended her banter with, "Call the minister and let's get this marriage on the books!" My mother would shake her head and say, "Sandra, put those hormones of yours on ice and stop trying to influence Alexandria's choices. It's hard to believe we are from the same set of parents!" When I stop to think about it, I believe my mother and Miss Jesus Sandals were sisters.

My parents had been married fifteen years when my dad was killed in an automobile accident. I was twelve and my brother was eight. That was a dark time in our lives that we rarely discuss. My father was a successful, but gentle, man who was totally devoted to his family. He was a successful educator. In fact, he was the assistant superintendent of our local school district. Mr. Morgan was also the recipient of numerous past academic and sports awards. My mother is the HR director for a major well-known foreign parts manufacturing plant in our hometown. She is a brilliant, but quiet, powerhouse. She is well-respected in our town for her community involvement and philanthropic undertakings. After my father's death, my mother spent years in mourning, but seemed to snap out of her fog all at once. There was never once in this dark time that she neglected my brother and me, nor any of her commitments to her projects. My father had planned and invested well, so we were not left impoverished by his death. In fact, my brother and I would be able to complete our post-graduate level education goals, without any financial imposition on my mother.

That was twenty-one years ago. My mother has never remarried. She has dated a little, on and off, but nothing serious. I believe her marital state is due to Taylor and his refusal to find anything or anybody good enough to be in the same room with my mother more than four or five times. As for me, I wanted my mom to find love again. This surprises me somewhat, due to the fact that I was truly a daddy's girl. My father was my hero. He is the person who started calling me Xandy, and it stuck with my whole family. He was so much fun, yet nurturing and protective of his family. Just as sweet as he was…he was strict and did not tolerate nonsense. According to him, education, good manners, respect, good friends, and church were not optional. He and my mother were church leaders and Sunday school teachers, and most of my and my brother's activities were centered on the church. So…as you can see, I came from a wonderful background, and my parents tried to do everything right to guide us in the right direction. Their parenting skills worked with me in every aspect of my life, EXCEPT my relationship choices. Ralph was the first serious evidence that supports this discovery.

Being with Ralph had a negative effect on my total college experience. I missed out on so much of the social part of college life, because I was so absorbed in everything he expected me to do. I chose to forfeit enjoying this phase of my life, because after all, I was in the "major league!" Plus, by doing so, I avoided those dreaded tantrums and cold shoulder treatments that Ralph was so good at, disappearing for days at a time.

Well, as you know, Ralph and I broke up. It was during my senior year that he delivered the final blow to my heart. His behavior had changed dramatically. We spent less time together, and the times we were together were strained and filled with petty disputes. My belief that we should be moving toward an engagement was always met with flimsy excuses. He even went so far as asking me- "Why is it that you keep insisting on turning our happiness into mere tolerance and boredom?" Followed by, "I might need to look at trading you in for a newer model that thinks just like I do!" That's exactly what he did. I soon realized that our "cold spells" were becoming more frequent and lasting longer than usual. Our dates were distant and our intimacy (as phenomenal as it was) had become nonexistent.

One evening during Greek week, my sorority sister and I were in the mall shopping for pledge gifts and ran into Ralph and "company" sitting in the food court. Amazingly enough, his face did not register any anxiety at all when he saw us standing there. He said, "Hey schoolgirl (referring to HER), let me introduce you to a friend of mine." I was in such a state of shock that I could barely make an audible sound. I vaguely remember extending my hand to receive her limp handshake, while he sat there quietly smiling at me. My sorority sister came to my rescue by grabbing me by the arm and snatching me from the spot in the floor I was glued to- saying, "Well, we are going to run along now…it was good to meet you!" Ralph simply answered, "Okay, you two take care." While bidding us farewell, he was unashamedly looking directly at me. I was in a state of shock for the rest of the night and week. Ralph never called! I eventually called him about two weeks later and asked if I could get my things from his place. Neither of us mentioned the night in the mall. He informed me that all of my stuff was in a wicker basket in his guest room closet and that I knew where the key would be. His final words were, "You won't encounter a problem. The coast is clear. Just lock up when you leave…See you, Alexandria." That was it…I was now Alexandria! I was no longer schoolgirl (at least not the current one in his life)

After a couple days of depression and denial, I mustered up the courage to do what needed to be done. I went to his apartment to pick up my things, while he was at work. Upon entering, I saw two empty wine glasses on the fireplace hearth, a pink netbook and anatomy and physiology textbooks on the coffee table. My heart nearly jumped out of my mouth. I feared that I was not in this apartment alone. However, after standing frozen in time for what appeared to be an hour…the tomb-like silence convinced me there was no one there but me. Immediately, Miss Red Pumps started chattering in my ear. "Girl, take that laptop and throw it as far off the balcony as you can, torch those books in the fireplace and get the bleach spray out of the laundry room and sanitize his clothes before you leave!" Boy, did she have a master plan of revenge, but thank God, Miss Jesus Sandals was on duty. She quickly brought me to my senses by simply saying… "Alexandria, don't be a fool! You know this man will not hesitate to press charges against you; besides, you deserve better than him."

I quickly went to the guest room closet, opened it, and picked up my basket. In the process, I happened to notice the Coach overnight bag with a yellow see-thru nightgown lying on top of it. It was placed right next to my things. I'm sure that was compliments of the "new and improved schoolgirl." It's nothing like your replacement rubbing the fact that you have been replaced in your face. But, amazingly enough, I continued to follow the guidance of Miss Jesus Sandals. As I was about to leave, I stood there, taking one last long glance around the place that held so many fun and wonderful memories for me for the past two and a half years. I was totally immersed in my memories, until I caught sight of the empty wine glasses. That snapped me back to reality, and I then realized that I was crying. It was at that moment that I realized how much I truly loved Ralph. I walked out carrying my wicker basket and closed the door on two and a half years of my life. As I was striding to the elevator, Miss Red Pumps was screaming in my ear, "You should have smashed the flat screen or at least broken those frigging wine glasses!"

In the next months, I mourned the absence of Ralph in my life. I found myself feeling displaced in my own dormitory, among my own peers. The major leaguer had been demoted to the minor league. As my father would always say, "I was as lost as a golf ball in high weeds." No one could have convinced me that Ralph and I would not end up married. It turns out that Ralph was the first and only man I had loved, other than my father and younger brother, Taylor. In my mind, we were destined to be a successful upper middle-class couple with two children, a dog, Benz, BMW, and a house to- die- for in suburbia. Those times spent daydreaming about our wedding and life together had been very real for me. I had managed to convince myself, somehow, that he loved me just as much, but his skills at expressing his love for me were not as good as mine. So I settled for the "me too(s)" that I got when I expressed my love to him. We spent all of our free time together (except for the weekends, and sometimes weeks, he was teaching me a lesson about bringing up the subject of marriage).

Well, just so you'll know, Ralph never called me again. My family and I ran into him and his family at my graduation. They were there supporting his cousin. Everyone exchanged forced, but polite, greetings, except for his grandmother. She gave me the biggest smile, followed by a bear hug. She said, "Hi baby, how have you been? I'm so happy to see you and congratulations on your graduation. You are going to do well in life, because you are such a good girl." Upon saying this, she frowned at Ralph and went "Humph!" At that moment, everyone's frozen stances dissolved, and all of them gave me a congratulatory hug, including Ralph. His hug was impersonal. "Hey Alex, girl you are about to look as good in the cap and gown as I do in my suit." Everyone laughed, except my mother and Miss Red Pumps. My mother was sawing him in half with her eyes, and Miss Red Pumps was saying, "See! If you had trashed his place like I told you to, he wouldn't have the nerve to be standing here in front of you grinning and sounding stupid." Before I could think of something ugly to say, Miss Jesus Sandals said, "Alexandria Rae Morgan! Be the lady that he'll never have. This is your graduation day. Move on!"

Move on is exactly what I did. Despite my longing for his presence, his lovemaking, his laughter, I closed that chapter of my life. I saw him several times with that same young lady. The last time I saw them was at a production of *Cats*. My friends and I were sitting in the theatre when they arrived. One of my friends recognized her. She happily reported that she is a pre-med student, who started at the university about three years ago, but had to drop out and return home due to a serious family situation.

My closest friend and I exchanged glances, and it was obvious we were thinking the same thing. She said, "This calls for an investigation." A couple of days later, she returned with the obvious verdict. This young lady and Ralph had been involved the entire time. Those times he was supposedly giving me the cold shoulder and punishing me with distance...he was gone to see her. According to the gossip report, she has a submissive personality and is absorbed in her studies and her future career as a physician. Marriage and a family are at the bottom of her list of priorities. Therefore, she was perfect for Ralph. And let's not leave out that the reports say she idolized him, almost as much as he idolized himself! I can't say this new-found discovery didn't hurt me. I shook it off fairly quickly, but in doing so…. I vowed to never trust a human being that can be identified as a male. "Shut up, Miss Jesus Sandals!"

After taking a year off for R & R and submitting many applications and resumes all over the country, I accepted a job in Philadelphia as a headhunter for a company that provides personnel for Fortune 500 companies in the eastern section of the U.S. I was excited about the income potential and that I was not too far from my family in Virginia. I found a fantastic townhouse with a view and immediately started work and grad school (with the help of my family). That was twelve years ago!

# CHAPTER 2
## ◆ ALL ABOUT ME ◆

What's happening since then? Well, I'm glad you've asked! **NOTE:** (As it commonly said… "to make a long story-short," I will condense my life and male involvements for the past twelve years into a compact series of events.)

I am now thirty-three years old. I am successful by today's standards. I have attained a Masters in Human Resource Management, and I am working as a senior personnel recruiter for a well-known company with international contracts. I live in a beautiful condominium in a gated community and drive a Panarmera (Porsche). I guess some would say…I am in the major league! I have several girlfriends, who share my free time. I devote some of my time to charities, and I maintain occasional attendance in church. One would think I am happy and enjoying life to its fullest. Well…let me put it like this…I'm not unhappy. I'm unfulfilled. I have reached my education and career goals. I am healthy, vibrant, and have all the material trappings that most people would want. Yet, there's so much missing.

I drive to Virginia to see my family quite often. I'm not sure I do so because I miss them or it's because I'm trying to escape the emptiness I feel here in Philadelphia. Being at my childhood home gives me a lot of distraction from my life. My mom is seriously involved with a wonderful guy, named Jeff. They have been seeing each other for about eight years. Jefferson Onslow, III is, or was, Benson, Virginia's most sought after mature bachelor. He is a retired decorated colonel in the U. S. Army. Since retirement, he has been a chief instructor for the Officer's Training Course at the nearby military installation. Jeff is also a widower, who has devoted his life to community service and the arts, since the passing of his wife about ten years ago. He is the father of three accomplished children, one of whom is also an up-and-coming noted army officer. His daughter is a teacher and phenomenal cellist in the Virginia Symphony Orchestra, and his youngest son is completing his last year in law school. Though, well-refined and highly intellectual, his kids are absolutely wonderful people, who are a joy to be around. The best thing about them is that all three of them adore my mother and fully respect and support her relationship with Jeff. All of us, except for his daughter, are geographically separated, but when opportunity brings us together, it is always a loving fellowship.

Prior to dating my mother, Jeff was never seriously involved with anyone. Securing consistent companionship with Jefferson Onslow, III could be likened to the motto of the U.S. Marine Corps- "Many are called, but few are chosen." Many of the local ladies put in their bid for Jeff during the latter days of his wife's battle with cancer. In the words of my mother, Ms. Abigail Morgan, "True desperation has no shame." Even Miss Red Pumps agreed with her on that one.

Jeff and my mother met during a fundraiser auction for the Council on the Arts. They ended up bidding against each other for a beautiful painting done by a local artist, called *Virginia Sundown*. Jeff won the bid, much to my mother's dismay, because she is quite the nature aficionado. However, three days later, my mother's doorbell rang, and upon answering it, she found a private courier standing on the porch with a large package. Inside was the Virginia Sundown with a card with the following inscription "a beautiful painting for a beautiful lady." My mother immediately obtained Jeff's address and mailed him a check for the amount he paid for the painting. He returned her check and subsequently refused to take the gift back when she offered it. Somehow, this bartering back and forth resulted in a coffee date, and they have shared eight years of sundowns since that time.

Their union has not been without some minor opposition. After having been escorted by Jeff to several local events, one of the city's most popular socialites had set her sights on him with permanency in mind. This woman happens to be the sister of Jeff's best friend and colleague. She used this connection to her advantage. She was present and made herself obviously visible to Jeff at every event she could manipulate her way into. She even went so far as to attempt to cause discord by planting seeds of suspicion, regarding Jeff's fidelity, in his relationship with my mother. However, Ms. Abigail never acknowledged any of her childish efforts with as much as an ugly look or a snide remark. She has never been one who lacked confidence or grace. A blind man could see that Jeff loved my mother, completely and exclusively. Ms. Socialite, by the way, soon got the message and turned her laser beam on another retiree target.

Whenever I quiz mother about her refusal to marry Jeff, she responds by saying, "Xandy, why should I get married? I have had and raised my children, and I am financially secure. What do I need a husband for?" My response to her is always, "What about love and companionship? Don't you want someone to share your life with… someone to grow old with?"

She said to me, "Honey, Jeff and I love each other very much and we do share our lives together. He would marry me tomorrow if I would say yes, but I think things are fine just the way they are."

We've had this verbal exchange many times. Surprisingly enough, my brother, Taylor, likes and accepts Jeff and has badgered my mom about marrying him. He gets the same speech that I get every time the subject comes up. During one of our "Jeff and marriage talks," Miss Red Pumps said, "Xandy, ask her is fornication no longer a sin, since she's having sex outside of marriage. You remember all those lectures she once gave you about pre-marital sex being sinful. Haven't you noticed that those lectures have ceased, since she met and got serious about Jeff?" She ended with, "Go ahead and ask her, it's only fair." It was at that very moment that I knew Miss Red Pumps had to be completely out of her mind. I would never have the courage to say that to my mother. Ms. Abigail Taylor Morgan would have rearranged my expensive veneers. During my trips home, my mother, Jeff, Taylor and one of his many girlfriends, and my Aunt Sandra would get together for cookouts, dinners, and movie outings. Everybody seemingly fulfilled...with one exception- me!

Speaking of Taylor, he finished college. He has his MBA (are you surprised?) and is enjoying the bachelor life. He's quite the ladies' man. He's working for a local brokerage firm in Richmond, Virginia and doing really well. I don't foresee a wife in his life in the near future. Taylor, like me, was hurt badly during his junior year at the University by the woman he thought was going to be his wife. As life would have it, she turned out to be his child's mother and not his wife. It was only after a lot of confusion and family feuding that a forced paternity test revealed Taylor as Joshua's father. The story--- Taylor and Lisa were college sweethearts in every sense of the word. They were like Siamese twins. When you saw one...you saw the other. Lisa was cute and popular, and Taylor saw her as his prized trophy, which I believe, was the problem. Lisa was outgoing and a bit too flirtatious if you ask me. I never did reach the 100 percent mark of liking her. There was something there that I couldn't quite put my finger on. Whenever she was around the family, she was the center of attention. She put forth a little too much effort in keeping the attention of the crowd, especially the men. Jeff and my Aunt Sandra's current boyfriend were no exception. Taylor would sit there beaming with pride. Too bad he didn't have a Mr. Wingtip and Mr. Jesus Sandals standing on his shoulders!

I approached him with my concerns about Lisa, one day. Oh boy! It was as if I was questioning the Virgin Mary's purity. He said to me, "Xandy, you've got a problem with Lisa, because she's not all conservative and restricted like you! She's outgoing and funny and not to mention pretty, and all men are drawn to that. You should try it sometimes!" The nerve of him to say that to me. Miss Red Pumps muttered, "You ought to put that joker in a head-lock, right now, just like you use to do when you were kids!" I ignored her and stood there, shaking my head. He must have experienced some guilt, because he came over to me and put his arm around me. "Look sis, I'm sorry. I know you're trying to watch out for your little brother's heart, but trust me; everything is okay." His final effort to convince me that all was well was when he said, "Xandy, you know that mother likes her, and if Abigail Morgan likes a girl that Taylor chooses…she's got to be all right." I simply replied, "Okay, little brother, whatever you say…it's your life!"

Well, here's the rest of the story. Lisa was a senior, therefore graduating before Taylor. On Lisa's graduation day, she walked across the stage at about three months pregnant! Taylor had reluctantly broken the news to my mother and me earlier. He had texted me and asked me to drive down for the weekend and, subsequently, told mother that the two of us were coming home. When my mother and I talked and discovered that the spontaneous visit was being orchestrated by Taylor…we knew something was not quite right in his world. As soon as the two of us arrived on that Friday evening and were corralled in the kitchen, Taylor blurted out his news, while pacing the floor like a caged lion. I thought my mother was going to go into a coma. She sat there staring, without speaking or moving a muscle, for what seemed liked hours. Taylor and I sat there, neither one of us meeting the other's gaze.

When mother managed to find her voice, she murmured, "This is an untimely situation, but Taylor, you will be the man your father would have you to be, and you will do the right thing by Lisa and your child." Then she continued to say, "First, you will finish college, and I will help you as much as possible in the interim period until you can find a good job. I will help you pay for a nice place for your family, until the two of you can get on your feet." Mother ended her speech with, "When are the two of you planning on getting married? Before the baby- Right?" Taylor sat there with his head down, and all of a sudden, he looked like he was ten years old. His response was nothing like we expected. He said, "Lisa doesn't want to marry me. She doesn't want to be with me anymore." At that point, I could tell he wanted to cry, but the man in him would not allow him too.

My mother quietly rose from her chair. "Taylor, what's going on? This is not making any sense." Why doesn't she want to get married to you or, at the very least, be with you to have and raise this child?" He got up and walked to the window and stood there staring out at the backyard for a while without speaking. Finally, he said, "Mother,

Xandy, Lisa is upset about all of this. She never dreamed she would get pregnant, but it's the pregnancy that has brought the real truth to the forefront. You see, Lisa has been cheating on me! It seems as though, while I was away at all those games and tournaments, Lisa was keeping herself entertained by someone else. She never factored in getting pregnant. Finding out she is pregnant made her tell me the truth." My mother and I just sat there in silence. Believe it or not, I commented before Miss Red Pumps could. I said, "If she wasn't pregnant I'd put my foot so far up her...." "Alexandria! Be quiet!" My mother intercepted my expletive.

Taylor continued by saying, "I guess, I should thank her for not deceiving me any further by letting me think that the child is mine. Lisa is sure the other guy is the child's father, so we are not seeing each other at all anymore." "I'd appreciate it if we don't talk about this anymore. It's over." Well, we granted his request not to talk about it anymore. We all agreed that it made no sense to dwell on it. In my mind, I was glad it was over, because I felt like Lisa would bring Taylor a lot of disappointments if he had married her.

Well, as life would have it, it was not over. Lisa married the other guy and had a little boy. Taylor graduated and began his career in the finance industry. He and Lisa were a thing of the past, and if the number of girls he was dating was any indication that he was healed then...the boy was doing fine! At least... until a chance meeting of my mother and Lisa in the Mall one Sunday afternoon.

Lisa was in town visiting some friends and out for an afternoon of shopping with Joshua, her son. The three of them ran into each other, rounding the fountain in front of Saks. Lisa looked startled. "Well, hello Ms. Morgan, how are you?" My mom politely responded, but was caught off guard by Lisa's son. My mom was almost speechless. She couldn't take her eyes off Joshua. Standing there in front of her was a mini replica of her husband, Alexander Morgan. Lisa couldn't ignore the intensity of the moment. "Ms. Morgan, what's wrong? I know you are still upset with me about what happened with Taylor but..." My mother, raising her hand with a gesture signaling stop, interrupted her and quietly said through tears... "Lisa, this child is my grandson." Lisa stood there with her mouth gaping open and looking at my mother wide-eyed. "Look Ms. Morgan, Joshua is my husband's son and don't say that again." "Lisa, I understand how difficult this is for you, because it is equally as devastating for me, but Joshua is Taylor's son. There is no doubt in my mind. I'm standing here looking into the eyes and face of my late husband and Taylor's father." Lisa marched over, grabbed Joshua's hand, glared at my mom and stalked off.

My mother called Taylor and me and told us to come home… it was important. Upon our arrival that weekend, she told us all the details. Taylor jumped up, said that was impossible, and stormed out of the house. After a weekend of frustration and denial and Mother's non-stop insistence, Taylor agreed to contact Lisa. He did so through one of her friends. Surprisingly enough, she was calm and agreeable when she called Taylor. She convinced him that she knew Joshua was not his son. She told him the timing was wrong, and that unlike her and Taylor, she and her then "other man" did not always use protection.

She asked Taylor to give her some time to talk with her husband, and she would contact him soon. She said, "Taylor, this test thing is going to kill my husband, Mark, but I'm certain that Joshua is not your son." Well…she was wrong! Ms. Abigail Morgan knew her grandchild when she laid eyes on him. The paternity test revealed that Taylor is Joshua's father. After a period of feuding and eventual adjustment, being that Lisa lives in Maryland, Taylor gets his son one to two weekends a month and rotates holidays and summers. Word has it that Lisa and her husband are separated, and the chances look slim for reconciliation. We discovered that Mark knew nothing about Lisa's simultaneous relationship with Taylor at the time of Joshua's conception. I know one man who couldn't care less what Lisa's relationship status is, and that's William Taylor Morgan. Taylor is such a great father, and he is currently enjoying life with his son and a respectable collection of female suitors.

By the way, my Aunt Sandra is still Aunt Sandra. She is a single, successful woman, who owns the city's most popular florist. She has never been married and probably never will marry. She dates quite a bit, and sometimes, her taste in men leaves a lot to be desired. She has two sons by a childhood sweetheart, and they live down south and are married and doing well. They don't visit that often. It appears as though Aunt Sandra makes the trek to see them each time any visiting takes place. Say what you will, Aunt Sandra is an attractive, independent woman, wo doesn't mind telling you what's on her mind -but everyone loves her. She's a joy to be around. I think it was Aunt Sandra and her unique way of handling life and that contagious personality of hers that brought us sanely through the death of my father.

So now, you have a pretty good snapshot of my family background and what's happening in their lives to date. Just like all families, we have our ups and downs, but my family is the stabilizing factor in my life. My life has been full of God's blessings and favor, except for my love life. For the past twelve years, I have dated a lot of men. Let me be clear about this…dating a lot of men does not equate to having slept with all of them. I enjoy a variety of experiences that one man has not been able to give me. I guess it's because I have not found that right man. Or shall I be biblically correct? The right man has not found me!

Dating some of these men has meant going out to dinners, movies, plays, concerts, and even church with several of them. However, the six that I am sharing with you were different. I have tried to condense each of these relationships into its own compartmentalized story, but they span a course of twelve years. I refuse to be bored and to confine myself to the house or sentence myself to constant female company, just because Mr. Right has not come along. I think the reason that a lot of single women are experiencing loneliness and boredom is because they put too much emphasis on being asked out on a date. Does it really matter how good he looks or his financial status- just to go out to have a good time? My goodness, the man is generally only asking you out for an evening of activities. Women need to stop acting like every man who says something to them is asking them to "come to my cave, cook my food, have my babies and wait on me hand and foot until I die." The problem is they would be willing to do just that if they felt the man doing the asking -met all of their "my- man- MUST- have" criteria. So what if the man asking is short, or overweight, or not as handsome as you'd like? It's just a date, ladies!

I do not like to be bored. Therefore, I try to keep myself mentally stimulated, socially involved, and community connected. Sometimes, my efforts in doing so render me over engaged, overwhelmed, and always unfulfilled. I spend a lot of evenings and some weekends involved in some kind of sorority gathering or community service endeavor. I enjoy the company of many of my sorority sisters, and it is always fairly easy to rally a group for a girl's night out or a day of unbridled shopping. My continued involvement in my sorority's activities is really my effort to avoid being bored or idle for too long. To be honest, I experience more aggravation than enjoyment most times due to it always being 20 percent of the sorority's active membership roster doing all the work, especially during Rush. When it comes to rolling up your sleeves and committing some elbow grease to an endeavor, most of these ladies pull disappearing acts. When the curtain opens on the night of the event...everybody is present. My ability to ignore this is waning rapidly.

I am committed to giving back through service to others. Therefore, I continue to support the sorority's community efforts, but I have become more selective with the projects that receive my commitment. Lately, the time I spend with my sorority sisters has been purely social. I've never been the type of female who thrives on running in packs, like wolves. From my observation, this kind of social habit is always fertile ground for unspoken jealousies, competition, and drama. Occasionally, I enjoy meeting a couple of girls from the office or the sorority house for brunch, cocktails, or a movie. It seems that, whenever we get together, the subject matter inevitably will end up being men. More times than not, somebody in the group will be experiencing relationship dysfunction and wants the opinions of the self-proclaimed experts, who happen to be present for the evening. It's amazing how much good advice is spoken, but ignored, during these "support group sessions. It appears as though the damsel in distress, at the time, just wants to vent and is never serious about considering the solicited advice given.

I've always been a private person. I don't ever share the intricate details of my relationships for fear it will end up in the local gossip mill. I definitely don't want to be the subject that everybody is talking and cackling about behind my back. So, no matter what dumb decisions I've made when it comes to men, mums the word. I only have one real confidant, and that is my best friend, Carmen. She was my partner-in-crime for about five years, until she relocated to St Louis due to a job change. I would say she is the only woman I've been close to in my life, other than my mother and my aunt. She and I have a lot in common, except for our taste in men. I think that is the reason we mesh. Carmen has basically three requirements for her men and they are: 1) They must have nice teeth, 2) they must be tall, and 3) they must go to church. That's it! You may agree with me that her short list covers a lot of men. Believe me -Carmen has done her share of trying to audition them all. She is the most likeable person that anyone could meet. Her personality is magnetic, and her humor is so corny but habit -forming.

We met at a jazz concert in the park that I was attending with the most boring date I've had. It turns out that my boring date's boring friend was Carmen's date, so we ended up spending the entire evening chatting, while our dates sat there bobbing their heads to the beat. The rest, as they say, is history.

Carmen is always in love with almost every man she's with for more than three dates, but her relationships never last. She says that she's still sowing her "wild oats" and will do so until she's thirty, and then she'll consider getting serious. She is twenty-eight years old. So look out world…Carmen's got two more years on the prowl. She says to me, "Alex, you are way too uptight when it comes to men. Too many qualifications." It doesn't matter that I differ with her about that. She simply shrugs and laughs when I tell her that being tall with good teeth is just not enough to base a relationship on. She will always remind me that "at least my men go to church!" My coined response to her is "Satan is also in church every Sunday, and your point is?"

No matter what's going on in Carmen's life, you will find her in church on Sunday mornings. Sometimes, she's there bright and early after just getting in from pulling an all-nighter on that Saturday night. When asked about her commitment to Sunday worship, she simply says, "It's the way I was raised. In my parent's house, church was mandatory and never optional." The rest of the story is that Carmen promised her deceased maternal grandmother that she would always go to church, and no matter how promiscuous, intoxicated, or exhausted she would get, that part of her life was non-negotiable. There were times she'd be sitting in church, looking like Rocky Raccoon, with dark circles around her eyes, but she was there. It was as if she felt her grandma would know and be disappointed if she missed church.

It was Carmen's commitment that helped me stay actively involved. We attended the same church and tried to hold each other accountable for attendance. Her attendance record was always far better than mine. I tend to find excuses for not going. My common one is, "I've had a hard week. I just need to relax." "Sister Carmen" makes every effort to guilt trip me by telling me, "God never relaxes when it comes to blessing your butt" or "Dang, Alex, can't you just spare two hours of your time for God?" I usually cut her off by saying, "Enough Carmen! If you think I'm a heathen… shut up and pray for me, okay?" She'd laugh and hang up on me.

We continue to talk a lot on the phone, and we get together as often as time and our hectic job schedules will allow. We text and email daily, and she's always sending me pictures of different guys with the accompanying text, "Alex, check out this smile!" with a smiley face at the end. I always tease her that I need to compile a file for her and her male conquests, so I can keep up with her exchange pace. When I visit her in St. Louis, I'm caught in a whirlwind the whole time I'm there. She has made lots of friends, and as expected, she has a harem of admirers who appear to be on-call to entertain her whims. When we are together, it's like a week or weekend long slumber party, where we break to interact momentarily with others. It goes without saying…we go to church every Sunday I'm there. Sometimes, when we get in her car on the way to church, I'll look over my shoulder in the backseat and say, "I hope you are happy, Grandma!" She squeals and hits me and off we go to worship. No matter what she does, Carmen is my best friend, and I miss her dearly.

Due to my job, I spend quite a bit of time at intervals on the road, including trips abroad. These days, when I am assigned to a contract that requires travel outside of the continental U.S., I cringe. Why? I've spent many of these trips with many people accompanying me to avoid being alone. Recently, my mother has been my companion. The decision to take my mom is not solely due to my enjoying her company. It's because she is drama-free and safe! Over the years, I have made these trips with guys I was dating at the time, and each time, they turned out to be a source of aggravation and regret. With one exception—

# CHAPTER 3
## ◆ BRENT ◆

B rent was my one and only attempt at having a "cougar" experience. Brent was barely legal. I was thirty, and Brent was twenty-one and three quarters years old.

**Age**: Twenty-one (nine years younger than me)

**Occupation**: Engineer

**Marital status**: Single

**Children**: none

Family Background: Has no siblings. He was raised by both parents. Parents are extremely involved in his life. In fact, they are well-to-do and are the greatest influence on his life.

**The Details:**

I met Brent at a city-wide job fair that my company had agreed to co-host. The event was extremely successful. All the junior recruiters present had acquired some really great prospects, and I had been successful in securing about four potential contracts. It was truly a good day. As always, it was a day to dress to impress, so I was in full uniform-meaning a dark, but feminine, business suit, pumps, hair in a bun, and my maternal grandmother's real cultured pearl necklace and earrings.

As the day progressed, I was on my way back into the arena for the third time, carrying a sizeable box of pamphlets and brochures. As I was rounding the corner heading to our display, I heard a voice next to me say, "Please let me carry that for you." I turned to my left and looked up into a pair of the most beautiful eyes I've ever seen. I must have been motionless and silent, because he said, "I don't mean to be forward, but you look like you could use my help." I just silently passed the box to him. In the process, he passed his portfolio over for me to carry. We walked silently through the crowd to my display. When we arrived, I pointed to the cart behind the table. "You can set it there if you don't mind. Thank you very much." He said, "Sure, no problem. You're welcome. It's just another opportunity for me to prove that chivalry is not dead. By the way, I am Aaron Brent Girard. I prefer just Brent."

I extended my hand saying, "Hello just Brent. My name is Alexandria Morgan. (Both of us chuckled.) It's a pleasure to meet you and thank you for restoring my belief in chivalry." He responded with a really big smile and stuck out his chest. He then looked at the display and looked at my now visible nametag and said, "So Alexandria, you are a senior recruiter, I see. If I hadn't already accepted a position, you could have helped me start my career." I responded, "Well, Brent, let's just see where things are when the dust settles on your new job." He immediately said, "Will you and I still be communicating when the dust settles on my new job?" Once again, I was speechless. He broke the silence by saying, "I truly hope that we will." I found my voice. "Sure Brent, I'd love to stay in touch, just in case things don't' work out for you." He gave me a "yeah right" look. Before he could comment, I said, "Here, take my business card and stay in touch to let me know how things are going. Thank you again for helping me with my box." He took my card and extended his hand. "I will most definitely be in touch, Alexandria. Meeting you has been the highlight of my day. Take care." We stood there with a lingering handshake and fixed gaze into each other's eyes for what seemed like minutes. He then picked up his portfolio, turned, and walked away.

There was no denying the encounter with Mr. Aaron Brent Girard was having a lasting effect on me. One of the female staffers at the table looked at me. "My, my, my, now that's what I call eye-candy to the tenth power." I hadn't realized anyone had paid any attention to my interaction with Brent. Before Brent had turned the corner, Miss Red Pumps was in my ear saying, "Did you see those eyes? Girl, you should have given that hottie your cell number. Today is Friday!" Not only did I see his eyes, but I saw the whole package, including dimples deep enough to hold water when he smiles. His curly brown hair, his voice, his demeanor, his confidence, and did I mention his eyes? He was quite a handsome man. As I was lost in my flashbacks, Miss Jesus Sandals quietly asked me one question. "Alexandria, why are you trying so hard to ignore the most obvious thing about Brent?" I snapped out of la-la land. "ALRIGHT! He looks like a baby!" This was true. He looked young and the fact that he did say, "you could have helped me START my career", confirmed my suspicion that he IS as young as he looks.

Miss Red Pumps was right about one thing.... I gave Brent my business contact information on a Friday. This meant I would have to wait until Monday to find out if his interest was as intense as mine was. When I found myself getting too immersed in the Brent replays, I recalled Miss Jesus Sandals' reality check. This man was probably not old enough to buy my pomegranate martinis for me, yet. Well after a weekend of volleying Brent's eyes, dimples, and youthful looks back and forth in my head.... Monday finally arrived. Upon exiting my staff meeting, my assistant greeted me with a handful of resumes, faxes, and messages. Everything in the stack of papers requiring my attention disappeared when I saw the While You Were Out message from Brent Girard. He had left every telephone number assigned to him in his message. Miss Red Pumps was saying, "You Go girl!" Miss Jesus Sandals was saying, "Don't waste your time or his." Well, I sat at my desk pretending to be in limbo. It didn't last long, because I reached for the phone and dialed his number.

When Brent answered, I immediately said, "This can only mean that you are unhappy in your new position already." He laughed. "No, Alexandria, I haven't even started my new job. To be honest, meeting you caused such a disturbance in my weekend until I called you, hoping we could have lunch today." This man was forthright and obviously didn't believe in wasting time. I explained that Mondays are a working lunch day for senior recruiters, so I had to decline his invitation, but surprisingly, I said, "We can meet for dinner this evening instead." He readily accepted. He asked me to meet him at the Platinum. I absolutely love that place. It has awesome food, relaxing ambiance, and a live jazz ensemble that sets the mood for intimate liaisons. We met, talked, ate, drank, laughed, and even danced until the place closed.

Brent then followed me home, and we parked at the park across the street from my house. I listened to the nonstop chant that Miss Jesus Sandals had flowing in my ear. "Alexandria, don't take this boy inside the security gate. You don't know him." After parking, Brent got in the car with me (I could hear Miss Jesus Sandals say, "My God, what's wrong with you?" and we sat there and talked until almost daybreak. I called into work that morning and signed out to do prospecting calls and slept the whole day, except for the five times I talked to Brent on the phone.

Most of the time I was awake and not talking to Brent was spent in an internal debate over our age difference. You see, our lengthy encounter resulted in me discovering that Brent is twenty-one years old. He is nine years younger than me. Upon divulging his age, he put those eyes of his on high beam, looked into mine, and asked, "Alexandria is my age a deal breaker for you?" Without hesitation, I answered, "No!" Now I was having second and third thoughts. When I finally dragged myself out of bed, I called Carmen and filled her in on all the details. She saw absolutely nothing wrong with our age difference. She quickly reminded me, "This, by the way, is the era of the cougar." We both laughed, and she encouraged me to relax and see where this relationship goes. I decided to do that. Brent and I became quite the item. It took me a while to get used to and comfortable with his "baby face" appearance. I was even asked on one occasion if he was my little brother. Brent was such a gentleman and so supportive and thoughtful. He put all of my other suitors to shame in many ways, especially his energy and stamina (um Hmm!).

In spite of all the positive attributes Brent had, there were a couple of things I found irritating. Brent is the son of a minister. In fact, his father is a well-known spiritual leader on the east coast. It is because of this that Brent led a double life. Under the radar, he partied, drank, and fornicated on a regular basis. I know, because all three were done with me. He had his parents convinced he was celibate and totally "living for the Lord." They knew he wasn't a virgin, because he was busted at the age of sixteen in the parking lot of the movie theater with his Sunday school teacher's daughter. He promised his dad to remain celibate until marriage after seeing and hearing how disappointed they were over his "fall from grace." Brent traveled with me, when his job permitted, to job assignments in and outside of the U.S. During the times we were together, Brent never acknowledged it with his parents. If he was ever on the phone with them, I had to be quiet while he pretended to be doing nothing. Brent also tried hard to keep us apart from his friends. Every time I voiced my opinion about this behavior, he would convince me that everything takes time and asked me to be patient with him, as he prepared his family and friends for the eventual unveiling of our relationship.

Other than this being a nuisance, Brent was perfect. He was kind, thoughtful, romantic, generous, and a great listener. Brent met my family once during Thanksgiving. I hosted the dinner, and he came by while they were there. My mother and Aunt Sandra were quite taken by him. Taylor said, "Hey sis, got milk?" laughed and left the room to join Joshua for another round of video game competition. Miss Red Pumps said, "Listen, don't let anyone discourage you from keeping your boy toy! They're just stuck in a time rut!" Brent and I spent a lot of time together, with one exception; he would never attend church with me. He was afraid he might be recognized as his father's son. He was convinced that, if any of his family and friends met me and saw or learned our age difference, they would automatically know he was not celibate and living the life of sainthood he pretended to live. You see, Brent's father was determined that Brent was going to follow in his footsteps. He tolerated, but never fully accepted, Brent's work as an engineer. Brent was a man, until it came to his father. Just a mere conversation about his dad caused him to regress mentally at least five years.

Well, after about a year or so of flying under the radar with Brent, I grew weary of his failure to be man enough to bring me out of the shadows. After all of this time, he still begged me for patience. He said, "These things take time." In the meantime, he would pretend to be interested in the young ladies at church that his mother approved of and continued the "Saint Brent" persona his father expected. I will admit that Brent never changed as far as the way he treated me, supported me, and listened to me whenever I needed him to. Miss Jesus Sandals had even been swayed by his uncommon relationship skills as far as how he treated me. "Alexandria, that boy has potential to be a good husband for somebody. Could it be you?" she asked. I said, "No if he can't stand up to his father at twenty-one, what makes me think he will ever be able to stand up to him when he's older?"

Her response was, "You must surely understand that his father is a well-known public figure, who is rapidly gaining notoriety and trying to build a spiritual empire and legacy. Brent doesn't want to do anything that can be perceived as immoral to shine a negative light on his family." I turned my head, looked at Miss Jesus Sandals and said, "That sounds good. It even sounds right, but is it right for me?" I had grown weary of sitting idly by, while Brent dated all of his parents' "church girl picks." I was never totally sure that some of those church girls were not laying hands on my Brent during these so-called "fake dates" as he called them. I began seeing other people. Brent was hurt by my decision to apply the brakes on our relationship.

He is currently dating women his age, but still contacts me to this date, hoping I'll sneak around with him again. There are times when he calls that I'm tempted, because I do miss his energy and that he always treated me like a queen. Miss Red Pumps always chimes in and says, "Now girl, you know that's not all you miss about that dreamy-eyed, deep-dimples Brent!" At that time, I looked back and wondered if I ended our relationship too prematurely. Oh well, I refuse to live handcuffed to "what ifs and the shoulda, woulda, coulda(s)." Miss Jesus Sandals quickly interjected, "Xandy, something tells me that you haven't heard the last from Aaron Brent Girard, and I personally feel that's a good thing." I responded with, "Who knows?" and left it at that.

# CHAPTER 4
## ◆ RALPH (AGAIN) ◆

A s you can see, I've had quite an interesting life, socially. It's been twelve years since I graduated from college and from the dysfunctional relationship that I had with Ralph. By the way, speaking of Ralph, I actually ran into Ralph last year at a conference in Boston. He still looks amazing and has maintained all the charm and finesse he had twelve years ago. Our meeting was like something in a movie. I was walking by the escalator in the host hotel on the eighth floor, when I noticed the third person out of the six people riding up towards me. Something about him made me notice him out of the corner of my eye. When I stopped turned and focused, I realized it was Ralph, the major leaguer.

He seemed to have noticed me at the same time. I waited at the top of the escalator and our eyes locked and that million-dollar smile of his lit up the room. "Alexandria!" His voice caused those around us to take notice. I said, "Well, hello Ralph!" We both extended our arms and engulfed each other right there on the spot. "My goodness, Alexandria, you look beautiful!" "You are still quite the eye candy yourself," I quickly replied. As we finally moved and started walking down the hallway, he turned to me. "Eye candy is definitely not what I'd expect you to call me -all things considered. I expected to be called something ending in "hole"! We both laughed. "Look Ralph, I'm a big girl now, and that was over a decade ago. I'm deciding to let bygones be bygones." He quickly responded, while showing all thirty-two teeth, with… "Well, that's the best news I've heard in a long time. Let's blow this boring place and get dinner and drinks." I said okay, but I told him I needed a few hours to secure a couple of contacts and then I would give him a call. "That's a date!" He handed me a card that included his cell number. He then gave me a quick hug and disappeared around the corner.

I had such mixed emotions about running into Ralph and making a date with him. Miss Jesus Sandals confirmed my foggy feeling by quietly saying, "Proceed with caution, Alexandria. How sure can you be that this leopard has changed his spots?" Almost before she could finish her statements, it was if Miss Red Pumps all of a sudden woke up, because she started shrieking… "My Goodness woman, he's not asking you to marry him and bear his children…dinner and drinks are ALL he asked. Give the man and yourself a break, Geez!" As usual, Miss Red Pumps made more sense to me, at the time, so I sped through my work and went up to my room to find the right outfit.

I called him when I was almost ready, and he answered his cell on the first ring. "I'll get a cab and be there in about thirty minutes." He was true to his word. In about an hour, we were seated with a bottle of our favorite Cabernet Sauvignon, awaiting our meal service. The evening went really well. We shared many evenings after that one. Ralph still lived in Virginia, but happily commuted to Philadelphia once or twice a month for about six months after we returned from the conference. We never really discussed our break up in great detail. He did admit to being thoughtless and self- indulgent. I almost choked on a glass of wine the night he admitted that. Many things had not changed about Ralph's vain personality, but overall, he had become quite a mature and accomplished man.

My questions about his family seemed to be avoided and every time I mentioned coming to Virginia to see him and possibly reconnect with his family, especially Grandmother Ames, he didn't think it was the right time because something else was always conflicting. When he was in Philadelphia, we spent a lot of time relaxing at my place with occasional dinners and movies. One thing that did surprise me was his willingness to accompany me to church. We went several times, but after each of those times, he would become somber and seemed to withdraw into himself. He would cuddle with me, but silently. When I would question him, he always said he was just "Absorbing the day and mentally preparing for tomorrow and the trip back home." During those times, he wasn't even interested in talking about himself. When it comes to Ralph Ames-that fact was unbelievable.

During what turned out to be his last visit at my home... something really strange happened. I awoke at 2:30 am that Sunday morning to find Ralph sitting up in the bed, staring at me. I could see him by the light from the balcony. "What's wrong, baby?" I asked. "Are you okay?" I reached for the bedside lamp, and he quickly said, "No, leave the light off. I'm ok. I'm just sitting here looking at how beautiful you are and thinking what a fool I am." "Ralph, stop it. It's okay." Before I could say anything else, Ralph slid from the bed to the floor on his knees and turned to me. "Alexandria please forgive me for then and now. I deceived you back then, and I have been lying to you and deceiving you ever since we reunited six months ago."

I reached for him, but he pulled away. "Please don't say anything... just hear me out. Alexandria, you mean so much to me. I know now that I loved you before and love you now. I was just too stupid to push past my fear to tell you and show you. My fear is that if I allow myself to love someone, she will naturally want marriage, and marriage terrifies me. I was raised in a house where two people are married, but did not love each other. My father acquires things and people. Everything and everyone is a trophy for him that he takes care of, but ignores when something else of interest or another challenge presents itself. I was raised in a tomb. We had all the finest tangible trappings, but nothing emotional. My sisters were raised to be too materialistic to care. My mother was once loving, but somewhere along the line, she went into an internal cave and never came out. I vowed, never will I live this way and do that to a child of mine. So the easy thing for me to do was stay single." I then understood that all of his behavior was his effort to stay distant and protect himself.

I said, "Oh Ralph sweetheart, it's okay. I appreciate you being open and honest with me. Honey, we can start from here and get it right this time." I felt him pull even farther away from me. In fact, he sat back on his legs, still in a kneeling position looking at the floor. "Ralph? Why don't you answer me? Come back to bed, honey; we'll sleep in, go out to brunch and talk about all of this. I can even take a few days off and fly back with you, so we can stay connected while working things out." He quietly murmured, "We can't! I'm getting married!" "What did you just say Ralph?" I yelled as I sprung out of bed and stomped around to stand in front of him. He looked up at me with a face of agony. "I'm engaged to someone else, Alexandria. My wedding is taking place in four months." I staggered backwards and plopped onto the bed. Miss Red Pumps and Miss Jesus Sandals were awake and screeching in my ears at the same time. All I can remember that was very distinguishable in the auditory chaos was Miss Red Pumps saying, "Oh hell no! Girl, go get your pepper spray!"

I managed to get enough oxygen back in my lungs to say, "How could you?" Ralph came over to me. "Alexandria, please believe me when I say this was not intentional. I had finally made up my mind to give marriage a try and became engaged to this woman I've been dating for the past three years. She's a wonderful lady, and she loves me dearly, and I believed I could be a good husband to her. The problem is, I never factored meeting you again into the equation. Something happened inside of me that I didn't expect, and since then, I've been lying to and cheating on both of you. What do I do now, Alexandria? I know I love you, but I care about her too.

She and our families are so busy planning what they describe as the wedding of the new millennium that I don't believe she's even focused on the distance I've put between us." I was sitting there, speechless. Ralph looked at me with tears in his eyes… "Say something, Alexandria. I don't want to hurt her or our families. But right now…I'm so torn." Somewhere out of the vast confusion in my brain (probably from Miss Jesus Sandals) I said, "I have something to ask you, Ralph, and I want nothing less than the truth." He said,

"One hundred percent truth from now on." I then looked him directly in the eyes and asked, "Before you ran into me six months ago, did you ever cheat on her with anyone else?" The look on his face gave me my answer. He dropped his head. "Yes, several times." Before I realized it, as I was yelling, "You cheating sack of shit!" I slapped him across his face so hard that my hand felt broken. "Alexandria Morgan!" screamed Miss Jesus Sandals, "You are a lady, not a gutter rat!" Miss Red Pumps just stood there, nodding her head and smiling from ear-to-ear. He grabbed his face and hung his head even lower and murmured, "I deserve a whole lot worse."

I then jumped back in the bed, turning my back to him saying, "Ralph, I can't believe this. I want you out of my bed and out of my life. Now take your sorry, lying, manipulative ass across the hall to the other bed or the couch -just somewhere out of my sight!" He came to my side and dropped to his knees again. "Alexandria, please don't throw me away, I've never opened up and told anyone what I've shared with you tonight. Please give me some time to figure this out." Miss Jesus Sandals ordered, "Xandy, get this man out of your face before you get weak and fall for his manipulation AGAIN!" She knows when she calls me Xandy that it really gets my attention. I reached for a pillow and tossed it at him. "Close my bedroom door when you leave."

I didn't sleep a wink for the rest of the wee hours before dawn. It shocked me at how much this hurt me. I realized, as the hot tears soaked my pillow, that the roots of this reunion with Ralph were deeper than I realized. As much as I wanted to lie there with a made up mind about what just happened, my thoughts were in conflict. Miss Red Pumps' tone was comforting, although confrontational, when she softly said... "You are no angel; you haven't been Mother Teresa since you've been seeing Ralph again. Give the guy a break. He could have kept lying to you, got married, and never told you a thing while continuing to see you the whole time." Miss Jesus Sandals butted in with, "This man was a liar and cheat in the past and still is and will probably always be." Miss Red Pumps wasn't having it. She seemed to have heard what her opposition said to me and accused, "How can anyone who wears a halo, robe, and Jesus sandals be so judgmental and unforgiving?" I grabbed my head and screamed internally.

I leaped out of bed and stomped down the hall to find Ralph sitting in the dark on the sofa. "So when is the big day?" I asked. He couldn't even look at me when he quietly said, "May thirteenth." I don't think I've ever wanted to choke a person as much as I wanted to at that moment. "I'm done! It's over!" I yelled. Ralph jumped up and grabbed me and managed to wrestle me into the tightest bear hug imaginable while saying, "Alexandria, please, please don't do this. I never planned this. I never meant to hurt you, but I don't want to hurt her either. Please try to understand." I struggled out of his arms, despite Miss Red Pumps smirking and saying, "Girlfriend, if you were really done with this man, you wouldn't have lingered in his arms as long as you did, nor would other parts of you have responded the way they did. Get real!" I looked at his pleading eyes. "What part of I want you out of my life don't you understand?" I turned stomped back down the hall and slammed my door.

I stood on the other side of the door listening to Miss Jesus Sandals say to me, "You did the right thing, Alexandria." I managed to fall asleep somewhere during the morning. When I awoke, I discovered that Ralph and his things were gone, without a note or a farewell. I comforted myself by saying, "I will not allow this man access to my heart." Let him get married in 4 months to whoever she is…Good riddance!"

After that horrible night with Ralph, I called Carmen, and she immediately zeroed in on my emotional state. "Okay Alex, tell me." That was all I needed to hear. I told her every little bitty detail since my reunion with Ralph. We were on the phone for about four hours. She just basically listened as I vented. She was quieter than usual and seemed to be guarded in her responses to me. She kept saying, "I don't know about this one, Alex. If I didn't know any better, I'd swear you've got "Home wrecking" plans on your mind." "Aw, come on Carmen, you of all people should know me better than that." I replied and went on to say, "I'm just still reeling from the shock of my not knowing or suspecting anything. Wouldn't you think that my intuition should be sharper than that? I'm not some dumb college freshman anymore." At that point, surprising to both of us, I burst into tears. I told Carmen that I'd call her back during the weekend. I obviously needed some time to get myself emotionally in check.

The following Friday evening, after days of moping and sulking, I had settled in for a weekend of overindulgence in food, chick flicks, and sad love songs. I had made up my mind that I was going to leave a message on my home and cell phone that I was away at a conference and would not be returning my calls until the beginning of the next week. Just as I had popped my supreme thick crust pizza in the oven and turned on Lifetime Movie Network to be my companion for the evening, my doorbell chimed. I instantly went into orbit, because one thing I do not like and acknowledge is unplanned visitors. It's rude! (although it had to be someone with my gate code). I did not budge from my sofa. After the third chime, there came a knocking that one would associate with an FBI raid, followed by a bellowing voice. "Alexandria Morgan, if you don't open this door, I'm going to use my key!"

"Oh my goodness, it's Carmen!" I squealed as I jumped up and ran to the door and yanked it open. We both stood there for a few seconds staring at each other until she said, "Are you going to get out of the way, so I can come in or do I have to perform my therapeutic magic out here on the porch?" As she stepped over the threshold, I said, "Hello my friend" and lunged into her arms for the meltdown of all time. Once I could pull myself together, I said, "I can't believe you're here. You should have called me so I could have planned…" She put her finger to her lips and said, "Sshh, this is not a social call; this is an SOS call. Alex, I heard the things you were not saying, and the sound of your voice told me that my friend needed me. So here I am!"

We spent the entire weekend at my apartment. We didn't even go to church (which was highly unusual for Carmen). Something told me that Grandma understood we were engaged in a high priority girlfriend therapy session, so Carmen showed no signs of feeling guilty for not going, and I was relieved. The whole weekend was not dedicated to my reaction and failure to accept Ralph's unexpected revelation. A lot of the time was spent having a soul-to-soul talk about our lives. Carmen told me, "Alex, I honestly don't desire to get married and settle down. I love a life of challenges and variety, and that includes my love life." When I gave her a look of disbelief, she said, "Okay, I know I told you that I'd consider settling down when I turn thirty, but that's only if my Mr. Right falls out of the sky and lands on me with a smile full of good teeth, with a bible in his hand, on his way to church!" "Carmen, you are truly out of your mind, which makes me a certifiable mental case, because you're my best friend.

Laying all humor aside, I think you want to believe that nonsense you're saying, but no one wants to go through life alone…. not even you." She quickly attempted to correct me. "Alex, I said absolutely nothing about going through life alone. I am going to have myself a man until the day I die, but not a husband. Every woman in this world is not in pursuit of a husband, children, and a condo with an impressive wall street investment portfolio." "What happened to husband, children, and a house with a white picket fence?" I asked. My comment didn't get as much as a smile from her. I then saw she was in the "This- is -too- deep -to- be -joking mode."

Well, despite spending that entire weekend delving into each other's hearts and minds, Carmen and I agreed to disagree on the importance and benefits of marriage. She admitted that she would like to have a child, one day, but stated she preferred to do it as a single mom. The "confinement" of marriage was not something she wanted to deal with. I threw up my hands, while sticking to my opposing beliefs. One thing Carmen was successful in doing was getting me to see that I still cared very deeply for Ralph and that he obviously still cared for and wanted me-despite him getting married. She kept telling me over and over… "Alex this man has hurt you, and he's made some bad choices, but that's where forgiveness comes in. He constantly tries to see you and is always checking on you. All you've got to do is say the word, and he'll stop his wedding or get a divorce and come running, bringing great looks, great sex, great job, and promising future along with him." "Maybe you are right Carmen," I said quietly. "Maybe this thing with Ralph is salvageable, but not right now…the wound is too fresh; plus, I've got other fish in my net to check out."

Carmen jumped up from the floor and ran toward me, seeking a high-five, while saying, "That's my girl! Check out your options, let him know you are doing just that, while he waits and suffers." While we were laughing and giving each other a rousing high five, Miss Jesus Sandals spoke up for the first time during the whole weekend. "Alexandria, how can someone as smart as you act so dumb?" Naturally, Ms. Red Pumps had to have her say, too. "Leave the girl alone. It's nothing wrong with her exploring all of her options before selecting the right one. Plus, it's always good to have a ram in the bush, while you're doing it." Miss Red Pumps and I were finally in complete agreement, and that's scary!

Well, to satisfy your curiosity, Ralph did get married. However, they are separated, but together, if that makes any sense. Both of them seem to be sharing the same shelter and occasionally the same bed, but little else. From what I have heard, it has been a social and emotional tsunami for all parties involved.

# ◆ MY (OTHER) OPTIONS ◆

W ell, here we are. It's been a while since my second encounter with Ralph. He has stayed in touch and kept me abreast of just how unhappy he is. It seems his wife wants to have a baby, which she thinks will bring them closer together. He told me that he would have a vasectomy before he would risk impregnating her. He still admits he loves her, but he is not in love with her, and their marriage is a mistake.

When I ask him why he won't divorce her, he says the divorce would be nasty, and that it would hurt his career and give his family a moral scar, BUT in the same breath, he tells me that he would do it in a heartbeat and relocate if I would commit to being with him. I will admit that I did allow him to come up and take me to dinner one evening, but that's as far as it went (in spite of temptation calling my name to take his visit to another level).

In the past twelve years, I have had quite a dating smorgasbord. My job requires travel and participation in a wide variety of social events. The HR field offers a variety of men from the corporate executives to the yuppie white-collar success seekers all the way down to the blue collar determined to make it guys, with less brains, but lots of brawn. I have had my share of experiences with someone in each category. If there's one thing I've learned as a HR professional, if nothing else, is not to discriminate when seeking candidates to fill an opening.

In the following chapters, I will share with you the guys in my life, whom I feel I should give careful consideration during the elimination phase of my lifetime partner pursuit. I've decided to seek input from others, who may possess better skills than I obviously do when it comes to picking the right men (man!). I am thirty-three years old and would love to settle down, get married, and start a family BEFORE I am thirty-eight years old. The men I have included are the ones I feel have the potential to be husbands and have continued to express an interest in maintaining some facsimile of a serious relationship with me.

My mother always says that dating is like fishing. No matter how many you catch, there are some you keep and some you throw back! I seem to keep the throwbacks a lot longer than maybe I should and throw back the keepers. Please help me decide.

# CHAPTER 5
## ◆ EDMUND ◆

**Age**: Forty-six (thirteen years older than me)

**Occupation**: Former Attorney; Currently a Sales Executive-pharmaceutical company

**Marital status**: Divorced

**Children**: one daughter age eleven

**Family Background**: Oldest of four children. Has three sisters. Raised by both parents. Parents appear to be supportive of him and actively involved in his life.

**The Details:**

Edmund and I met at a surprise birthday party for one of my co-workers. It just so happened that Vince, our company's best rookie headhunter, was dating Edmund's youngest sister. She pulled off one of the most elaborate and best surprise birthday parties I have ever attended. Considering she and Vince had been dating less than a year, the party was far more than I probably would have done for someone I had been dating for years. The sad part about the whole thing is that she was not the only female Vince was dating.

He was quite the ladies' man. The guest list contained the who's who of Philadelphia, and one of those was Edmund. I was dancing with Vince as Edmund arrived and approached Vince with a warm smile and well wishes. Vince introduced us and soon left us in the middle of the floor as he walked off, talking on his cell phone.

Edmund is an attractive and distinguished looking man, who had what I found extremely alluring in any man-a commanding presence. When I extended my hand during our introduction, he gently, but firmly, grasped my hand and covered it with his other hand. I felt such an immediate attraction to his grace and warmth. Edmund has a twinkle in his eye that caught and kept my attention all night.

We ended up spending most of the party together. His sister, Isabel, made a few comments about our looking good together and suggested we do some double dating. Edmund said, "I'm sorry, you must forgive my sister for being so forward and presumptuous. She shouldn't assume that you would be interested in seeing me again after tonight." I found myself saying, "Well, your sister is right. I would love to see you again if I get the invitation to do so." Ms. Red Pumps said, "Hmmm, you're a little quick on the draw tonight, aren't you Miss Alex?" Edmund turned that twinkle on high beam. "Well consider yourself invited, Alexandria, for many evenings and days to come." And that's exactly what happened. We spent a lot of time together. Edmund and I had a lot in common, despite the difference in our ages.

I met him when I was twenty-eight years old, and he was forty-one. In spite of the existing generation gap, we enjoyed the same kinds of movies, books, and music. We spent many weekends at the symphony, plays, and varied museums. We also would take trips to New York to catch Broadway openings and concerts. (NOTE: The only thing we grossly differed on was his obsession with trips to the tanning salon. Although I went occasionally, I never quite understood his obsession. Granted, he and I are maybe considered pale in contrast to some, but his complexion was beautiful. I'm sure the tanning salon staff looked at him strangely as he would go and come.)

During some of our trips, we were not alone. We were accompanied by Edmund's eleven-year-old daughter, Olivia. These were trips that I did not enjoy, because Olivia was and will always be the center of attention anytime her daddy is occupying the same physical space with her. She is a beautiful child with an above average command of the English language and knowledge of current events. She knows she's pretty, smart, and the apple of her father's eye. She is polite to me, but never really accepting. When she's with us, a great deal of her time is spent on the cell phone with her mom, giving her a blow-by-blow account of the day's activities. The trips that the three of us have taken together have consisted of she and her dad sharing a room and me in a separate room until the wee hours of the night when Edmund sneaks to my room for about an hour- TOPS!

He has Olivia every other weekend, but also goes over to see her during the week when she or her mother calls saying she's having a bad day or night and missing him. There have been times when he's actually spent the whole night at his ex's house, because "Olivia is having one of her really hard times tonight." According to him, he sleeps on the chaise in Olivia's room during these occasions. He and I have had several knock-down-drag-out arguments about these times, but he refuses to be open to the possibility that he is being manipulated. Claire, his ex-wife, would always convince him that three years was not nearly enough time for his daughter to adjust to her parents being divorced. Edmund truly was not still in love with his ex. That was obvious in his conversations and interactions with her.

◆

At the beginning of our relationship, Edmund said to me, "Alexandria, I will never talk negative about or disrespect my ex-wife, because she is the mother of my child, but I owe you some background information about my marriage and divorce. Claire and I were high school sweethearts and married right out of college. We are both high achievers and workaholics and focused on our jobs and careers right out the gate. I went on to finish law school and to begin my tenure as the Assistant D.A. We grew apart early and were about to consider divorcing when Olivia was conceived."

As I sat there staring at him and listening intently, he continued. "Both of us committed always to do what was best for our child, so we continued in a partnership…not a marriage. Well, human nature played its trump card, and Claire found the romance and attention she said she was missing in the arms of another man- A man that I had opened my home and life to on a frequent basis. When I discovered this affair, I did something I had never done in my life…I physically assaulted her. I grabbed her, pushed her, and she fell, breaking her arm. She never pressed charges against me because of the impact it would have had on my career, but she has had me at her beck and call ever since."

Miss Jesus Sandals almost leaped off my shoulders at this revelation. "Xandy, this man has a problem controlling himself when he's angry; don't you think this is a flashing red light, instead of a red flag?" Miss Red Pumps responded before I could even give the comment any thought. She countered with, "C'mon Alex, what man wouldn't lose it when he discovers he's been cheated on and lied to by his wife and that the other man is someone he considers a friend? Give this man a break!" I hesitantly agreed with Ms. Red Pumps. I knew that a lot of men would have probably beaten the crap out of both of them or shot them both and turned himself in.

The situation with Edmund and his ex-wife and child was our only serious area of conflict. There were some minor things that caused spats. One of those was the fact that Edmund was insistent on knowing my every move and that my cell phone was always answered. I was smart enough to realize this was residual baggage from his marriage. This man had been hurt and was having a hard time trusting again. I was trying to be patient and understanding, but sometimes, it was overbearing. Edmund would also go through periods of extreme insecurity when it came to my association with men my age or a little older. He thought they were his biggest competitors. And it didn't help that, one night, we were out dancing and this jerk who wanted to dance with me approached us and said, "Hey Miss lady, do you think your sugar daddy would mind if you danced with me?" Edmund became unglued. He let the expletives flow freely to the point the younger guy threw up his hands. "Hey man, calm down. I just wanted to dance with her, not have sex with her…you need some therapy!" Edmund was infuriated. We left the club, he dropped me off, and left without saying anything other than "Good night, Alexandria."

He later apologized for being "so wired." He told me that was one of the reasons he stopped practicing law because of the courtroom antics that kept him over the edge. He went on to say that his current Fortune 500 position paid him more with far less stress. It made rational sense to me. So be it! Edmund and I dated for quite some time, and I truly cared for him tremendously. He and I were so close, despite the baggage from his marriage and his insecurities. He was always so thoughtful and supportive of me. My family met him on one occasion. They came up for a company awards program, where I was the guest honoree for recruiter of the year. Edmund was my date for the evening. He was there looking ever so handsome and distinguished as usual. My mother, her boyfriend Jeff, my brother, and Aunt Sandra met him, and the five of us went out for drinks afterwards. We had a wonderful time. Of all times, Olivia and her mother called during our social time, and he sat there giving them a complete replay of the evening, including everyone presently sitting at the table. Aunt Sandra's eyes were burning a hole right through me. My mother, Jeff, and Taylor were distracted by someone in the restaurant who looked like someone all of them knew.

Edmund eventually excused himself from the table to continue responding to the interrogation. Miss Red Pumps said, "Girl, you should have kicked him so hard under that table and gave him such an evil eye that he would have hung up that frigging phone immediately. Enough is enough!" It seemed as though my aunt had heard Miss Red Pumps, because she said, "Come on, Alex, show me where the little girls room is located." I knew the last thing on Aunt Sandra's mind was using the bathroom. When we entered the women's exterior lounge, she checked to see if we were alone, and then she crossed her arms on her chest and gave me the laser beam look, while asking me… "What in the hell is going on, Alexandria? First of all, you are smitten with someone that I should be dating, not you, then you sit patiently by while he and his ex-wife and child monopolize our evening on the cell phone."

My efforts to explain to her that Edmund's daughter was having a hard time dealing with her parents' divorce fell on deaf ears. Aunt

Sandra said, "Alex, it's obvious that you really care about this man and that he makes you happy, because you've allowed him to meet your family, but this divorce recovery nonsense has got to stop, and only you can stop it." She continued with, "Men have to be trained how to treat us, and you are not doing a good job training this one." Miss Jesus Sandals, let out a big sigh of relief. "Thank goodness somebody else is trying to talk some sense into you. Are you listening, Alexandria?"

I did not want to go into the details of Edmund's former marriage and breakup with my aunt, so I simply said, "Don't worry, Aunt Sandra, it's not as bad as it may look. We are working all of this out. I promise you." She gave me that I'm -not-sure-I believe-you–look, but reached out to hug me as we made our way back to the table. When we got there, Edmund had already returned to the table and ordered a bottle of their finest Champagne and toasted to my continued career success and to the continued success of our relationship. He ended the toast with, "Alexandria, meeting you has been the best thing that has happened to me in a long time. I love you!" I nearly fell out of my chair. He had never told me he loved me before. That warm, familiar hug and kiss he gave me and that twinkle in his eye reassured me that he meant every word. Needless to say, Edmund earned big brownie points with my family that night-including my aunt.

My mother and I talked on the phone after that night about my relationship with Edmund. She was quite taken by his charm and overall personality, but she did have one concern. She voiced her concern to me, without hesitation or stuttering. "Alexandria, you've had one father, and this man is not him. Edmund reminds me of your Daddy and I'm sure you see the same thing." "Mother! Don't be ridiculous!" I replied. "Edmund does not remind me of my father. If he did remind me of Daddy- there would be no way that I could…." I caught myself before I finished the sentence. Miss Jesus Sandals piped up, "You almost confessed to fornicating to your mother. If you'd exercise some self-discipline, you wouldn't have anything to confess." You-know-who in the red pumps quickly responded by saying, "Alex you and that roman sandals wearing chick have got to be out of your mind if you don't think your mama knows you sleep with that man!" Besides, Mommy Dearest is not being Mother Teresa herself!

After giving Miss Red Pumps a you're treading on thin ice look, I assured my mother, "Edmund and I have a wonderful relationship in spite of our thirteen-year age difference. We are more compatible than most of the guys that I date that are my age." After realizing she was not winning the age argument, she asked me, "Are things better with the situation with that ex-wife of his and his daughter?" After recovering from the shock of her question, I replied, "Mother, I see that you and Aunt Sandra have been talking, and I'll tell you the same as I told her…we are working all of it out." "Okay Alexandria," she said, "you are a grown woman, and I hope you are making wise decisions when it comes to your future. I like this man. It's just that I do have a few reservations about the differences that I am aware of that exist between you two. I'll leave it alone." I quickly thanked her and changed the subject.

◆

As far as Claire and Olivia are concerned, I was telling my family the truth. Edmund was not spending nights over there like he was doing at the beginning of our relationship. The episodes of Olivia calling and demanding his attention still occurred, but with less frequency. I trust Edmund completely around Claire. Since she feels that she has access to the biggest skeleton in his closet, she has the nerve to include her boyfriend on some of the occasions that all of us are together. Mind you that this boyfriend is a former friend/associate of Edmund's.

There was one event, in particular, that Edmund and I, Claire and her man, and Edmund's family attended. It was the first time I had actually met Claire face to face. We had talked a couple of times when she or Olivia called, and I was present. I was nervous about our meeting, because I had no idea how things were going to turn out, especially since Olivia was the focus of everyone's attention, being that it was her first classical piano recital. The way Edmund was acting, one would have thought we were going to a live performance by Mozart. Olivia arrived at the auditorium in a stretch limo, followed by her mother and her man in her car. The rest of the family and friends had arrived early to form what was supposed to be a red carpet entrance for Queen Olivia. After the "Queen's" exit from the limo and her stroll down the sidewalk, her mother and her escort made what appeared to be an entrance, seeking the same kind of attention.

Before my thoughts and response to Claire's appearance could register in my brain, Miss Red Pumps started laughing hysterically saying, "Oh my goodness, is this what all the fuss has been about? This woman looks like somebody from the wrong side of the tracks playing dress up in a rich woman's clothing. Was Edmund blind or crazy when he hooked up with HER?" Miss Jesus Sandals surprisingly said, "Hmmm not quite what I expected either." I agreed with both of them. Claire looked like a combination of Cher, Tina Turner, and Barbara Walters. Hard to imagine, isn't it? She was petite and muscular with big heavily made-up eyes, wild black hair, and conservative clothing.

After seeing her, Edmund's comments about my beauty really concerned me! Anyway, once we were formally introduced and she and I gave each other a slow and scrutinizing once-over, things went fairly smoothly. The tension of the evening was not between Claire and me. It was between Edmund and his former associate. Despite the discomfort it obviously caused him, he did not allow it to interfere with his effort to make the day special for Olivia. Olivia played beautifully and looked like a regal doll sitting at that grand piano under the spotlight. Her father and mother were beaming with pride, and at that moment, I loved Edmund for being the kind of father he was for his little girl.

Edmund's parents and siblings were nice people, who treated me with warmth and familiarity. Isabel was out of town for this occasion and was unable to be there. However, it was obvious by the things they said through the evening that Edmund had been talking about me. His mother was a stately woman, who appeared to tolerate little nonsense in her world. During the reception, she said to me, "You are quite young, but you are good for my son, Miss Morgan. He's happy with you. Just don't hurt him…he's been through enough." Edmund's father rolled his eyes and shook his head. "Here we go again!" I'm not sure what that meant, but he seemed exasperated by his wife's comments.

Edmund's sisters seemed to be glued to Claire's side and hung on her every word. My effort to interject a comment or two had little to no response or impact. Claire, on the other hand, seemed to watch me and listen to me purposefully. During a lull in the many conversations, she grabbed me by the hand and asked me to come over and sit with her. After nestling into one of the overstuffed sofas, she turned to me. "So you are the woman that is after my Olivia's heart? You obviously have her father's. Isn't' that enough?"

I was taken aback by her questions, but managed to say, "Claire, I'm not sure what you're talking about, but I'm not after anything but a friendship with Olivia. She's the daughter of the man I care very much for and spending time with her is a joy." I lied! Claire went on to say that Olivia really finds me interesting and that she talks about the way I dress, how pretty I am, and my make-up. "You've made quite the impression on my little girl," she went on to say. "Maybe it's because the two of you are so close in age, but that's neither here nor there. Edmund and I are devoted to our daughter, and you and I will get along just fine as long as you don't try to interfere with that." Miss Red Pumps said, "I know Cruella Deville did not just say that to you! Please give her a piece of your mind before I find a way to do it, myself." Miss Jesus Sandals quietly said, "Alexandria, you can't control this woman, but you can control you! You are a lady with class…Remember that!" I almost bit my tongue in two as I managed to say… "Claire, it is not my desire to interfere with anything. Edmund and I are together, and nothing is going to change that. I need for you to accept that, and we'll get along just fine." Claire shrugged. "Touché'!"

Edmund knew nothing of any of the conversations that took place the entire evening between me and his family or his ex-wife. He was totally engrossed in Olivia. The evening ended with everyone still alive and reasonably well. I think the person most uncomfortable was Claire's boyfriend. I think she purposely rubs that man in Edmund's face as payback for their altercation. He was relatively quiet throughout the occasion, with only a few noticeable exchanges of glances between Edmund and him. Edmund told me that he just holds his tongue to keep the peace and to avoid upsetting his daughter. Although Edmund has professed to being in love with me, I am not silly enough to think anyone will ever come before his beloved Olivia. I think I'm okay with his devotion to his daughter, because I know what it's like to not have your father in your life, although my situation is due to my dad being deceased.

Overall, my relationship with Edmund is fulfilling. He makes me feel secure and valued, and most of all, I know I can trust him. He is handsome, accomplished, physically, emotionally and financially generous, and has strong family values. At his age, he is still quite a "head-turner", but he only has eyes for me and constantly reminds me of that. I'm not sure if I've fallen in love with Edmund, but I do know that I care very much for him. If only he could be as trusting of me and as secure with me as I am with him. He continues to be clingy and suspicious of everything and everybody. I believe he feels that, if he is with me all the time and if he maintains the unbelievable stamina and frequency that he does with me physically, that I won't have a reason to entertain the thought of being with someone else. In fact, when it comes to stamina…I'm the one begging for mercy. Miss Red Pumps always says, "Alex, you got yourself a champion; he must definitely eat his Wheaties EVERYDAY!" Miss Jesus Sandals doesn't bother to respond. She just shakes her head.

Edmund and I dated for a little over a year and a half before I decided to ask him for some space to think and decide if I wanted our relationship to continue toward something more serious. He was devastated with my decision. Edmund even went so far as to tell me that he had been thinking a lot about us being together for a lifetime. He said, "Alex, I know my situation has been trying, but you know in your heart how much I care for you, and you know that I would give you the kind of life that most women would kill to have. If you and I were to marry, your choice to work and continue your career would solely be for your pleasure and not a need, because I will make sure you never need or want for anything, including a devoted friend, husband, lover, and father to OUR children."

The thought of being married to Edmund has crossed my mind, but the thought of having a child with him had not. After he planted that seed, I have to admit that I did begin to fantasize about the all-American lifestyle I would have with Edmund and how devoted he would be to our child. Ms. Red Pumps cast her vote early in my mental debate. "Xandy, this is an ideal opportunity for you. What woman in her right mind would let this kind of man go? He is a total package in the looks department, financially, socially, and he is CONSISTENTLY great in the sack! What more do you want, girl?" Miss Jesus Sandals answered before I could. "Look, Miss Red Pumps or whatever your name is, Alexandria needs to slow down and take a realistic look at this "total package" you are speaking of and consider the negatives too, and you and I both know there are some negatives now and some potential ones to come." Ms. Red Pumps responded, "Well, you want Xandy to go through her life looking at the glass half empty. There are negatives involved in every relationship. I say when a man is good in the bank and good in the bed and generous with both- GO FOR IT!" I yelled, "Will the two of you stop the bickering. I've got to figure out how to get rid of the two of you!"

After about a month of Edmund pulling out all the stops to assure me of his devotion to me and his intentions toward me, I insisted on my space. I assured him that we would continue to go out occasionally, but for right now, I had a lot on my plate, and I wanted some time to sort things out. He argued that things had gotten much better with his situation with his ex-wife, being that she and Olivia only called about 3 times each week with a list of demands, instead of the initial ten to twelve times. Claire appeared to love it when she interrupted something that Edmund and I were doing. There were several occasions when she would tell Edmund to give me the telephone and she would say things like... "My dear...I know this is an intrusion on your plans, but as I told you- we are devoted to our daughter's happiness, and that will always come first. I do hope you understand this is just how it is going to be if you are going to remain Edmund's girlfriend."

That would just send Ms. Red Pumps into orbit, threatening to come off my shoulder and lose one of her pumps inside of Claire's butt cheeks. I will admit that Olivia and I have gotten closer. We've had several solo dates together that I really enjoyed. Regardless of his efforts to dissuade me, I decided to put Edmund on ice for a while. I knew he would be there when or if I decided to start seeing him again. Many times, since putting our relationship on ice, I have called on Edmund when I needed or wanted a companion of caliber to go on one of my extended work related trips or during those times when I was having difficulty at work. Edmund always comforted me in a way that no one else was able to do. I'll admit that my decision regarding Edmund was fueled, to some degree, by the fact that on one of my girls' night out with my sorority sisters, I became engulfed in the melodic sound of a beautiful keyboard player named...

# CHAPTER 6
## ◆ JULIAN ◆

**Age**: Thirty-three (same age as I am)

**Occupation**: Singer/Musician (IT specialist)

**Marital status**: Single-never been married (had a live-in relationship for six years)

**Children**: One son (deceased due to what was determined to be SIDS)

**Family Background**: He was raised by his father. His mother left when he was four years old- never to be heard from again, until the notification of her death by overdose when he was nineteen years old. She suffered with Bipolar Disorder that could never be controlled due to her refusal to take her meds, coupled with her eventual drug addiction. He has one older brother, who is a successful podiatrist. His father is still living, but they are estranged from each other.

**The Details:**

I t was a warm Friday evening in June when I hesitantly agreed to meet a small group of my sorority sisters for drinks and dinner. It had been a while since I had been out with them, and I was looking forward to being brought up to date on all of their issues and lives. We chose to meet at a place called Claude's. Claude's was a popular restaurant and lounge for the more mature preppies in the area. This particular evening, the five of us chose to sit outside on the patio, being that it was fairly crowded on the inside, and we didn't want to compete with the voices as well as the music from the band that would be starting later.

I was actually having a great time listening to everything from who's having the best sales, who lost weight, who got implants, and whose mate was cheating on them and with whom! The usual chatter among girls! I was sitting there, enjoying my second pomegranate martini and giggling like the rest, when my ears tuned into the most beautiful music I had heard in a long time. The band had started to play, and it was as if someone was skillfully playing the piano just for me. When the other girls noticed my withdrawal from the conversation and saw my head tilted to the side in the listening position and swaying with the beat, our table chatter ceased. They, too, listened intently. I opened my eyes and asked them if they had ever heard such beautiful music. They agreed that the sound was undeniably wonderful.

I needed to make a ladies' room trip, so I told them that I was going to check out the source of the sound during my trip to and fro. I left the patio and made my way through the tables and people to try to see the piano player. There was a four-piece band on the small stage that consisted of a sax player, bass player drummer, and last, but definitely not least, a piano player-Julian. He sat there appearing to be in a world of his own as he stroked the ivories. He appeared to be quite tall and slender, with beautiful long hair that reached below his shoulders with a wisp of curls in his face. He did a slow Stevie Wonder type sway back and forth with his head as he continued to play one of my favorite Celine Dion songs- *My Heart Will Go On.*

I continued my trek to the ladies' room that I soon discovered had a speaker. As I was doing my business in the stall, I heard the intro to *My Cherie Amour,* immediately followed by a beautiful voice singing the lyrics. I almost made a mega mess trying to get finished and out of the stall, and Miss Red Pumps said, "Well my goodness Alex, slow down. I've never met a man worth peeing on yourself for and neither have you!" I ignored her as I hurried out of the restroom. I came to a halt at the corner of the bar and never moved another inch.

I stood there looking and listening. For some odd reason, my current position gave me a direct face-to-face view of the piano player. He went on singing, and I realized he was looking directly at me. When he got to the part in the chorus that says, "*You're the one that my heart beats for…How I wish that you were mine!*" He gazed deeper into my eyes and smiled as he sang. Every time he got to that part, he eyes returned to me and his smile became mine. I was glued to that spot. It was as if I had totally forgotten my friends on the patio. (And the feeling must have been mutual, because none of them came to look for me). Somewhere in my trance, I heard the announcement by the sax player that the band was taking a pause-for-the-cause. "Oh my goodness," I said to myself, "he's about to leave the stage."

Miss Jesus Sandals perked up and adjusted her halo. "All right, Alexandria, don't go acting like some teenage groupie. That Kool-Aid smile you have on your face may give him the idea that you on the prowl and are easy prey!" I shrugged off that comment, as usual, and feigned surprise as he headed directly towards me. As he made his way through the crowd, several people stopped him for a handshake or a pat on the back. He never took his eyes off me in the process. As he reached me, he extended his hand. "Hi, my name is Julian. What's yours?" As I managed to respond, I took note of his height. He had to be at least seven feet tall. At least that's what it felt like standing next to him with my 5'5" frame. He then said, "Well, Miss Alexandria, will you please join me for a drink?" I followed him to a nearby table, and we exchanged general conversation for the duration of his break. He did tell me that he is only 6'4". His beautiful green eyes, sense of humor, and boyish charm was intoxicating.

Before leaving the table, he asked me if he could have my number, so he could call me to meet him for breakfast in the morning. I didn't hesitate, but told him I didn't have a pen and it didn't look like he did either. His response was, "Just tell me your number one time, and I'll never forget it." I gave him my number and away he went. I finished my drink as I listened to them play. Julian didn't do any more solo performances, so I made my way back to the patio. I waved to him as I was leaving. He managed to blow me a kiss from the stage.

When I arrived at the table, I loudly said, "Thanks a lot for coming to check to see if I had been slain by a serial killer or abducted by aliens!" They paused and looked at me incredulously as Myra said, "Alex, we saw you through the window at the bar in la-la land with that band member. You were so enthralled with him, you didn't even notice me as I walked past the two of you so close that I could have stepped on your foot." I laughed and crawled into my seat. Everyone was pretty sauced, tired, and ready to call it a night. We bid our farewells and parted company. I did not tell either of them of my breakfast plans.

On the way home, I called Carmen and obviously interrupted her in the midst of something that she had no intention of stopping to entertain my recount of the evening. "Alex, are you okay?" "Is your family okay?" I said, "Yes, my family is fine and I'm just peachy because I've just met an interesting guy." "Okay, okay!" she replied. "I'll hear about this later. Okay? I've got to go sweetie. Love you!" CLICK! I knew the deal, but I was still quite put off by her lack of interest in my world at the moment. When I got home, I quickly got in the bed, so I'd look refreshed in the morning, only to discover that I could not sleep. I laid there with my eyes open, listening to the negative talk that was going on between my ears.

I convinced myself that Julian was not going to call me, because he had forgotten my number. I felt really stupid to have fallen for the pick-up routine of a frigging piano player in a bar. What was I thinking? Miss Jesus Sandals was in agreement with me. However, Miss Red Pumps came to the rescue. "Alex, get a grip girl! That tall charming male specimen was just as taken by you as you were with him, and you know it! After all, you are a real prize, yourself. So stop the nonsense and go to sleep, so you'll be able to hear the phone ring when your call comes!" Unlike most times, I did exactly what Miss Red Pumps told me to do.

At 7:30 a.m., my telephone rang. My caller ID said unknown caller. I made myself wait until the third ring. When I answered, he said, "Good morning Alex, this is Julian and how are you this morning?" "I'm fine," I replied. I went on to say, "I will admit that I am surprised that you actually remembered my number." Julian hesitated for a moment then softly said to me, "Beautiful lady, one thing you will come to know and trust about me is that I am a man of my word." After the positive recoil I experienced, I told him how much I appreciate a man with integrity. We exchanged small talk that resulted in an offer I could not refuse.

He said, "Alex, what are your plans for the day?" I told him that I had not made any plans other than to spend the day hanging around the house relaxing. Miss Jesus Sandals said, "Even if you had made plans, you would have cancelled them at any cost. Desperation and impulsiveness is never good, Alexandria." Julian's offer was so appealing to all of my senses. He said, "Well, I'd love for you to spend the day with me. I thought that we could really get to know each other more today, being that I rarely have a Saturday off. I'd like to begin our day together with a hearty breakfast, then maybe a morning stroll through Independence Park, and after that, we'll grab a world-renowned Philly cheese steak sandwich at Geno's for lunch. The rest of the day is totally up to you. How does that sound?"

I was momentarily lost for words. I expected him to ask me to go to breakfast, but I was not expecting to spend any additional time with him. I said, "Okay that sounds good. What time should I be ready?" "Is 9:00 am too early for you? Will that give you enough time to be ready?" I didn't tell him that I had been up since the crack of dawn, preparing my best "first-time-eating-breakfast-look-with-him." "Sure, I'll see you at nine." I gave him my address and we hung up. As soon as I had pushed the end button, Miss Jesus Sandals demanded, "Alexandria Morgan! Have you taken leave of your senses? You just gave a total stranger your home address and are about to get in his car to go off to parts unknown!" I shrugged her off, as usual, and busied myself perfecting my look and outfit.

Julian arrived promptly. When I buzzed him through the gate and opened the door, he greeted me with a big smile and extended his hand to me. Inside of his hand was an envelope. "I know we are about to leave, but if you will pop that CD into your player, it will only take a moment." He came in and I did exactly as he asked. What I heard for the next couple of minutes was a beautiful piece of music with lyrics about ME! I didn't know what to say. He said, "It's just a little something I threw together last night after I got home and couldn't sleep." In my silence, I was thinking-Hmm, so he couldn't sleep either? "Thank you so much, Julian. I am beyond impressed. You are so talented." I really wanted to hug him and plant a big one right on his lips, but I controlled myself. Reading my thoughts as usual, Miss Red Pumps said, "Chicken!" We chatted for a moment and headed to breakfast. I must say that from the ride to breakfast until he returned me to my doorstep, I was thoroughly into Julian, his conversation, his presence-everything about him.

We talked non-stop. He made me feel so comfortable. Neither one of us appeared to be guarded when it came to sharing our lives. We sat in the park and talked in-depth about our childhood and families. I shared with him how my father's death had thrown my world into a tailspin at a young age, and he talked about the hurt he continues to experience about being abandoned by his mom, discovering her mental illness, and her later dying as a result of a drug overdose. These conversations took place over the course of the morning, until well after lunch. Around 2:00 pm, Julian brought me home, but only so I could prepare for our evening together. We had planned to go to a *Jazz under the stars* concert at Independence Park that night at seven. Julian warned me not to eat anything, because he was packing a powerful picnic basket for us.

As I floated around the house getting ready, I listened to the tune he had penned for me. The song and the events of the day were just too good to be true. While I was taking a moment to relax, Carmen returned my call. As soon as I picked up the phone, she said, "Hey, Don't ask me about last night! Now, tell me what's going on with you." I quickly responded with, "I don't ask questions when I already know the answer." She said, "Whatever!" I gave her a complete blow-by-blow recap of my meeting Julian and the day we had together up to the point of her call. She listened intently and finally responded, "Well, he definitely sounds like a good catch, but I don't know about musicians, especially those who actually perform in clubs... they tend to be slicksters."

She went on to say, "Alex, you do know that these performers have local groupies and a non-stop flow of women flirting with them, and most of them take advantage of the continuous opportunities. Just proceed with caution." I told Carmen that I heard what she was saying and that I felt that Julian was definitely not like your typical musician. Miss Red Pumps supported my decision to pursue a relationship with Julian. "Alex, don't pay Carmen any attention. After all, the laps on her track record, nobody has ever written a song about her. She's just jealous!" I didn't agree with her about the jealousy part, but I felt that I was right about Julian, so began a relationship that spanned far longer than I expected.

Julian and I initially spent a lot of time together. He worked a lot, and some of our time together consisted of me hanging out at the venues in which he performed. I'll admit that there were lots of times that I would get upset about all the attention he received from the women in these places. Some of the ladies were quite aggressive/borderline inappropriate with their flirtations. At those times, Julian would always introduce me as his lady.

There were several occasions when he would introduce everyone to his lady, "Miss Alex" in the audience as he performed. So that placated me quite a bit, but I still had some concerns as to what really happened when I was not there and he didn't come to my place afterwards. Julian and I had a lot of fun when we were together. There were times when we would be in the park, and we'd play on the playground equipment just like kids. He was usually always in a great mood. Even when we had disagreements, he tended to remain calm and would not allow himself to be lured into a high volume exchange of words with me. Our arguments always stemmed around the women at the lounges or his former relationship with his live-in girlfriend of six years that was also the mother of his deceased son.

There were times when Julian and I would spend time at his loft apartment. I did not like to be there, because I felt like I was in the shrine of two dead people. (One of whom was still physically living). Everywhere one looked in his place was a picture of his baby son or his son and his mother or the three of them. In an odd sort of way, His ex-girlfriend and I looked like we could be from the same family tree. When I asked him her name, he wouldn't tell me. It looked as if his son's nursery was still as it was at the time of his death. When I tried to question him gently about that, he would say, "Alex, I know it may seem weird to you, but that's just a part of me that I'm asking you to accept."

There were nights when I would wake up alone, and I'd find him in the nursery. This happened two years ago, and I felt it was time to put the hurt away. I felt like I could try to deal with the mourning of his son, but the pictures of his ex- girlfriend bothered me. During one of our conversations when I was there I found out that they were still close. He said that they continue to comfort each other when the memories get to be too much to handle alone. I had no idea what that "comfort" involved, but he did say that, sometimes, she would come over to spend time with the baby's things. Miss Red Pumps, Miss Jesus Sandals, and I chimed in unison, "They need some therapy!"

On a rare occasion, when Julian was actually openly talking about their split up, he divulged they could not make the relationship work after the death of their son, because they each blamed each other for not waking up and checking on the child in time. Their whole world seemed to have centered on this little boy. When I asked him why they didn't get married, he said they were going to, but everything changed the moment that little baby took his last breath. As frustrated as this situation made me, I still felt sorry for them. In my heart, I believed that they had continued to find solace in each other's beds from time to time, but I felt that they had stopped since our relationship began.

When it came to the "groupies," I could pretty much contain my displeasure with their flirtatious antics, except when they came from women who made it obvious that they knew Julian really well. He got frustrated with me and gave me the silent treatment every time I would try to delve into the details of his involvement with other women, including his live-in. He would say to me, "Alex, I don't ever try to pry into your past, and that is the way I'd like to keep things. It is you that I'm with, and that's all that should matter."

One night during a band break, we were sitting chatting, and this rather attractive woman approached our table. "Excuse me, I don't mean to interrupt." "Sure you don't," Miss Red Pumps interjected. The intruder continued with, "but Julian, I somehow lost my song you wrote for me, and I was wondering if you still have a copy you could give me. You know how much I love it." She looked at me and smiled and stood there waiting for him to reply. Smoke was billowing out of my ears and streaks of lightning were being ejected from my eyes.

Before I could say anything, Miss Jesus Sandals, to my surprise, said, "Now, Alexandria, this is one time you are truly being disrespected-don't be a pushover!" I placed my hands on the table about to get into my confrontational stance when Julian stood up. "Paula, I don't know what game you are playing tonight, but I don't appreciate it. I will not allow you to disrespect me or my girlfriend." As he was talking, he took hold of her arm and began leading her away from the table. I spoke up. "No! Julian, where are you going?" He turned and gave me a no-nonsense look. "I'm only making sure that Paula finds her way to the door. I am not leaving. I'll be right back." She again looked at me and smirked as they both walked away. I sat there steaming! Carl, one of the band members, came over to me. "I just saw what happened. That girl has always been trouble, but you don't have to worry Alex. Julian is not interested in her. That was one of his mistakes that shows up to haunt him now and then." His attempt to make me feel better did not work.

Julian returned rather quickly from his mission. He looked different somehow. I took it as his "I'm pissed, but trying to act civilized look." He sat down and looked and me. "Alex, I apologize for that. As Carl told you, she is someone I used to date, and she continues to have issues with us not being together. I don't want this to affect us. Please don't let it do that." At that moment, I wanted to slap his face off! I stood up and looked down at him with a piercing stare that was sharp enough to saw him in half. "Julian, I have been such a fool," I began, "Here I am thinking that I'm so special that you wrote a song just for me, and I have to find out like this that writing songs for women is just your M.O. for manipulating your way into their hearts and beds."

My venom then became deadly. "Even your band partner just told me that she is just ONE of your mistakes. God only knows how many of us you have swooned with your music and your looks. You are no different than any other musician whore." Miss Red Pumps said, "Now finish him off with that cold drink in his face, and make your grand exit. He deserves it!" Miss Jesus Pumps screamed in my ear, "Alexandria! You've said enough and made your point; now leave with class!" As I was picking up my purse, Julian grabbed my hand and tried to stop me saying, "Alex please don't leave. As insulted as I am by what you just called me, I want you to know the facts. Please stay until after my set, and we'll get coffee and talk." I yelled at him, "Shut up Julian! I know the facts. They just hit me in the face!" I made my exit at that point.

◆

I fumed all the way home and did not hear from Julian that night or for many nights to come. I was trying to convince myself that it did not matter. Truth be told, I missed him. I missed his calming presence, his sense of humor, and his putting in tracks serenading me upon request. I kept busy during that time with my job. In fact, I had preparation for a big career fair coming up in a week to keep me occupied. It was during that Career Fair that I ran into Carl. He approached me with caution, but did so nonetheless. "Alex, Julian ripped me a new one about the comment you told him I made, and I want to apologize for even opening up my mouth. I just didn't want Paula to be victorious in her effort to cause Julian some drama. It's not a secret that Julian has dated and gone out with a lot of women, but let me tell you this…he is not sleeping with all of them."

I interrupted him saying, "Look Carl, I know Julian has probably put you up to this, but save your breath." Carl responded with, "That's not true, Alex. Julian is not the kind of person to play games, and he has no idea that I'm at this fair job hunting. Listen, if you will just have lunch with me and talk about this situation, then I promise you that I'll be done with this whole thing." I reluctantly agreed to go to lunch with him, because my curiosity got the better of me.

Once we were seated across the street at the bistro, Carl began saying, "Alex, Julian is really a great guy. He's just someone who has experienced a lot of hurt and disappointment in his life and to try to cope with these unresolved feelings, he turns to his two vices." He continued, "I always tease him by saying, dude you need to stay away from the two "W(s)," one of them is going to get the best of you one day." He went on to answer my unspoken question by telling me that the two "W(s)" were women and weed. When I heard him say weed, it took everything I could do to control my outward response.

I didn't want him to know that I knew nothing about Julian having "weed" issues, although a bell went off in my head, because I had always wondered about his scent. He wore one of my favorite colognes, Abercrombie and Fitch, but it smelled different on him. The strange thing was that it was a scent that, though different, I liked. I have spent countless night nestled in the warmth of the fragrance. And now I find out that I was enjoying the odor of Abercrombie, Fitch, and marijuana! How naïve can one person be? I guess it's because I'd had little to no exposure to the drug scene. I think Taylor may have experimented, but he did so in a land far away from his mother! According to Carl, Julian smoked weed quite frequently, but he did not consider his habit to be out of control or anything that should concern me. Although I can say I have never seen him partake of his weed and have not smelled it in his home or mine when I was present, I now know why the fire escape outside his loft is one of his favorite spots to relax. My jury is still out on this situation.

Carl went on to say, "Growing up without his mother and not knowing much about her until he was told she was dead and they were going to her funeral is a deep emotional wound for Julian. His dad did a great job raising him and his brother, but it's the older brother who seems to have the better relationship with Julian's dad. His dad makes it obvious of how proud he is of the other brother, but has repeated over and over that Julian is "just like his mom" chasing the streets and pipe dreams. Therefore, the Grand Canyon exists between them. Julian is one smart guy, and few people, except those fortunate to be his IT customers, know this. He can take a computer apart and put it back together and create software and apps to meet his client's needs upon request. That's really how Julian makes his real money, but music is his love!"

I knew he had computer skills that he's used on the side, but nothing to this magnitude. Carl finished by saying, "Julian is someone

I trust and know I can count on. Sure he has his quirks, but don't we all have a few?" Although I was sitting there barely eating my food, Carl had managed to wolf his down in the process of his informative speech. I said to him, "Okay and now for the other "W." At that point, Carl dropped and shook his head while grinning. "Alex, Julian is a tall good looking talented man who does something that puts him in front of a lot of females. He has a voice unmatched and can make a piano talk, so other women find him attractive and irresistible, just like you did. They also see that eye-catching long hair, light green eyes, and that smile. When they hear the voice that comes out of that package, they become smitten, just as you were." What could I say at that point? Everything he said made logical sense, and I admitted that I understood the mega attraction women felt.

Carl stated that he wanted it to be clear that I wasn't thinking that Julian went after every woman who batted her lashes at him. He stressed that "Julian's biggest problem is that he does not like being alone" and that gets him into trouble sometimes. Since his relationship ended with Fran, his son's mother, he's only been in a couple of relationships, and one of those is you." I was expecting that. He went on to say, "He is and has been so different with you. Being with you has turned his frown upside down and I, for one, was glad." I told Carl I appreciated him telling me all of this and that I knew what he was trying to do, but the fact that Julian deals with the kind of women who make public scenes, while revealing a common trick of Julian's -the personal CD - was more than any woman should tolerate.

Carl responded with, "Alex, I'll admit that thing with Paula was off the charts, and yes, she is one of a few dingbats with whom Julian has found himself entangled. Also, that personal song thing was blown way out of proportion. Paula begged Julian to write a song for her for her birthday, and he did just that. The song he wrote for her could be dedicated to my grandmother. That's just how generic it was. The only thing personal about it was he called her name in it…. that's it!" I sat there dumbfounded thinking, "Boy, did Paula score a big one on me!" I caught myself and refused to succumb to almost being apologetic for my actions. "Carl, I've got to get back to the fair.

It should be Julian sitting here talking to me, not you. In fact, I have not heard from him since that night."

Carl immediately said, "The sad thing is you probably won't hear from him. He's withdrawn into his world of disappointment. Losing his mom, child, Fran, and now you- has him in overload, but if I know him, he'll emerge from his cave with some dynamite music. In fact, he's been contacted by a music producer who is trying to hook him up with M. Brenae to pen a ballad for her. Now, he had my attention. M. Brenae is a vocal powerhouse and rapidly monopolizing the Billboard charts. Carl went on to tell me that Julian actually had a meeting with her and her team, and he is considering saying no to the collaboration. I think it goes beyond the meshing of their music that's affecting his decision. You see, M. Brenae is quite smitten with Julian and making it known every chance she gets.

She is not one who takes no easily. Carl ended his speech with, "Alexandria, I'm afraid if you guys don't get your act together, the music carrot she's dangling before him, along with other things, may give her the upper advantage with him." I immediately asked him, "Is that a threat that Julian sent you here with?" Carl responded in an exasperated tone, "For the last time, Alex, Julian is innocent in knowing that I am here. I understand that you were embarrassed and highly annoyed by that stupid girl's behavior, but none of that had to do with Julian being unfaithful or purposely disrespectful to you. This guy is like my brother, and I love him and don't like it when he's hurting, but I understand your viewpoint too." Carl rose to his feet as he ended with, "Just know what you are giving up if you end things with Julian." I heard nothing after that because I was in a sea of confused emotions-drowning!

After a long-term mental debate and several "I told you so" conversations with Carmen, I decided to stop by the club one night in hopes of seeing Julian. Actually Vince, my co-worker, and I agreed to meet there for drinks. Vince just told me directly, "I'm not stupid! I know you are using me as smoke screen tonight, but since my social life is in the ditch right now, I'm game." He was right. Julian had heard me talk about Vince, the player, before and had actually met him during one of our staff's holiday events. We arrived at the club early and got a great seat at the bar...the seat that gave me a birds-eye-view of the keyboard player. Miss Jesus Sandals was alive and alert and as usual telling me, "Alexandria, please leave well enough alone. This guy is really nice, but he has some issues!" Miss Red Pumps cleared her throat. "Newsflash everyone, we've all got issues-so do you! So what's your point?"

I ignored their banter and turned as I heard the band start. Carl bowed an acknowledgement in my direction, but Julian obviously having seen me, diverted his eyes and fixated them on a distant place right inside the lounge. He played beautifully, as usual. At the break, he and Carl were making their way through the crowd, headed in my direction. I jumped down from my stool and opened my arms to hug Julian. Carl took the lead and hugged me first, followed by Julian. His embrace was warm and wonderful and oh so familiar. I inhaled his scent and all was well. At that point, I didn't care what ingredients were included in the scent.

Julian was actually wearing that gorgeous long hair of his loose, out of the normal ponytail, which made him even sexier. He spoke first. "Hi Alex, how are you doing this evening? It's a pleasant surprise to see you here. I hope you enjoy the show. Now, if you will excuse me, I have to get some music for my next set. It was great seeing you." I managed to say, "Okay, Julian it was good seeing you too" as he walked away. Carl shrugged. "Give him time." Vince looked at me as I returned to my seat and said, "When there's trouble in Paradise, life just ain't no fun, honey! Let's have another drink and let's make them doubles." Vince and I finished our drinks and left in the middle of the last set. I was not having a good time. I had even sat there and fallen prey to trying to look around the audience and locate Julian's new love interest. If I had been certain that one was there, I would have probably clawed her eyes out. "That's my girl," Miss Red Pumps cheered.

A couple of weeks went by after that night and Julian called. He wanted to do lunch the next day. I agreed and got busy preparing for my re-entry into the world of Julian. He picked me up, with flowers in hand, and we went to Geno's for old time's sake. During lunch, we made small talk, and as we were leaving he said, "We could both use some exercise after those big sandwiches, so let's get some." I asked him just what he had in mind. He told me that since both of us were dressed in comfortable clothes with tennis shoes, today would be a good day to do the museum. I agreed.

When we got to the front of the Philadelphia Museum of Art, Julian grabbed my hand and motioned towards the steps saying, "Come on, Alex, let's do the steps the Hollywood way!" I looked at him. "Neither you nor I are Sylvester Stallone." Besides, that was just a movie. After a lot of pretentious pouting and whining, I said, "What the heck, let's try it!" We looked at each other and sprinted for the steps. Both of us made it three-fourths of the way up and collapsed panting for breath and laughing at the same time. As long as I have lived in Philadelphia, I have never even considered trying to re-enact that scene from *Rocky* that was filmed on the steps to the historic museum. We sat down right there and talked for a while. He looked into my eyes. "Alex, I miss you, but I don't know what I want to do about it.

That night in the club opened my eyes to see the real me and what a mess I tend to make out of others' lives. I've got to re-group my thoughts and feelings before I will be the complete man you need me to be. Right now, I feel so fragmented." I replied with, "I'm sure that Carl told you about our conversation, and I want you to know that there is no pressure for anything regarding us. Take all the time you need. I understand." He reached over and hugged me, but it felt more platonic than anything else.

My heart and mind tells me that Julian really cares for me, but I'm not sure if his feelings for me can ever be strong enough to overcome his past. During one of the many times that we've been together since the scene in the club, I did apologize to him for calling him such an awful name. I told him I had allowed my jealousy to get the better of me, which to me was a big clue that I care deeply for him. He told me he understood. During this date, I noticed that Julian's taste in music seemed to have broadened. He had always shown himself to be strictly a jazz enthusiast, but I couldn't help but notice that his entire playlist in his car were M. Brenae songs. When I casually asked him about that, his response was, "Oh M. and I are in negotiation about a music venture, and I am familiarizing myself with her flavor and spirit before I decide."

Before I could respond, he continued with, "Alex, can you imagine how much my life will change if I go on tour with THE M. Brenae?" Seeing the faraway look of happiness in those beautiful eyes, just over the mere thought of this possibility, hit me in the heart like a brick. I quickly recovered. "Yes, Julian that would be the break you've always dreamed of-hopefully, you'll remember li'l old me when you make it to the top." After looking at me intensely for what felt like minutes, Julian quietly said, "Lady, if you only knew!" "Knew what?" asked Miss Jesus Sandals, "That you are too self-absorbed to see that you are breaking a woman's heart?" she ended. The thought of him in a merger with M. Brenae, which would involve lots of travel and togetherness, gave me so many mixed emotions-with sadness being the dominant emotion.

I have been back to hear him play at several venues and just as to be expected, the women were moving and grooving to the sound of his voice only. There have also been times that I have observed more than casual interaction with a couple of the ladies, but I held my peace. After all, Julian and I are no longer in a committed relationship. Once or twice he'll call me after he gets off and ask me if he could come over, and I know what those times mean. It means that Julian is trying desperately to avoid being alone with his memories, and he's not wanting to fill this void with another empty physical encounter.

The fact that he comes to me is special to me. My question to myself is whether this man can ever successfully move forward with his life. The ghosts of his past are winning the mental and emotional war he's fighting. The strange thing is, with all the baggage that Julian still carries, I seem to find a way to justify his actions, which tells me that my feelings run deep for him. I just don't know if I can ever come to terms with sharing him with the ghost of his deceased baby and the lifetime involvement (including what I suspect is physical comfort) he seems to allow with his child's mother. Miss Red Pumps and Miss Jesus Sandals are quiet on this one. When I want their input.... I get silence! Crap! But, oh my! How quickly things can change, when you are just minding your own business-walking to work and...

# CHAPTER 7
## ◆ DANNY ◆

**Age**: Thirty

**Occupation**: Retail Delivery

**Marital Status**: Divorced for four years at the time of our meeting

**Children**: none

**Family Background**: Next to the youngest child of six children. He has two brothers and two sisters older than him. He is the product of a single parent home. He was raised by his mother and grandmother. He's only seen his father a couple times in his life. The last time he saw his father, Danny was sixteen years old. He believes his dad is serving a long-term sentence in prison, but no one has ever confirmed it. He and his brothers share the same father, but his sisters are the product of a different relationship. He is close with his family. His close-knit family is one of the things I like most about him.

**The Details**:

Danny is …well…. Danny seems to be my Achilles heel. I say this to mean that I have and will always have a weakness for him. He is one of the sweetest, yet exciting, guys I have ever dated. If anyone had ever told me that I would give Danny the time of day, I would have argued until the end of time. Danny is a short (5'9") muscular, cute as pie, VH1 video looking kind of guy. He is

100 percent man in every sense of the word, yet sweet as honey. As you can tell, I have a real thing for him, and the feelings are mutual.

I met Danny on the sidewalk outside of my office building one beautiful Monday morning. I was returning from my usual dash across the street to pick up my custom ordered cup of java, when something grand caught my attention. Going up the walkway in front of me was a man carrying two of those water cooler jugs- one on each shoulder. Every part of his body that possessed a muscle was on display. From behind, his back muscles and broad shoulders was a sight to behold, not to mention the bulging arms that were holding the bottles in place.

I was totally in a trance, following him up the walkway toward the front doors. I believe, if he had walked right off a cliff that morning, I would have walked right off behind him and died with a smile on my face. Miss Red Pumps was awake and checking things out, as usual. "Hmm, Hmm, Hmm- what a man! What a MAN! That's enough to make me come down off your shoulder to give him a run for his money!" I laughed. Miss Jesus Sandals must have still been asleep, or was it that even SHE couldn't trust herself to speak? I'm sure she doesn't want to risk tainting that halo of hers.

As we approached the automated doors, he suddenly paused and turned around to face me. "Good morning, after you." With that, he stepped to the side for me to enter the doors first. I said, "Good morning, and thank you much. It's good to see that there are some gentlemen still around." He smiled. "Well, I try hard. You have a blessed day." "Blessed day?" Gosh, how extraordinary and with an accent to die for! As we entered the lobby, he went directly to the left as I proceeded to the elevators at the back of the building. As the day progressed, flashbacks of that encounter crept back into my head. I shrugged it off and busied myself with preparation for the next meeting, as usual.

I had a pretty uneventful week. I trekked across the street a couple of mornings after that and did not experience a repeat of the visual pleasure I had earlier. On that following Monday morning, I executed my same coffee-run routine without incident. When I'm really early getting to work, I will sometimes sit in the coffee shop and read the newspaper or work on my laptop until time for me to start my workday. I enjoy the aroma of the fresh coffee and the buzz in the atmosphere that is created by the morning flow of customers.

After a couple of weeks of my usual busy, yet mundane life, I walked into the coffee shop carrying my newspaper and laptop, prepared to settle into my morning routine. As I was about to enter the line to be served, someone tapped me on my shoulder. "Miss, your coffee awaits you." I turned, and it was the water cooler guy, sporting the biggest smile and pointing to the table closest to us upon which sat two cups of coffee. I said, "Excuse me." "I know this may appear to be too forward, but I took the liberty of having your coffee ready for you this morning, so you wouldn't have to wait in line, and it would also give us more time to talk." Miss Jesus Sandals was up and on duty saying, "Alexandria, you don't know this man at all; don't accept a pre-ordered drink from a stranger. You don't even know his name. This guy is a real weirdo." What she said made a lot of sense, because it was absolutely true, but though foolish- I followed him to the table and sat down.

I was just staring at him in amazement of just how presumptuous this man was being. He extended his hand. "By the way, I'm Danny and you are?" There was that accent again! I then grasped the strongest hand I believe I have ever felt. "My name is Alexandria." When we finally pulled our hands apart, I could still feel the heat and the lingering pressure of his touch. He never stopped smiling. "I took the liberty of asking the counter person to fix your usual coffee when I saw you walking out of the building." It was as if he read my mind or heard Miss Jesus Sandals, when he went on to say, "It's safe to enjoy your coffee. I only took it from the server and sat it on the table as you were walking in the door, so I didn't put anything in it to hurt you." I took him at his word and opened my cup and started to sip it. Miss Jesus Sandals dropped her head and threw up her hands!

After settling in for what was obviously a morning coffee date, I said, "Danny, how did you know to come here and order coffee for me this morning? What made you so sure that I'd be here?" He laughed out loud. "When you saw me weeks ago, it was not the first time I saw you. I've been admiring you for a while. It just so happened that particular morning we finally ended up in sync on the sidewalk. I had observed your routine." Miss Jesus Sandals said, "Sounds like the mind and actions of a serial rapist or killer to me." Miss Red Pumps came to the rescue. "Sounds like a man who knows what he likes when he sees it and does something about it." Miss Jesus Sandals shrugged. "Insanity at its finest!" Danny went on to say, "You see that I work for a water delivery business and your company is on my route for every two weeks, but the neighboring businesses are on the opposite weeks, so that means I'm in the neighborhood every week."

Listening to Danny talk sounded like his words should be accompanied by some sort of beat. He spoke kind of loud with an aggressive (for lack of a better word) undertone. As I said earlier, everything about him reminded me of one of those video dancers or rappers. He was looking so handsome and impeccably neat. He was wearing a Polo shirt with khakis and Sperrys, and everything about him was clean and crisp. I liked that!

We had small talk while finishing our drinks. Danny had a cup of hot green tea, because he insisted that it is better for your body than coffee. I discovered that he is serious about his health and fitness and the neatness of his surroundings. In fact, the whole time we were talking, he made sure the table was wiped of any spills. We basically held a general conversation about the weather, current events, and my company. It seemed as if both of us purposely kept our interaction light and impersonal. I enjoyed talking to him. He was funny and had such a raw command of the English language. He would use contemporary slang, but in a manner that sounded and felt appropriate. For example, when he agreed with something I said, he responded with, "that's what's up! This was something new for me, but I liked it for some reason. The time for me to get to work came before we both obviously wanted it to.

Danny and I were having a good time just hanging out over coffee. I admired that he had not tried to ask me out or flirt with me during our entire conversation. When I told him I had to run. He said that he understood, and we both rose at the same time. After doing so, he proceeded to remove our cups from the table and took a napkin to wipe of the table before pushing the stools under it. I stood there looking at this, thinking to myself, "What a neat guy!" I meant this literally and figuratively. He reached for my shoulder workbag and placed it on his shoulder as we exited the coffee shop. I thought we were going to say goodbye and part company once on the sidewalk, but instead, he walked me across the street, into the building and bid farewell to me as the elevator doors closed with me inside.

I realized after getting settled in that Danny and I didn't exchange numbers or any personal information. In fact, surprisingly, he didn't ask me for my number. I wrote the whole morning off as just a nice time shared with my new buddy. Inside, I was hoping to have a repeat of this morning one day soon. The week passed and with some concentrated effort, I put the coffee "meeting" on the shelf in my mind. I called Carmen that weekend and managed to ease Danny into the conversation. She said, "Sounds like someone who may be a lot of fun, but it doesn't seem as though it's too promising because he didn't ask you for your contact information." "Yes I know," I replied. We both agreed that seeing Danny was just a bleep on my relationship radar. Carmen, on the other hand, was actually seeing someone she referred to as my "friend" that was seemingly slowing her dating pace. She was unusually quiet about him and tried to avoid all of my inquiries. "Alex, give it a rest. You know me. If I was even considering being monogamous with someone and becoming serious…you would be the first to know." I simply responded with a quiet, "If you say so." We agreed to do a visit soon

Monday morning came, and I found myself taking greater pain in getting myself ready that morning. I found the cutest little outfit that I could find and still maintain my professional appearance. I walked slowly across the street toward the coffee shop. In my mind, my slow pace was an effort to give Danny time to get my coffee on the table, because I could tell it was fairly crowded. As I entered the shop, I began to scan the place as if I had a laser beam that would beep once it located Danny. Well, to my disappointment, he was not there. I got in line and ordered my coffee and sat down and pretended to read the paper. I got frustrated with my pretense, so I decided to return to the office to get my day started.

I made my way across the street, entered the building, and

joined some co-workers at the elevator who were headed to my floor. We laughed and made small talk as the elevator climbed to the eighteenth floor. When the doors opened, to my surprise, there stood Danny holding the cutest bouquet of Gerber daisies. Everyone on the elevator appeared to have frozen in the moment with me. He broke the silence and awkwardness by saying, "Good morning every-one-especially you, Miss Alex" Everyone responded to his greeting as we exited the elevator. I was the last to get off. I was greeted again with a "Hi, Miss Alex" and a kiss on the cheek. I responded by saying, "Oh My goodness, Danny, how did you find me? This is so special and so sweet." He was smiling from ear to ear and responded with, "Well, Miss Alex, I was late getting to the coffee shop this morning, so I decided to dash to the flower peddler on the corner and then beat you to your floor." "But how did you figure out my floor?" I asked. "Are you forgetting that I'm a delivery man for this building and I've got connections on each floor and that's what's up." I took the liberty to hug him at that point. I later realized that someone watching from the sidelines would have thought that we were a couple with quite a tenured relationship.

Danny and I chatted for a few minutes, at least, until we realized that we had to get to work. He told me he had to run back home and change clothes before starting his route. I had already noted that he was looking awesome as usual. He was always clean and crisp and upbeat. Just being in his presence lifted my spirits. Miss Jesus Pumps interrupted my moment of positivity by interjecting, "Alex, this Danny guy, as cute and physically pleasing to the eye as he may be, is obviously not your usual type, and there's still something weird about him." I ignored her as usual.

Danny was about to enter the elevator when it hit me that, in spite of all of his obvious efforts to express his interest in me, he had not inquired about contacting me or asking me out. Miss Red Pumps, hearing my thoughts said, "Girl, his technique definitely needs some tweaking, but his fineness makes up for the deficit. Stop kidding yourself. You want more- so go for it. Ask for his number." "Don't do it, Alex!" shouted Miss Jesus Sandals, "When a man really wants to contact you, he asks for your number. Slow down and get your hormones under control girl." I quickly said, "Hey Danny-wait! Since we're both in a hurry this morning, let me give you my number, so we can talk later." He looked at me for a minute and then grinned. "Okay, cool!" I grabbed a Post-It pad from the receptionist's desk and jotted down my home and cell numbers and handed it to him. He looked at the paper and then at me. "That's what's up, Miss Alex." After Danny had left, Miss Jesus Sandals just could not resist drawing my attention to the fact that Danny did not offer nor give me his contact information.

A week passed before I heard from Danny. He had not shown up at the coffee shop nor called. When I answered the phone that evening, he said. "Miss Alex, are you ready?" I wasn't quite sure to whom I was speaking, because the caller ID indicated caller unknown. As if he read my mind, he said, "It's Danny. You wanna go skating with me?" I was taken back, because this invitation came without any pretense of small talk. I started to think like Miss Jesus Sandals for a minute. I reminded myself that this guy was quite ballsy to call me for the first time and take for granted that I would go somewhere with him. But...he was right! Without any questions or chatter, I said, "Sure Danny, I'll go!" "Cool, meet me at the Palace in about an hour. Okay?" "Sure, I'll see you there."

I hung up and quickly busied myself selecting the cutest skating outfit I could put together, all the while ignoring Miss Jesus Sandals carrying on in my ear. I intentionally arrived at the Palace a little early to allow myself some "oh you caught me off guard looking sexy" prep time. I walked in, and the place was quite crowded, and the rink was filled with bodies in various strides skating in a circle to the beat. I moved around, checking things out, swaying to the music as I walked. I took the liberty of renting my skates ahead of time and throwing them across my shoulder, I found a spot alongside the rink to wait for Danny.

As I was standing there watching the activity, someone caught my eye sitting at a rink side table on the other side of the room. It was Danny, but something was different. He was sitting there smiling as usual, but something wasn't quite right. I made my way around the rink, never taking my eyes off of him. As I managed to get past the crowd, I got a clearer view of him. My heart stopped! There sat Danny at a table smiling, but in a wheelchair! My tennis shoes became concrete blocks-unmovable, even as other people brushed past me. I must have stood in this position for quite some time when all of a sudden, I heard from behind me. "Hey Alex, I've been looking for you. I'm glad you made it." I turned around, and there was Danny standing right there in front of me smiling.

Miss Red Pumps and Miss Jesus Sandals were gaping at each other in disbelief as I was staring at Danny with my mouth open. He said, "What's wrong, Alex?" I couldn't respond. I quickly whipped my body around to do a sanity check. Danny started laughing and said, "Oh, I didn't know he had come around here. Come on, let me introduce you to my brother." He grabbed me by the hand and pulled my numb body along with him. As we reached the table, the person I thought was Danny starting smiling even bigger and making an effort to extend his hand. His quivering voice said, "Hi Alex, my name is Joseph." Danny quickly said, "Alex, I see that I failed to tell you that I have an identical twin. But as you can see, he knows about you. Joseph is three minutes younger than me." I took Joseph's hand and managed a big smile. "Hello, Joseph, it's good to meet you!" Danny and I joined Joseph at the table.

Joseph was not able to carry on much of a conversation, but he was obviously having a good time being at the rink. He motioned toward the skaters and Danny nodded. With that, he managed to wheel himself closer to the rink. When he left, Danny explained to me that during the final hours of his mother's labor, he became entangled in the umbilical cord and his leaving the womb first cut off the oxygen to Joseph's brain to the point it resulted in him being born with mild cerebral palsy and a seizure disorder. Danny told me that he and Joseph are extremely close and that he spends all of his free time with him. Miss Jesus Sandals said, "Well, Alex, your dude here just scored major brownie points with me-finally." At that point, he asked me if I was ready to skate. I immediately looked toward Joseph, and Danny reassured me that he would be fine. In fact, he told me that Joseph would sit for hours and enjoy the skaters, and he told me to look for Joseph's response, once he saw us on the floor.

Well, Danny and I started to skate and as soon as Joseph saw us, he became so excited and started waving and trying to call out to us. "Dan, Alex, you look beautiful," as we skated over to him. Hearing that, we both laughed out loud, looked at each other, and kissed each other on the lips. We placed our arms around each other's waists and skated for what seemed like hours. Danny was quite the athlete. He performed all kinds of fancy footwork tricks for me, and in my effort to try to mimic him-I fell. He reached down and literally lifted me off the floor up into the air. I imagine, in that position, we looked like a couple of figure skaters. To say the least, I had a wonderful time that day with Danny and Joseph. We all had pizza and cokes before leaving. Danny had to help Joseph a lot, because sometimes, his spasms make it almost impossible for him to feed himself, although he did manage to do so to some degree.

Joseph kept trying to apologize to me for his spills and, most of all, for the times he drooled a little bit. I kept trying to assure him that I was not bothered at all. I walked with them outside to Joseph's van and waited as Danny got Joseph settled in and turned on the music. Danny then walked me to my car and told me what a great time he had. He also asked me what I thought about Joseph. I wasn't expecting that question, but my response was that I really enjoyed meeting him and hanging out with him and that I really thought that Joseph was exceptionally handsome. Danny said, "Oh really? But he looks just like me." I smiled. "My point exactly." "That's what's up, Miss Alex." Danny responded and pulled me to him and kissed me. When I say he kissed me, I mean he kissed me in every sense of the word kiss- right there in the parking lot.

Needless to say, I was quite smitten from that point on. Miss Jesus Sandals said I fell madly in lust from that point on. Danny and I became quite the pair, or should I say the trio, because all of our time together included Joseph. I didn't mind that. "Sure you don't," Miss Red Pumps would say. "You know that you want more alone time with this man, instead of babysitting and entertaining his brother." At the risk of sounding shallow, many times, I find myself saying to myself, "Alex, you could definitely do better than this relationship with a man AND his brother" or "It sure would be nice to spend time with my man ALONE." As soon as one of these thoughts enters my head, I correct myself, because Danny is awesome and so is Joseph. I find myself enjoying Joseph's company a lot, because he is always so positive and encouraging. I don't think I have ever seen him down or frustrated. It is Joseph who comes to mind when I'm having a bad day or find myself sweating the small stuff.

Now, don't get me wrong; there were times when Danny and I were alone, with and without Joseph. When Joseph accompanied Danny to my place, we spent the initial part of the night watching movies and playing cards with him, but once he took his meds after dinner…he was down for the count until morning. It was in these stolen moments that Danny and I shared some of our best intimate times. During some of these times, I have had the privilege of learning just how sound Joseph sleeps, because we have unintentionally tried to break the intimacy sound barrier on several occasions, and Joseph did not hear a thing.

Miss Red Pumps reminds me during these times that, "You go girl. It's nothing like having a man that lets you know in more ways than one that he's… in the room!" She is such a force to be reckoned with at times. Miss Jesus Sandals had been quieter than usual during my time with Danny. I believe her silence is mostly due to Joseph. Carmen always says this experience is giving me a first- hand look at what it would be like to marry a man with a child.

Dating Danny and Joseph, though trying at times, has been good for me. Danny keeps me on my toes as far as my health/fitness and neatness is concerned. He is quite OCD about all three of these things. Even though there are times when his obsession with order and routine drives me nuts, it makes me a better person in the long run. When he's at my place, he is constantly wiping and swiping at something, and every morsel of food, dirt, and meal residue must be non-existent after a meal BEFORE he can move on to the next thing on the agenda- including me. This guy vacuums and does laundry every day. The first time I visited Danny at his place (or shall I say his mom's place), it was not what I expected. The whole house was in chaos, except for the "wing" that Danny and Joseph lived in. I guess

I did forget to mention that Danny lived at home with his mom to take care of Joseph.

Danny's mother was an awesome woman. She was very warm and personable and a wealth of support and encouragement for all who crossed paths with her. She was forthright in her interaction with everyone, and if you looked up the phrase "no-nonsense" in the dictionary, you would see her picture. Miss Jesus Sandals was impressed with her, except for the cluttered living environment that she created in her home. She readily acknowledged her cluttered, chaotic surroundings, but quickly warned anyone and everyone that, "This is my house and this is how I choose to live in it, so either accept that or don't come in." Every time I walked through her door, Miss Red Pumps would say… "I understand why that poor man of yours is the way he is…he was raised in a landfill." Miss Jesus Sandals would readily come to her defense by saying, "Stop judging this woman; she's happy, and that's all that matters. It's not hurting anyone, including Xandy." How quickly Miss Jesus Sandals forgets her judgmental tirades. She suspected Danny of being a serial killer or rapist…remember?

Danny's grandmother was truly the "godmother" of this clan. Her name was Edna, and she was nice, but quite a force to be reckoned with. The first time I met Ms. Edna, she didn't hug me like Danny's mom. She looked at me over her glasses. "So you are the little woman that's got Daniel walking around here in la-la land…huh?" "That boy hasn't been the same since he met you. He's been better honey!" I realized I had been holding my breath ever since she started to talk to me, and then realized I could actually exhale. She constantly made comments about Eve's (Danny's mom) poor housekeeping skills, while praising her for everything else.

This was a close-knit family. When all the pickup trucks with the gun racks in the back and minivans arrived with all the siblings and nieces and nephews, it was never the possibility for a dull moment. I don't know if growing up in Brooklyn had anything to do with their "carrying-on" or not. By the way, Danny, all of his siblings, and his mother are named after people in the Bible, and religion played a huge role in their family. Danny and Carmen would have really made a good connection, because there was no such thing as missing a Sunday worship service and the family feast that always followed at Ms. Edna's house.

Attendance at both places was mandatory. One Sunday, I was late getting to church after everyone else was seated and service was underway. I eased in the back and sat on the last pew. Ms. Edna stood up with her hat of crimson flowers and motioned for me to come forward to take my rightful place between Danny and Joseph. As I was walking down the middle of the aisle, Miss Red Pumps was laughing and saying, "Child, I sure hope your skirt ain't caught up in your thong or nothing, because all eyes are on you from head to toe!" Miss Jesus Sandals countered with, "That sounds like something old Miss Red Pumps would enjoy-tug your skirt a little Xandy, just to be on the safe side!"

On several occasions, I tried to get Danny to accompany me to St. Louis to visit Carmen, and he always refused. Danny and Carmen got along really well. Carmen fell for him when she first met him, although she said he was way too short for her liking. She never failed to remind me of how fine and well- dressed he was and that he had a great smile. Coupled with the fact that he was an every Sunday churchman…I was not surprised when Carmen asked me if I thought Danny was going to be my husband. My response to her was, "Girl, you'd walk down the aisle with me to marry Adolph Hitler if he was tall, had a pretty smile, and went to church every Sunday!" She threw her flip flop at me. "You forgot one thing on the list, Ms. Smart butt-he's got to be able to curl those toes and make them eyeballs roll back in your head too-on a regular basis!" "Carmen, you need Jesus!" I responded. Ms. Jesus Sandals mumbled, "You can say that again!"

Aside from trying to get Danny to go with me to visit Carmen, I tried also to get him to go on a couple of my recruitment trips. He always said no. When I finally asked him for his reason, he told me that he did not want to leave Joseph's care solely on his mother. I quietly reminded him of his other siblings and older nephews, who could help his mom; he responded with, "That's not their responsi-bility." Once, when I was at his mom's house, Ms. Eve said to me, "Alexandria, I heard Daniel telling Hannah that you had asked him about going out of town with you to one of those nice resorts you are always going to. I told her to try to convince him to go, because the Lord knows that man could use a nice break." I told her he said that he had to take care of Joseph. Her response was, "I know. I know." She went on to say that, "Daniel has left Joseph only one time in recent years, and wouldn't you know it? When he got back from that deep sea fishing trip with his brother, Isaac, he found out that Joseph had to be taken to the hospital for a mild seizure; he cried like a baby and hadn't left him since."

At that point, she got up, looking like she had aged ten years in the last ten seconds, and went to the kitchen and called me in there to share a piece of cake and coffee with her. I sat with her, but passed on the food, because I have a hard time eating anything out of a kitchen where there is no space on the counters, walls, or table. Miss Red Pumps said, "Alex, this woman is not just a holy roller; she's a holy hoarder and don't even know it!" It's such a shame, because I really like her and her company. It's just her house that gives me nervous tics. "Me, too," said Miss Jesus Sandals. "This place makes me want to trade in my sandals for some wading boots that cover my whole feet and legs!" What's funny is...her house doesn't look totally dirty; it just looks like a junk pile. I guess that's what makes Danny so obsessive. The homes of the other siblings that I visited were middle of the road between Miss Eve's and Danny's extremes.

Danny and I became so close. We did a lot of things together, and I went so far as to take my family over to Miss Edna's house for the Sunday afternoon circus-oops! I meant family gathering. I would have never taken my mom, aunt, and Jeff over to Ms. Eve's house. My mother would have hyperventilated and fainted at the sight of all the magazines, boxes, books, crafts projects, sewing materials, etc., etc., etc. I would have been proud to let her enter Danny and Joseph's area, because it was immaculate. It looked like a whole different planet from the rest of the house. During the mingling of the families, everyone hit it off really well, especially Taylor and Danny's youngest sister, Rachel. I had to pull my obviously hormonal brother to the side and remind him that she is married with kids. Her husband is a long distance trucker and gone most of the time. Rachel flirted, but

I'd bet my paycheck that it would never go any further, because that girl, though young, could rattle off some scriptures that would rival the efforts of Billy Graham.

Jeff and Joseph were quite involved in a video game session. Joseph loved them, although he had great difficulty with the controls…he played them his way, which proved quite entertaining for him and those around him. My Aunt Sandra and Ms. Edna were quite the pair. They spent the whole time arguing back and forth about the state of America's youth these days. Ms. Edna said, "Kids just don't have any parents with sense to teach them how to talk, walk, and dress anymore." And Aunt Sandra was determined to convince her that young people need the freedom to express themselves to avoid all the pent up anger. Ms. Edna said she discovered the solution for pent up anger in young folks a long time ago and that's "the bible and a belt!" Miss Jesus Sandals said, "Let the church say amen" and, of course, Miss Red Pumps said, "That woman is a candidate for death row when it comes to disciplining children…Alexandria, please don't get pregnant by Danny!"

Getting pregnant by Danny would never happen, because Danny had a vasectomy done during his marriage. That was the largest contributing factor to his divorce from his high school sweetheart. He did this without his wife knowing it and later told her during one of their regular arguments about having children. Danny has never told his family about his choice to do this. Other than Joseph, Danny was the only person in the family without children. His oldest sister has five. Comments about his getting married again and having kids are frequently made during family times. He looks at me, but never comments. I smile sheepishly on the outside, but on the inside, my heart is feeling stabbed, because I want, one day, to experience pregnancy and motherhood.

On one occasion, Danny's sister, Hannah, and I were talking alone during one of Ms. Edna's cookouts, and she asked me had Danny and I ever talked about a future together, and I was honest with her and told her no. She said that she was not surprised, because as wonderful as he is- she doesn't think he will ever get married again, and she also said she didn't believe he would ever have kids. I asked her for the reasoning behind her beliefs, and she looked at me and asked, "Can't you see it? Danny has taken on the lifetime responsibility of taking care of our brother, Joseph.

He will never leave him. He lives with mama in order for him to be able to work during the day." She leaned over and whispered, "All of us knows that he feels responsible for Joseph's disability, and he has devoted his life to trying to make up for what he feels was solely his fault. We wish Mama had never told him that the umbilical cord was wrapped around his knees, which caused Joseph to be oxygen-deprived for too long." I looked over at Danny and Joseph, and I had to walk away to hide the tears that had welled in my eyes. Hannah followed me and apologized for upsetting me. She said, "Look, Joseph is my brother and I love him with all my heart, but caring for him can be physically and emotionally tiring. You don't have to say it, and I respect you for that, but I know you get tired of Danny bringing Joseph along for most of your dates and times together. I'm a woman before I'm a sister!" With that being said, she hugged me and walked off.

Later that night, while Danny and I lay on the bed talking, with Joseph snoring in the next room, he picked up on the change in my mood. I wasn't aware I was distant, but he asked me why I was so far away. I turned and looked at him and before I realized it, I said "Danny, where is our relationship going? We've been seeing each other exclusively for a long time now, and you never say anything about the future." He sat up and walked over to the French doors, opened them, and walked out onto the balcony. I didn't follow him. I just laid there until I eventually fell asleep.

I'm not sure when he came back to the bed. He was up bright and early that next morning with my apartment smelling like IHOP. Joseph was dressed and sitting at the table, as I walked up to a table covered with whole grain pancakes, egg white omelets, and turkey bacon, and fresh squeezed orange juice and, of course, green tea. Joseph greeted me with his usual big smile and, "Hey Alex, you look so pretty!" and Danny seconded what he said. I stood there, looking like Medusa in wrinkled gray sweats. That night had not been one of those nights where I put my best foot forward in the looking-cute department. I joined them for breakfast, and needless to say, Joseph was the only person trying to hold a conversation.

After breakfast, I told Danny that I would clean up, because I had a job fair to prepare for, so I was just going to hang out at home all day. He refused to leave until my place was spic and span, including vacuuming, and then he and Joseph left. As always, because my condo is not handicapped accessible, I'd baby sit Joseph in a regular chair, while Danny takes the wheelchair down, and he then would return to physically carry Joseph down the short flight of stairs. As he was leaving with Joseph in his arms, he leaned over and whispered to me, "You are far too special, Alex, for me to complicate your future. And that's what's up." He kissed me on the cheek and left. A rare thing happened as he was turning to leave; Ms. Red Pumps and Ms. Jesus Sandals agreed with him and each other. They both said in unison, "He's right, Xandy." And…Ms. Red Pumps never calls me Xandy.

I called Carmen to talk to her and bring her up to speed on everything that had transpired between Danny and me. After listening intently to me talk and even cry about my feelings, to my surprise, she agreed with Ms. Red Pumps and Ms. Jesus Sandals. That's also rare, because she's usually in sync with one or the other, but never both. By the way…Carmen doesn't know about my two little constant companions. They've been around ever since my father passed. I always tell myself that they were sent to me by my dad, being a man with such an analytical mind…I figured he'd always want me to look at everything from both sides before making decisions. I put every effort into trying to convince Carmen that I could live my life with Danny AND Joseph, but she was not having it. So I came up with the perfect solution to keep what I perceived was the perfect man for me. I was going to show all of my naysayers that what I had for Danny was unconditional. "Please, Xandy, don't do anything foolish" was the only response I got from the audience that sits on my shoulders.

Danny and I continued to spend a lot of time together, and we never talked about the night I brought up the future. The three of us went on picnics, to the movies, to games, and of course, to the skating rink. Nights after Joseph was asleep was still my favorite times with Danny. He was such a generous- though not gentle man (if you know what I mean). "See there, that's the hold he has on you, Missy!" Of course, you know who said that- Miss Jesus Sandals. Things were going really great. I even managed to start having coffee with Ms. Eve. "You are a brave soul," Ms. Red Pumps reminds me each time I take a sip. "I wouldn't be surprised if there were some staples or paper clips in the bottom of that cup!"

One Saturday morning, Danny was about to load Joseph up to take him to the gym with him for his regular workout. I somehow convinced Danny to let Joseph stay with me while he worked out. After all, he'd only be gone for a couple of hours. Danny resisted profusely, but I convinced him to do it. Reluctantly, Danny left, and Joseph and I settled in for a Sponge Bob marathon that morning. About forty-five minutes into our cartoon time, Joseph let out this yelp, and I almost jumped off the couch. I said, "What's wrong, Joseph?" He wouldn't look at me. He dropped his head and said, "I'm sorry, Alex, I'm soooo sorry, Alex." I said, "Sorry for what, Joseph? You can tell Alex." Well, I didn't have to wait for my answer. My nose gave me the answer that I didn't want to receive. Joseph had soiled himself in the worst way. He just sat there looking down, and I sat there frozen! Ms. Jesus Sandals said, "Okay, Xandy, this is reality…you've got to deal with it. He can't help himself." All of a sudden, I was zapped out of my frozen state by a voice from Joseph that I didn't recognize. He still wouldn't look at me, but his voice became deeper and demanding as he said, "I don't like it, Alex. It's on me, Alex." Miss Red Pumps cupped her hands around her mouth and yelled, "Paging Ms. Unconditional!" Joseph started flailing and repeatedly saying, "It's on me; it's on me!" getting louder, without looking up each time. I jumped up and grabbed his wheelchair and started pushing him toward the bathroom. I stopped in my tracks, because I had no idea how to change him. I ran to the room and looked in his bag, and sure enough, it was full of adult diapers.

I grabbed one and ran back to him. I pushed him into the guest room, instead, and managed to get him out of the chair, which was no easy task. I literally dumped him on the bed and immediately thoughts of my destroyed $675 bed ensemble flashed before my eyes and then my tears began to flow. Instead of Joseph being nice and sensitive, he finally looked at me like the exorcist and said… "It's on me!" Ms. Red Pumps said, "Alexandria, stop the madness, and call Danny to come change this man's diaper!" I said, "I got this!" I unbuckled Joseph's pants and managed to pull them down to thigh level. When I did this, the sight and the enhanced odor made me throw up on my bed ensemble. I fell on the bed next to Joseph, and that's where Danny found us—both of us bawling!

Needless to say, things changed after that day. Danny was not angry with me for my failed attempt to provide respite care for Joseph for him. He repeatedly said, "Alex, this is my cross to bear and mine alone. I am not going to ask or expect anyone to share this with me. It's not fair." My efforts to convince him that I did not see Joseph's care as a cross nor a burden did not register in his brain or heart at all. I even went so far as to tell him that I was willing to be professionally trained to care for Joseph. His response to that was, "Alex, I love you because you are a good woman, but I also love you enough to refuse to give you a load that's not yours to carry." He and Joseph and I continued to spend time together, but the frequency changed. Joseph was much quieter around me and didn't actually initiate the fun we use to share. Danny said that Joseph was really embarrassed about that day, and even though he doesn't always remember things-it seems as though that day was chiseled in his memory.

I eventually told Carmen and my mother what had taken place in my efforts to grow closer to Danny by being a caregiver to Joseph. My mother told me, "Alexandria, you can't make someone love you the way you want them to. They can only love you the way they know how, and it seems like Danny's decision not to want a future with you is his way of showing you he really loves you." My mother's analysis really hit me like a ton of bricks, but it was something I did not want to accept. Carmen, on the other hand, was not as gentle in her assessment. She said "Xandy, get a grip! Just what does Danny have to offer you? You are a professional. You are also an accomplished young woman with a six-figure salary and a promising future. This man has no formal education, delivers water for a living, and has a die-hard never-ending attachment to his handicapped brother that supersedes anybody or anything else in his world."

I quickly reminded Carmen to be politically correct by using the term disabled or physically challenged, rather than the word handicapped. To my surprise, Miss Jesus Sandals chimed in and commented, "Alexandria, you know I don't particularly care for that Carmen, but I must agree with her 100%. Danny is a nice guy with a big heart, but you cannot overlook the obvious." My head and my heart were in a monstrous battle over my relationship with Danny. To make matters worse, I had to contend constantly with Miss Red Pumps reminding me of just how fine, handsome, and PHYSICALLY SKILLED Danny is, and the one thing he has demonstrated to me is that he can be counted on to be committed to those he loves.

Danny, Joseph, and I continued to see each other occasionally, but things were different. In our alone time, Danny would rather talk about bottled water or global warming or anything other than our relationship. I cared so much for him. He had had such an impact on my world, although it was privately. Danny didn't care much for mingling with my colleagues or attending business events with me. He called that the "stuffy society." I did everything I could to make him want to be a part of my world, including letting him see some of the texts I got from my female colleagues, telling me how awesome and, not to mention, fine he is. Danny and I had discussed (due to my initiation) the possibility of him going to school. This discussion always ended with him telling me that he never liked school and that he is happy with his life. Plus, going to classes would mean having to rely on his mom more to take care of Joseph and that was not going to happen.

One night, Danny said to me… "Alex, it's not fair for me to occupy so much of your time, especially when you and I want different things in our futures. I just want you to know that it's okay with me if you see other guys." Miss Red Pumps responded before I could. She said, "That sneaky rascal! He has his eyes on another female! And to think I liked his deceitful behind." Her comments fell on my fertile eardrums. I jumped up from the table and told him just to cut to the chase and tell me that he met and wants somebody else. Danny said, "Alex, stop yelling before you wake Joseph. I haven't met anyone. I've just been thinking, that's all." Miss Jesus Sandals adjusted her halo and commented, "Xandy, I believe him. Think about it…he has been honest about not wanting a future with you, even though he feels it's for your own good. So I agree; it's not fair to you for him to monopolize all of your time and attention."

After a moment of reflection, I agreed with Miss Jesus Sandals. Miss Red Pumps stuck to her analysis. She said that no man recommends and condones his woman being with another man, unless he has another woman in the wings. Although I agreed with Miss Jesus Sandals, I still told Danny I didn't appreciate him continuously telling me what was best for me. Needless to say, all three bedrooms in my condo were occupied that night. For the first time, Danny and I parted ways in the hallway.

Even though I occasionally continued to share in Ms. Edna's Sunday feasts…things were not the same. As fate would have it, before I could talk things over again with Danny regarding our distance and dim future…the unplanned happened. As I mentioned earlier that Julian, my mesmerizing musician, would call me sometimes late at night and would come over for a nightcap and familiar company. Well, this particular weekend, I was without plans, except for the possibility that Carmen might stop through on the way back from a Philly rendezvous with her mysterious friend. So…. I made the decision to let Julian come over when he called this rainy Friday night after his gig.

I had not heard from Danny in quite a while, and I was lonely, bored, and needed Julian to take the chill off of me and my mood. He got to my place about 12:30 am with my favorite bottle of wine under his arm and what he described as a big surprise. I poured us a glass of wine, while he fumbled with my CD player. In moments, the room was filled with some of the most beautiful music I have ever heard that included beautiful vocal accompaniment. I listened without speaking and almost hyperventilated when I heard the song he had written for me on this cd, entitled "Only You." I looked at him with my mouth opened. He said, "Xandy, you have just heard my new CD that's slated to take the world by storm. Sony Records is interested in a piece of this rock!" I screamed, "Oh Julian!" and leaped across the floor in his arms. Miss Red Pumps was equally joyous... yelling, "What in the world am I going to wear to the Grammys?" Miss Jesus Sandals quickly responded with, "What about a red strait jacket?"

Julian and I spent a wonderful night together that night with all the trimmings! When we finally woke up late in the morning after a whole bottle of wine and wee hour aerobics...Julian told me he would fix us breakfast, while I hopped in the shower. Unlike my usual rushed showers, I took a long hot shower and gave long overdue attention to my skin. The smell of bacon and fresh brewed coffee filled the air, while Julian's music provided a soothing background for relaxation. I was deep into the thoughts of what a wonderful world it is at this moment, until the voice yelling at me from the kitchen snapped me out of it. I quickly grabbed my sexy little see through robe on the door, wrapped my hair in a towel and barefooted it to the kitchen. As I rounded the corner, I came face to face with Julian standing there, slice of toast in hand, (looking like Michael Bolton dressed only in his boxers) and DANNY! Unbeknownst to Julian, I had given Danny the gate entrance code to simplify things for him and Joseph. Julian knew that Carmen was the only person with the code, other than my mom and brother. So when the knock came at the door, I knew Julian assumed it was Carmen. Well, if there was ever a time in my life that I wanted to be swallowed up by the earth... this was it. Miss Jesus Sandals and Miss Red Pumps screamed at the same time, "Oh my God!"

After what seemed like an eternity, Danny was the first to speak. He said, "Well I see I'm interrupting something, and I apologize. I should have never stopped by without calling." With this being said, both men stood there looking at me, and I stood there with my birthday suit in clear view through the robe and barefooted with my toes frozen in a curl like the Lollipop Twins on the Wizard of Oz. I managed to say, "Danny, Julian, I am so sorry. I don't know what else to say." Danny turned quickly toward the door and said, "You don't owe me any apology or explanation," and Julian said, "Yeah me either," and turned and walked into the bedroom, saying he must get dressed, still with toast in hand. Danny and I looked at each other, not speaking. Miss Jesus Sandals was yelling hysterically on my shoulder, "Alexandria, are you deaf? I've been yelling at you for five minutes to cover yourself!

I managed to reach over and grab my coat off the rack and put it on. There I was, standing there naked, in a Chanel coat, barefooted with a towel on my head, staring into Danny's eyes. Julian emerged from the bedroom fully clothed, stopped to grab the CD out of the player, and hurriedly exited. He said, "Sorry Alex," as he was leaving. Danny turned back to me after staring at the door that closed after Julian and said, "Alex, I never thought you were sleeping with someone this soon. But from the looks of things, this is nothing new. So this must be your "stuffy society" boyfriend, while I'm your charity case. I never thought I would ever say this to you, but even with all of my baggage, I love you, but right now, I want you and your slutty behavior to go straight to hell!" He threw the papers he was holding on the floor in front of me and bolted out of the door. I didn't try to stop him or call after him. Miss Red Pumps quietly said, "Xandy, what in the world is going on?" I picked up the papers, and to my amazement, I saw a syllabus and a graded math exam with the number ninety-eight written in the corner. Danny had been going to college!

# CHAPTER 8
## ◆ JULIAN, DANNY AND EDMUND ◆

Well, it's obvious that, eventually, paths will cross! The scene at my home with Danny and Julian really resonated deep within my soul. I am still reeling from the emotional confusion and guilt from that morning. Not to mention the embarrassment of having my body on display in the midst of the fiasco. Miss Red Pumps had the audacity to remind me, "Girl, are you forgetting that those men didn't see anything that morning that they already hadn't seen?" Miss Jesus Sandals piped in to set the record straight by saying, "Xandy, as unfortunate as this situation was...one thing you are not guilty of is being involved with Danny and Julian at the same time. What you had with Danny had pretty much fizzled out, and Julian's reappearance, though bad timing, was just happenstance."

Miss Jesus Sandals was right. Julian and I never really permanently disconnected. He was allowed to come and go, in and out of my life, whenever it was convenient for both of us. We have a connection that only the two of us seem to understand. His music career is about to soar to major heights, and he wants me to be a part of that. My only question to myself is if I can share Julian with the ghost of his dead child and the woman who once shared that child with him.

Julian and I met a couple of times after that morning we all wanted to forget. Julian admitted he was hurt to be face to face with the current man in my life. He said to me, "Alex, I know you don't trust me because of my career, and I know my continued commitment to Fran bothers you, but neither one of us can deny the chemistry we have and the obvious feelings we have for each other. I admit you inspire me and soothe me like no other woman." My response to Julian took him and me by surprise. I said, "Julian, you forgot to add your drug usage to the baggage I have to consider when it comes to you."

Julian looked at me as if I had two heads and one eye, but he responded calmly with, "Alex, I know my friend Carl told you about me smoking weed, but you never mentioned it, so I thought it was no big deal with you. I try hard not to impose that part of my life on anyone, but that's something I've done since I was sixteen. I seem to write my best music and solve my most complicated computer problems when I smoke." "What about the fact that it's illegal, Julian, and you could go to jail?" I replied. Julian smiled and shook his head saying, "Come on, Baby, let's not over dramatize this. It will be legal, one day, and it's not something that has a negative effect on any part of my life- including you."

In his effort to sway me to agree with legalizing marijuana, he hit me with another bombshell that he thought Carl had disclosed to me. He said, "After the death of my son...I started using cocaine quite heavily to medicate the pain I was in emotionally, but I was eventually able to get myself back on track with weed, instead, and I'm proud of myself for that." Miss Red Pumps quickly said, "What the hell?" Miss Jesus Sandals just threw up her hands and said, "Did he just say he was proud of smoking weed?" Julian and I agreed that some thinking space would be a good idea for us and sealed it with what we do best. Miss Red Pumps said, "Alex, that hair, that body, those eyes, those skills, and most of all, that Grammy potential is an opportunity you are stupid to let go of!" Miss Jesus Sandals said, "Dear Lord, that woman in red truly has no shame, and it's because she has no morals!"

Danny, on the other hand, was not as open to communicating about that morning. The following Sunday after the fiasco, I took it upon myself to show up at Ms. Edna's church, because I knew that Danny and the clan would be there. I got there a little late, and this time, I did not get an invitation to come up front by Miss Edna. Miss Red Pumps whispered, "Well, looks like we've got to sit in the heathen section today, girl." I saw Danny sitting between Joseph and Rachael, and he was holding one of her little boys. My heart melted just looking at how wonderful he looked and how family focused he is. Someone entered the church rather loudly after I was seated, which made many people turn around in their seats to check out the disturbance. Danny turned and saw me in the process. Our eyes locked in what I felt like forever, but then he turned back around, and it was as if he needed security at that time, because he put his arm around his sister, Rachael, and held her close through the service.

Once it was over, the whole family, except for Danny, greeted me with hugs and professions of having missed seeing me. Miss Edna and Ms. Eve came up to me and hugged me saying, "Alex, how are you? It's good to see you. You look so pretty!" At that time, Danny was trying to scoot by inconspicuously, and his grandmother reached out and grabbed him, saying, "Doesn't Alex look beautiful today, Daniel?" Danny, though uncomfortable, said, "Hey, Miss Alex, you do look beautiful this morning and that's what up!" With that, he turned to leave saying, "I'll see you guys at the house, I've got to get Joseph" ignoring his mother, saying that his brothers already had Joseph taken care of. Danny was already gone.

Both of them looked at me and said, "Take care of yourself, baby!" Hannah caught up with me at my car and said, "Hey, Alex, Good to see you. I'm the only one in the family that Danny confided in and told what happened. He's really hurting and has withdrawn into a shell that none of us can seem to penetrate. The good thing is he is totally committed to school and doing well in his studies. I just want you to know that I'm not angry with you. As I've said before, I'm a woman and my brother, as wonderful as he is, promises no woman a future- just the present, and I know you and anyone else wants more. He loves you, Alex. Take care!" She hugged me and left. I cried all the way home.

Danny called me a couple of days later. When I answered the phone, he said. "Just listen to me. I am sorry for what I said to you that morning. I was in a bad place. I remember and realize after I've had lots of time to think that I told you to see other people. I guess I just thought you loved me too much to do it. When I saw that, not only were you seeing someone else, but that you were giving him what I felt was mine too...I lost it. I miss you Alex, and I love you, but I still can't tie you to the burden of me and Joseph and to the fact that I can never father a child. With that said...I don't know what to do with all of these feelings and desires I have for you and you only. I guess time will tell." After a long silence, I said, "I miss you too, Danny, and I am just as confused as you are. I am not confused about my feelings for you, though." Danny interrupted me and said, "But what about him?" I immediately said, "Danny, please don't!" He responded with, "Well, that's what up then. I understand. See you later, Alex."

There was silence on my shoulders. It was at this time I took a week off from my job and went home to Mother. I needed the comfort of my family and my old familiar surroundings. My mother recognized my need without me saying a word. She devoted the entire week to catering to my every whim. My aunt popped in and out, because she was in the throes of a new romance with one of the master gardeners who serviced her greenery during the summer months. It was obvious from the glow on Aunt Sandra's face that more than her greenery was being serviced. The timing of my visit was perfect, because Jeff was away on a month long certification in some kind of new military strategic course. Miss Abigail Morgan and I spent the whole week pampering ourselves and giving in to all of our guilty pleasures.

Taylor brought Joshua down to see me while I was there, but was called back due some kind of account glitch, which cut my fun time with Joshua short. Taylor lived about seventy-five miles north of my mom's home in Benson, so my mother and aunt got to see Joshua quite often. I threw a temper tantrum about Joshua having to leave early, so Taylor shocked me when he asked me if I'd like to be a full time aunt for the summer. He was offering to allow Joshua the opportunity to spend the summer with me. He assured me that it would be fine with Lisa, since she had two other children and a husband vying for her attention these days. This would also free up

Taylor to increase his summer harem, without restrictions. I shocked myself by saying "Yes!" to having my eight-year-old nephew spend the summer with me.

Well, Taylor kept his word and made all the necessary arrangements and when school ended in May, he and Joshua showed up on my doorstep, luggage, sports equipment, and video games in hand. My nephew also possessed every new electronic gadget and gizmo currently on the market. This was all compliments of my mother and Jeff, who both believed that children who are exposed to technology at a young age have a greater advantage as they get older. I believed that everything this boy owned had an apple on it, except for his clothing, which sported its own trendy designer insignias.

Joshua and I quickly made whatever adjustments were necessary to accommodate him during his stay. I had already arranged for Josh to attend the summer cultural arts academy, as well as sports camps at the YMCA, during my work hours. I had even arranged for *Kiddie Kab* to transport Josh back and forth between his activities and home.

I believe Joshua added a much needed piece of sanity to my life. Much to my surprise, even Miss Red Pumps and Miss Jesus Sandals were content. I believe they took a vacation a couple of times during Josh's stay. Miss Jesus Sandals commented on several occasions, "Motherhood really fits you well, Xandy. This child has been suffering in the attention department for a while, and a mother's love and focused attention is what he has been yearning for, and you are doing a wonderful job with him." Miss Red Pumps agreed, but could not resist adding her unsolicited two cents to the end of her comment. She said, "Well, it's not hard doing this kind of job with a child that's only temporarily yours."

Joshua was making quite a name for himself with all of his instructors and had even placed in a small technology fair at the cultural arts center. He had also taken a liking to playing the violin and had asked for one. Wouldn't you know it? Fed Ex showed up at my door one week later with a beautiful violin from his father. Joshua was a natural. His music instructor stated he was already more skilled at playing the violin than a lot of his classmates who had been studying for years. I would hear him at night playing for his father and grandmother via Skype on his laptop.

Josh and I had seen every new movie out and were making our way through all the famous sites in Philadelphia. On several occasions, Edmund had called, and we had gone to lunch together, and during one of these times, I told him about Joshua spending the summer with me. He insisted on Joshua meeting Olivia, and I thought that would be a great idea. Joshua and Olivia hit it off. The four of us began spending a lot of time together. Josh and I would go over to Edmund's house and hang out on the weekend when he had Olivia and Josh and Olivia managed to put together a couple of impressive duets. Olivia's skill on the piano was wonderful.

If she and Joshua were older…one would say they make a perfect couple. Speaking of perfect couple, Edmund and I had begun to grow close again. He doted on the three of us. Being with Edmund was confirmation that I was truly approaching the serious desire for marriage and a family. Edmund's maturity and financial resources make those thoughts appear easy to manage. Edmund still had his moments when he would question my "real" interest in him, and on one occasion, Josh innocently remarked how much he enjoyed an outing he and I had shared with "Uncle Ralph", which only made matters worse.

(For the record…Joshua is quite fond of Ralph and sees him often, because Taylor and Ralph are good friends.) And Yes! I still see Ralph occasionally. He's a hard habit to break. He's asked his wife for a divorce, but they have not progressed to telling their families or seeking legal counsel. When he discovered that Josh was spending the summer with me, he made it his business to come a few times to offer us entertainment opportunities that no eight-year-old could resist, nor the eight-year-old's aunt. Edmund was livid, to put it mildly, when the comment was made, and he got me alone to talk about it. He reminded me of how faithful he is to me, even to the point of keeping great distance between his ex-wife and me, now that we had "reconnected."

I reminded Edmund that I did not see our "reconnection" in the same light that he did. I thought we were just hanging out, having fun with the kids, and taking things one day at a time. He seemed to be quite hurt by my response and hit me with one of his own. "Alexandria, you know I'm the best man for you. I offer you everything a woman could possibly want and more. I don't understand, for the life of me, why you insist on entertaining these losers. I am husband material. They are not." Miss Red Pumps responded with, "My, My, My, Mr. Posh and Pizazz just called all your other suitors -losers! He's definitely not lacking in the self-confidence department. In fact, what department is he lacking in?" Miss Jesus Sandals spoke just above a whisper, "Xandy, your heart knows if he speaks the truth." On that note, I turned and quickly left Edmund standing there, poised for a debate, and gathered Josh and left. All the while- all three voices, Edmund and my two female nuisances, were playing over and over in my head. Feeling as if I was relationally overloaded, I jumped back into my job and returned to being a full-time focused aunt for my adorable Joshua until…

# CHAPTER 9
## ◆IAN◆

**Age**: Thirty-two

**Occupation**: Teacher

**Children**: None (that's not definite)

**Family Background**: Raised by both parents. He is the eldest of two children. He has one younger brother and a younger cousin, who was raised in the household with him as a brother. His mother is a successful physical therapist, and his father is a former army chief warrant officer, currently employed as a security service supervisor. His family dynamics are strange at first appearance. They are not close, but seem supportive of each other's choices and goals. From brief conversations with him about his childhood, he reports some challenges with his parents having separated a couple of times due to what sounded like some alcohol abuse and infidelity issues.

**The Details:**

Meeting Ian began as one of my life's most embarrassing moments. It was a beautiful Wednesday afternoon, and I was in the process of picking up Joshua early from the YMCA, en route to Boathouse Row via Schuylkill Expressway. Joshua and I had planned to take part in an interactive art exhibit for kids in the park and to stay long enough for night to fall, so he could see the famous lighting from our return trip on Kelly Drive. Joshua and I were leaving the registration desk at the Y when he remembered he had left his camera in his locker. I told him to run back and get it, and I would wait for him at the car. Joshua dashed off in the direction of the gym, and I bid the receptionist farewell and headed for the door. The entrance to the YMCA has two sections of stairs leading to the first floor foyer. I was descending the steps rather quickly, knowing that I was looking really cute in my capris, halter, and my Pour La Victoire sandals.

I was about to begin to descend the second set of steps- in fact my right foot was in mid- air, just as I heard Joshua yell, "Aunt Xandy!" I immediately jerked around toward his yell, just before I began to topple head over heels down the steps. One minute, I saw Josh standing at the top of the steps pointing his camera in my direction. The next thing I knew, I was lying flat on my back, looking up into Josh's face, wet with tears, and a caring male face that I didn't recognize. If Joshua hadn't been in the scene, I would have questioned whether I had just opened my eyes in heaven.

I was okay, other than having the breath nearly knocked out of me, and my left leg was scraped and my pants were torn. It was hard for me or the stranger to focus on me, because Joshua was crying inconsolably and apologizing profusely. I was then sitting up on the sidewalk, and poor Josh was wrapped around me like an anaconda. The stranger said. "Are you okay? Don't move I've called for the paramedics to check you out." I hadn't realized he had made a phone call. I guess it was because of my focus on Josh. I assured him and Josh that I was fine, but I did sit tight until the paramedics arrived and checked me out. They told me it looked as though I had a pretty nasty sprain, but wanted to transport me to the hospital for x-rays. I declined the ambulance transport, saying that, since it was my left leg and foot, I could drive myself.

In the midst of all the confusion, the "Y" staff had been summoned. They were so apologetic and expressed genuine concern for my condition and assured me they would cover all of my medical expenses without hesitation. I told them that I had mega insurance coverage and everything would be fine. Well, my strange caregiver volunteered to drive me to the medical center for X-rays. His car was within six feet of where I landed from my fall. He had just pulled up as I was making my landing. In light of the fact that my ankle was really starting to hurt, I accepted his offer. I told Josh to call Vince at my office to grab a ride to come and get my car later. He knew where I kept my spare keys at the office.

The stranger picked me up from the sidewalk and carried me to his car, where Josh had the back door opened and waiting, and Josh jumped in the front seat and away we went. Of course, Miss Jesus Sandals was paranoid as usual. She said, "Alexandria, do you realize that you may have just placed you and your nephew's life in jeopardy by getting in the car with a complete stranger, who is well aware that you are defenseless at the moment?" Miss Red Pumps said, "Shouldn't you be thankful for the kindness of this gentleman and be praying, instead of worrying? I'm beginning to wonder if you don't need a new headpiece!" We arrived at the hospital, and I was wheeled in for x-rays after all the customary questions.

My knight in shining armor was so respectful of my privacy that when he wheeled me up to the desk to begin the process, he stepped outside of the door to allow me to answer the clerk's questions confidentially. Joshua was glued to my side, like wallpaper, but his spirit was lighter, because he could see that I was alive and going to be okay. By the time I came out of X-ray, to my surprise, Vince was already there looking concerned and ready to take charge. The ER doctor confirmed that I had a badly sprained ankle and gave me some crutches and an RX for pain medication and bid me ado.

When Vince and Josh and I returned to the waiting room, I was looking around for my knight, and he was nowhere to be found. As Vince was about to wheel me out of the ER, he appeared out of the elevator. I said, "There you are. I was beginning to think you had left." He said, "Of course not. When I saw that your friend had arrived, I took the liberty of running upstairs to obstetrics to see one of my co-worker's new bouncing baby boy." I said, "Aww that was sweet of you, and I want to thank you for everything you did for me and Josh. You were truly a lifesaver."

He immediately said, "No problem. You definitely looked like you needed some help, and I was the first person on the scene, so I stepped up to the plate." Miss Jesus Sandals piped in with, "Xandy, for God's sake, introduce yourself to the man." Miss Red Pumps couldn't wait. "EXCUSE ME! Aren't you the same person who just suspected the man of being Charles Manson or somebody? Now you want her to introduce herself to him?" Miss Jesus Sandals responded with, "please be quiet. All I'm doing is reminding Alexandria to mind her manners in return for this stranger's kindness." While they were carrying on, I extended my hand to him and said, "By the way, my name is Alexandria Morgan, and this is my nephew, Joshua and my co-worker and close friend, Vince." "Oh," he said. "Your close friend? I was under the assumption that this was your boyfriend, so I made sure I made myself scarce when he arrived."

"Ian, uh Ian Sommers is my name. I almost forgot." He smiled sheepishly when he realized, instead of responding with his name when I introduced us, he focused solely on Vince's position in my life. I said, "Well, Ian, I am forever indebted to you. You literally scraped me up off of the pavement and became my knight in shining armor. As soon as I'm at my best again, please allow me to show you my appreciation in some way." Ian smiled and said, "Alexandria, you don't owe me a thing other than to be careful, so that that ankle of yours will heal properly. I will check on you through the staff at the Y to make sure you are okay, if that's alright with you?" Vince cleared his throat to remind us that he and Josh were present. He quickly said, "Hey Josh, you want to run up to the canteen with me to grab a soda before we leave? I'm really thirsty." Josh said, "Sure, but I'll have to get juice…I'm not allowed to have sodas." Off they went and left Ian and me in the hospital waiting room surrounded by awkward silence.

While Vince and Joshua had Ian distracted with Vince's awful pretense at being suddenly thirsty, I was able to make my first real physical assessment of Mr. Ian Sommers. He was average height with somewhat of an athletic build, but not one that boasted a daily gym regimen. He was cute, but not anyone that would turn your head a second time during a walk-by. I guess I would describe him as attractive in a nerdy way. I continued where we left off before Vince interrupted us. I said, "No, Ian let me give you my number; that way, you can check on your damsel in distress personally, without having to go through the staff." He said, "Are you sure? I'm the new baseball coach at the YMCA, and I'm sure they wouldn't mind giving me updates on you through Joshua."

I assured him that giving him my number was the least I could do in return for him being so noble. I gave him by number, and he immediately dialed my cell phone, so I would also have his. While we waited for the guys to return, I began to get a bit woozy from the pain meds, and he immediately took off his hoodie and folded it for a pillow in an effort to make me comfortable. We were making small talk when Vince and Joshua returned with drinks in hand. They even had a drink for Ian at Josh's insistence. Josh had selected some apple juice for him, and Ian told him that apple juice was actually his favorite fruit juice and gave him a high five.

We exited the hospital and Vince drove my car around to the ramp to get me, and Ian picked me up from the wheelchair and put me in the back seat and offered me a handshake and bid us goodbye. The three of us watched him go across the parking lot and get into a beautiful new Infiniti. Vince said, "Your knight has a nice horse, doesn't he?" We both laughed as we drove off with Joshua in the front seat saying, "Horse? What horse? I don't see any horse!"

Needless to say, I was off from work the rest of the week, because I was so sore, and my ankle was quite swollen. Taylor drove up and stayed with us to help out with Josh during my down time. My mom and Aunt Sandra kept my telephone hot with calls about my level of pain and progress. Josh told Olivia what happened, and of course, she told Edmund who, in turn, had food delivered each evening for dinner until I made him stop. The way everyone was carrying on, one would have thought I was recovering from being hit by a speeding bus. Carmen was also checking in, and I took advantage of the calls to tell her about Ian. Her response was, "Well, he sounds like a nice guy, but I can tell from the tone of your voice when you were describing him that you are not really attracted to him." I think I agreed with her. Miss Jesus Sandals didn't fail to remind me, "Character goes much farther than the physical." Miss Red Pumps informed her, "Yeah, that's true, but you can't see character when it's on your arm walking down the street. Women want to have some eye candy!"

Ian called the second day of my recuperation. Joshua answered the phone and ran over to me saying, "Aunt Xandy, it's your knight in the shining Army on the phone." Taylor looked at me with a confused grimace on his face. I just simply said, "Details later li'l brother." Ian greeted me with "Hello Alexandria, this is Ian. How are you feeling? Is your ankle better? Are you able to walk without the crutches yet?" "Hi Ian," I responded after he finally paused. "Now which question would you like for me to answer first?" We both laughed. He said, "I'm sorry. I guess it's a combination of being exhausted and anxious to talk to you at the same time." "No need to apologize. I'm doing really well. If you don't mind my asking, why are you so exhausted?" There was a moment of silence, and when he spoke, he was almost whispering. He said, "Alexandria this call is not for you to ask about me; it's about me checking on you, and now that I see that you are okay.... I'll let you get back to convalescing. Take care, and I'll be checking on you." I reluctantly said okay.

When I hung up, I had to give Taylor a step-by-step- account of the way Ian and I met, and he thought it was quite comical. It was the weekend and Taylor informed me that, since I was up and about, he was going to take Joshua home for the weekend to see his mom and siblings and bring him back on Sunday. I agreed, and they left with Joshua asking me a hundred times if I was going to be all right without him. Taylor and Joshua had me stocked up with groceries and all of my necessities, so I settled in for a relaxing weekend.

I had been doing a lot of my work from home with help from Vince and my assistant. So I had some resumes to review and a recruitment schedule to set up. Needless to say, I had plenty to keep me entertained during my three-day sabbatical from Joshua. On Friday morning, as I was in the process of wrapping up some directives via phone with my assistant and arranging for a courier to drop off my planner and scheduling options, my call waiting tone went off. I looked at my phone and saw the name Ian Sommers. I quickly switched over and answered it. He said, "Hello Alexandria, how's that ankle coming along?" I told him that I was doing fine, except for a little discomfort after being up and about for a while.

He quickly said, "Well, there's no reason for you to be on your foot for any length of time, because you have your trusted sidekick Josh to take care of you." When I told him that Joshua was gone with his father for the weekend, he became quite anxious about my welfare -to put it mildly. I assured him, or at least I tried to… that I was okay and that I was about to test drive my boot by driving for the first time to my office to expedite getting my hands on the papers that I needed to complete my recruitment project. Ian said "Absolutely not, Alexandria! I will go to your office and bring those papers to your home within the hour. I am through with my classes for today, and I don't have "Y" duty, so I can make this happen for you."

Miss Red Pumps responded with, "Well, the knight rides again." Without much thought, I agreed to allow Ian to bring the papers to me. We hung up, and I was making the effort to get off of my chaise when my phone rang back. When I answered it, I heard laughter on the line first, and then Ian said, "Alexandria, we forgot two major things…I don't know where you work or live." At that point, we both burst into laughter. I gave Ian my work information and my address and asked him to buzz me from the gate when he arrived. Miss Jesus Sandals reminded me as usual, "Xandy, this man is still a stranger. A nice man, but still a stranger." I disregarded her paranoia.

Ian arrived about an hour and a half after we spoke. When I hobbled to the door and opened it, he almost dropped everything right there on the stoop. He was in a big hurry to empty his hands to help me back to my chaise, despite my efforts to assure him that I was able to navigate solo. After getting me settled down, he went back to pick up the items he was carrying. He then presented me with the document portfolio from my office. When I opened it, I discovered a get-well card inside that said, "Get well soon, and until you do…I am at your service." On the cover was a picture of a good-looking butler. I said, "Awwww, Ian that was really sweet of you to go through the trouble of not only playing the role of my courier, but also taking the time to buy me a card." There were two large binders filled with papers that he placed on the bar, but didn't mention. He sat on the chair opposite of me, and we settled in for what was our first real conversation. He kept interrupting by asking me if I needed anything.

Miss Red Pumps whispered, "I really think this guy meant that card literally, but don't knock it…enjoy it." We talked for hours about our families, and I discovered that Ian had a really quirky, but cute, sense of humor that I enjoyed. He has such a comforting spirit about him that I missed my scheduled pain pill and didn't take it. He told me stories about growing up with his two brothers (one whom was a cousin) and how he actually felt more fatherly toward them, instead of brotherly, despite their close age difference. When I questioned how that happened…. his response was that his parents' careers kept them away or pretty busy, and the three of them had to be independent. I shared my family of origin dynamics with him, and he surprisingly said… "I look forward to meeting them." "Who said you are going to meet them?" mumbled Miss Jesus Sandals. Miss Red Pumps quickly reminded her that she had just previously commented that Ian was a nice man, so why is it that he can't meet the family? Just as I expected…there was no reply from the halo.

After what seemed like only a short time, we soon realized we had talked right into the dinner hour. Ian asked me if I was hungry and what my dinner plans were. Miss Red Pumps said, "Did you notice he used the word "were" instead or "are?" Hmmmmm!" I took note of that and informed Ian that Taylor had left me with a plentiful supply of all of my favorite foods and snacks, which included guilty pleasures that I really did not need. His response was, "Alexandria, please don't see this as me trying to impose on your plans, but I would love to provide dinner for you this evening if I may." I told him that I was the one who felt like the imposition in this situation, ever since "landing" at his feet on the day we met and didn't want to take up any more of his time.

Ian's response was, "Me providing and sharing dinner with you this evening is about as far away from being an imposition on me as the distance between earth and the sun!" "Wow. Well in that case, I accept," I said, while sporting a big happy face smile. To be honest, I was not looking forward to spending this Friday night alone with work and sitcom reruns. Ian told me that he would be right back and proceeded to grab his keys and head for the door. As he opened the door, he turned and asked me if I needed anything special while he was out, and I told him that I had everything I needed. "Do you really?" whispered Miss Jesus Sandals.

While Ian was out, I laid back on the chaise and replayed everything about today's interaction with him in my head. I guess I was trying to make an assessment as to whether I was really attracted to Ian. Miss Jesus Sandals chastised me by saying, "Xandy, why are you sitting here trying to determine your attraction to this man, when he has not indicated that he is interested in you, other than being a friendly and helpful human being, due to the circumstances under which you two met?" I admitted to myself that she had a point, BUT I proceeded with my assessment as planned. Honestly speaking or thinking…I was not attracted to Ian as physically as I was spiritually (for lack of a better word). There was something about his spirit that I liked. Other than his car…he appeared to be an average, simple, and kind of corny, but sweet, guy. He was definitely a gentleman, and because of his chosen career, I know he has compassion and patience. Ian fit the bill perfectly for a good friend.

In less than an hour, Ian was back at the gate waiting to be buzzed in. When he came through the door, I was expecting maybe some sort of take out or fast food bags. Much to my surprise, he was loaded with grocery bags and a wine carrier. He said as he passed me, en route to my kitchen, "I hope you don't mind Alexandria, but I've decided to serve us a home cooked meal this evening. I figured, since you've been shut in and incapacitated, it had been a while since you had one." I sat there speechless as Miss Jesus Sandals said, "Tell him you had a home cooked meal yesterday that was prepared with love by your nephew."

I shrugged off the comment, because I truly did not want to make Ian think I would be putting the ramen noodles and microwave brownie that Josh prepared in the same category as what was about to take place in my kitchen tonight. I just sat back on the bar stool with my foot up in another stool and watched the culinary orchestration take place. He was at home in the kitchen. He prepared rosemary lamb chops, roasted new potatoes, broccoli and cauliflower with cheese sauce. The aroma had me salivating before he actually finished. What amazed me was that he had not asked me whether I ate any of the foods he selected, and even more amazing, I loved everything he cooked.

Once the meal was ready, he asked me if it was okay to play a CD while we ate and poured us a glass of wine to accompany our dinner. I reminded him that I was taking pain medication and would have to forego the wine. His response was, "Okie Dokie, I will fix you a pomegranate spritzer then-alcohol free, of course." "Wow," was all I could think, because I was wondering how he knew that pomegranate anything was my favorite. Ian went to the entertainment center and selected a CD, and immediately the room was filled with the sound of Julian's music. Out of all the music in this room…he selected that one. I had not listened to it since that dreadful day of the unexpected triangle that unfolded in my house with Julian and Danny.

I pushed the memory and the thoughts that music usually evoked back into the recesses of my brain and focused on Ian's mouthwatering creation. Both of us almost inhaled our plates with brief attempts at conversations throughout the meal. The food was absolutely delicious, and the spritzer, of which I was not familiar, was exquisite. When I finally came up for air, I couldn't help but question this man's culinary skills. He said, "I told you that I was primarily responsible for my two brothers while growing up, and they had to eat, and most nights, that was left up to me." There was sort of a sadness to his voice when he said that. He said that his mom had taught him a few things and most he had learned through experimenting with various recipes. Miss Red Pumps perked up and said, "Alexandria, this is truly a keeper -a man willing to run errands, grocery shop, and cook the food too? It doesn't get any better than this! Let's see what he does with the mess he made of your kitchen."

As soon as she said that, it was as if he heard her, because he said, "Alexandria where is your dish detergent?" I said, "Oh no, Ian throw those dishes in the dishwasher, so we can continue to chat." He responded with, "We can continue to chat while I wash the dishes. I don't have anywhere to be. Do you?" Miss Jesus Sandals said, "Yes, tell him you have to be home alone for the rest of the nigh!" "What was up with her?" I asked myself. She really doesn't seem to care much for Ian, although he has been nothing less than a gentleman.

After the dishes and having made general conversation in the process, we settled down on the couch to watch some TV at his suggestion. I told him that I should be focusing on my paperwork, instead of watching TV. To my surprise, his response was, "You are right, and me too." With that, he got up and retrieved the two large binders of papers that he had brought with him that I had forgotten about. He said, "Now Miss lady, you do your thing right here, and I'm going to go over there to the table and do mine." Turns out, his thing was grading papers. Of course, I should have known. Ian is a teacher and all teachers have plenty of papers to grade. The thing was...he was grading them at my house, and even more puzzling, he didn't ask me, and I was happy to have him here doing it.

Ian and I spent most of the night into the wee hours in our own zones doing paper work, with a few verbal exchanges scattered throughout the process. There was something so comforting about being with him. This was illustrated when he said, "Alexandria, please don't consider this forward or weird, but why don't I just stay here with you this weekend to help you until Taylor and Josh return on Sunday?" Before I could answer, Miss Red Pumps said, "My, My, what have we here?" Miss Jesus Sandals was quick on the draw and said, "Maybe a presumptuous pervert."

Ignoring them both, I said, "Okaaay...I guess that will be all right. You can sleep in Josh's room." He quickly said okay and sprinted for the door. When I asked where he was going, he responded with, "To my car to get my bag." When he saw the color drain out of my face, he smiled and walked over to me and said, "Okay, let me slow down and explain. As you know, I teach and coach on the same day several days a week; therefore, I always keep a bag with a change of clothing and toiletries in my car. Please don't think this is some kind of pre-meditated sexual offense in the making here. Pretty please?" I said "okay." At that point, Miss Jesus Sandals started screaming, "Somebody please call the people with the white jackets and the butterfly net... this child has lost her mind!" The shocker that followed was when

Miss Red Pumps said, "Believe it or not, I agree with you, Miss Jesus Sandals!" That confirmed it for me. This man was an enigma, just asking to be explored.

Ian returned to the house with his bag, and I pointed down the hall and off he went. He got his stuff settled and joined me on the couch. We chatted for a while and then both agreed it had been a fun, yet productive, evening and we should turn in. I went to my room and Ian to the guest room.

As you can see, I've made the story of a short weekend very long and the reason is that I want you to understand the origin of Ian in its entirety. We shared that weekend together in my home as if we were a couple that had celebrated several wedding anniversaries-minus the intimacy. Yet, there was something very intimate about the time Ian and I spent together. He prepared the meals and only requested that I keep him company by sitting at the bar talking to him and making note of the many cooking tips he passed on. We laughed a lot, although I don't think many would find his humor funny, and I'm not sure I do either, but it's too corny not to laugh.

On that Saturday after breakfast, Ian suggested we go for a ride, just to break the monotony of me being in the house. I readily agreed to go, and in less than an hour, we were off to see the sites and places of special interests in Philadelphia. We stopped at the park and managed to score two ice cream cones from a street vendor and shared them at a picnic table that was close to the parking area, but under a beautiful oak tree. That whole day was so relaxing. I did not feel the need to be anybody else, but me, with Ian. I realized I had on no makeup, my hair was pulled back in a ponytail, and was dressed casual, though still cute. Ian had on a really nice Nike sports suit that matched his tennis shoes to the letter. In fact, for the first time...I thought he was actually handsome, especially when he put on his sunglasses.

We grabbed some sushi to go and spent the rest of the day at home. We watched a couple of movies, and Ian prepared some burgers to die for. I told him that he was spoiling me. During that weekend, each of my family members called to check on me, including Carmen. Each time, I told them that Ian was stopping by to see about me and to run whatever errands that I needed done. I did tell Carmen the truth. When I told her that Ian was staying over with me for the weekend until Taylor returned, she said, "Say what? Girl you didn't waste any time with this one did you?" "Hold your horses, sister," I said. "Ian and I have not touched each other this weekend, nor have we talked about touching each other in the future." "Ouch! I'm sorry," she replied. "I was wrong to assume...I see that this must be a really nice guy and someone you really like in order for you to be spending the weekend with him so soon, even platonically." I agreed with her. She continued to drill me about Ian for a long time on the phone, until I told her that I had to go, because he sounded as if he was done with his paper grading efforts in the living room.

I told Ian about losing my dad and my childhood and even about Ralph. I found him soooo easy to talk to, Miss Red Pumps whispered and said, "I see you left out one small detail about Ralph, and that's that he is still very much in love with you and still comes in and out of your life." Miss Jesus Sandals finished the commentary by saying, "And he's very much married to someone else and making a fool out of both of you." Ignoring them and moving on. Ian did open up to me a little more about his childhood and family. These revelations took place on Saturday night after about his third glass of merlot. (We bought another bottle during our morning ride).

Apparently, Ian's Dad was a career army man, who spent a lot of time deploying alone to different duty stations, leaving his family behind. His mom was somewhat resentful of him always leaving, although she chose not to go because of her job and the two boys. Ian's cousin was actually the son of Ian's mother's sister, who had been killed in a car accident that resulted in the child becoming a permanent resident of the Sommers' household. Ian obviously cared for his two brothers, but there was something different about him when he talked about his parents. We brought the night to a close after watching a few episodes of reality TV and a discussion about the foolish things people will do for money.

Sunday was pretty uneventful. We had a laidback day with some TV watching and Ian helping me put some final touches on my career fair plans. We were sitting out on the balcony sharing the newspaper and drinking some apple juice when one of my neighbors across the way also came out on her patio holding an infant who was pretty upset if crying was any indication. I said, "My goodness, that baby is loud. I don't know if I could deal with a fussy baby, but I guess, one day, I'll find out if I have what it takes." Ian responded quietly with, "Yes, I imagine you will." I said, "What about you? Are you planning on having children, one day?" I was not expecting the response I got. He said, "The jury is still out on whether I already have one, but I doubt I'll ever know." He was in a zone for a moment and just as he came out of it and looked at me in astonishment.... the doorbell rang, and Josh was screaming from the other side.

Ian jumped up, went inside, and let in my two rambunctious male family members. Taylor introduced himself to Ian and Joshua swept right past the two of them and dashed right into my outstretched arms. I had truly missed him. He had a thousand questions about my weekend and wanted to get a close up of my ankle. When he was convinced that I was okay, he retrieved his bags from the foyer and went to his room to unpack all of his new clothes, video games, and gadgets.

I stayed on the balcony and eavesdropped while Ian and Taylor chatted. They both did a quick rundown of their jobs and interests. Somehow, investments monopolized the conversation, and they exchanged numbers and agreed to follow up later. Ian finally came to hug me and then proceeded to take his stuff to the car. Miss Red Pumps noticed that, "Girl, he hasn't directly addressed you since making that weird comment on the balcony." Miss Jesus Sandals said, "It's really none of your business any way, Alexandria, so please don't turn this into a Barbara Walters special."

Well, things returned to normal. Taylor stayed with me until Wednesday, which was my day to return to work. I was excited about going into the office and driving again. I was up bright and early and got to work with about thirty minutes to spare. My mother called me when I arrived at my desk, just to make sure I didn't cause any fatalities en route. I assured her that things were back to normal. She asked me how my knight was doing. My response was surprising to me. "I haven't seen nor heard from Ian since Taylor and Josh returned on

Sunday. Hmmm, that's odd." My mom replied, "Yes, it is; you ought to be ashamed that you haven't taken a moment to call and thank Ian for the grand display of concern and chivalry he has demonstrated since you fell at his feet."

She was correct, so I didn't argue with her. I promised I would give him a call. I kept my promise and called and left a voice mail for Ian, because I knew he was already in the classroom. Strangely enough, Ian did not return my call that week. It bothered me, but not enough for me to call him again. It worked out for the better anyway, because Josh and Olivia had re-connected, which automatically brought Edmund back in the picture. The four of us went to a Justin Bieber concert and out to dinner on that Friday night. During this night out, Olivia told Josh and me that her daddy was taking her and her mom on a seven-day Disney Cruise this summer, right before school starts. "Her and her mom?" said Miss Red Pumps, "I know where he needs to send that ex-wife of his, and it's certainly not to Puerto Vallarta." Edmund wouldn't look at me after Olivia made her big announcement. Miss Jesus Sandals said, "I wonder, did that mother of hers put her up to making sure you knew?" "Of course she did," Miss Red Pumps responded. "You can't be that naïve."

Anyway, at the end of the night when the kids were in Josh's room playing his latest game, I asked Edmund for the details. He looked at me sheepishly and said, "Olivia really wants to do this, and she doesn't want to be on that big ship on all of that water without her mom. This was supposed to be a father-daughter trip, but I'm trying not to spoil it for Olivia, so now I'm bringing her mom along." I didn't even respond. I just stood there and shook my head. He said, "Alexandra, you are a fine one to talk. Don't think for one minute I haven't heard about this Ian character, who has been at your beck and call, including overnight. Claire and I are not sharing a bed or anything else for that matter- just a child."

Miss Red Pumps whispered, "Did you notice he said a bed...not a room. Ask him." And that I did. "Edmund will the three of you be in the same suite on the ship?" He fell silent. I had my answer, despite his profession of, "Alex, nothing is going to happen." "Edmund, it's time for you to go, and we'll talk some other time." He grabbed me by my shoulders and pulled me in for one of the best kisses I've ever had. Despite our age difference, Edmund was awesome in pushing all of my physical buttons, and he was one of, if not the best, kissers in the world. It was at that moment that I knew I really cared for this man and that I was jealous of his ex-wife. When we finally disconnected, he looked down at me and said, "Alex, kisses like that don't happen without feelings, and you know how I feel about you, so don't blow this out of proportion." I didn't say a word. I couldn't because I was concentrating on trying to mentally extinguish the fire in my body that he had just ignited. He and Olivia left with him promising to call me in a day or two, once I've had a chance to process things.

Well, I didn't waste much time in thought about it. I will admit that I am seriously jealous of Edmund's allegiance to his daughter's every whim, which obviously includes his ex-wife. I truly care about Edmund, and something tells me that we could have a meaningful and long-term relationship but…

◆

Mr. Ian Sommers called me and asked me if he could come over to see me the following day, which was Saturday. I quickly responded with, "How about me coming over to your place, instead? I have cabin fever and could really use the break." I could sense his hesitancy, but he responded with, "Sure Alex, I will cook for you if you'd like, or we can order in or something…your choice." I jumped at the offer to have more of Ian's cooking, but told him to keep it simple and light. He said, "Is 4:00 pm okay?" I agreed, and we hung up. Immediately, we dialed each other back laughing. I answered the line with, "I know, I know…what is your address?" He laughed too as he proceeded to give it to me. When I hung up, I was shocked when I looked at Ian's address. He lived at Meadow Lake. Meadow Lake was one of the most picturesque and prestigious waterfront areas in the suburban Philadelphia area.

I dressed casually to impress, and off I went. When I drove up to the address Ian gave me…I was blown away. His amazing home sat in a beautiful setting, nestled amidst majestic old oak trees sitting atop a slight hill overlooking Meadow Lake. Visitors were greeted by a well-manicured landscaped lawn that included a large circular driveway, prelude to a beautiful colonial-style house that included the southern veranda and stately columns. I sat there in the car admiring this estate in all of its grandeur. I managed to get out of the car and continued to stand there, looking around and enjoying the wonderful breeze that was blowing in off of the lake. This was the epitome of beauty and peace.

Miss Red Pumps was grinning and mentally packing her bags, saying the she would love to be the Scarlett O'Hara of this modern-day Tara. Miss Jesus Sandals was quietly taking it all in, but by the look on her face…she was taken with the peacefulness of the surroundings, just as much as I was. I was jolted out of my thoughts when Ian opened the front door and came down the steps to greet me. He hugged me and said, "My, don't you look beautiful this Saturday afternoon." I responded, "Well, considering this house and grounds, I feel a bit under-dressed for the occasion." "Don't be silly, little girl," he said. "Bring yourself right on inside, so we can begin enjoying each other."

When we entered the house, I soon discovered it was just as beautiful on the inside as it was on the outside. It was not ornate, but it was tastefully done, and it was obvious it had been done expensively and professionally. Ian took me by the hand and led me to the love seat in front of a large picture window overlooking a magnificent deck and view of the lake. He said, "Alexandria, I am accustomed to getting this reaction when people come to my home the first time, because I know when you see me first, then see my home…the two don't match, huh?" I smiled, but remained quiet.

He went on to say, "You see Alex, my paternal grandparents were well-to-do people. My grandfather was a skilled automotive engineer way before his time. His skills and know-how far exceeded his BS degree in engineering. He worked his way up to top management status in the car industry in Detroit and remained there until his death. He died in an accident on site at the plant. A belt broke holding one of the motor casings that hit him, knocking him against another machine, causing his death from a massive head injury. I guess I don't have to tell you that my grandmother became a wealthy widow as a result of that.

She returned to Philadelphia, built this house, invested a bunch of money, blessed her siblings and grandchildren, and eventually died peacefully in her sleep upstairs one night in the bedroom I now sleep in. Everyone, including the doctors, said that my grandmother died from a broken heart. She lived eleven years after my grandfather's death and spent most of that time right here, when she wasn't serving in her church or in the community in some capacity." I didn't speak because it was obvious that Ian had been holding on to this story to this degree for a long time. I reached for his hand, and he held on tightly as he continued.

"You see, Xandy, (first time he had ever called me Xandy) my father is an only child, and my brother and I are my grandmother's only grandchildren, and being that I am the oldest of the two…she left this house to me with enough money set aside in a designated account to maintain it." He saw the puzzled look on my face, so he said, "I know you are wondering why she didn't leave this house and property to my father. Well, as much as we don't talk about it…my father has a drinking problem that had cost his parents quite a bit of money-bailing him out of the alcohol induced shenanigans he always managed to get himself into. When he went into the military, my grandfather was well aware of the dire consequences involved when the army discovered your infractions as a result of drinking, so they continued to clean up his mess.

◆

In the daytime, my dad was an exemplary warrant officer with many medals and accomplishments to show for it, but at night, he was a different person. As a result of my dad's non-stop work ethic and commitment to the Army and the bottle, my mother found solace in other things. According to my dad and his parents, her main comforts were casinos and men. She also maintained a dual existence, because by day, she was the persona of a good mom and professional woman. So as you can see…my grandmother did not trust her son and daughter-in-law to do the right thing with her money and property. My brother is a lot more impulsive and a daredevil than I am, so he has to go through me to get to his inheritance. And he hates me for it. My cousin, whom I refer to as my brother, is my mother's sister's child and is smart and pretty independent and doing a great job supporting himself and his family as a pharmacist."

"So now, you know I have a dysfunctional family, and I think they hate me for being so predictable and stable. I'm almost sure my dad resents me because of my grandmother's faith and belief in me and the fact that she left me in charge of her small fortune." I then said, "Ian, you shouldn't think that way." He placed his finger to my lips and said, "Shhhh, it's true, but it's okay, and I've gotten used to it." With that, Ian Sommers pulled me to him and kissed me ever so gently for the first time. I was truly not expecting it, but I'm not sure how I felt about it or if I enjoyed it. But I do know that I was connected emotionally to Ian at that time.

After the kiss, we sat back, just holding each other in silence looking at the view outside. Miss Jesus Sandals was whispering in my ear. "Xandy, I now believe this is truly a nice guy, but there are some deep issues here, and I'm not sure what they are…but I like him." "Yeah, so do I," Miss Red Pumps offered. "I could definitely get use to this lifestyle. This place makes a girl feel like somebody real important." Miss Jesus Sandals and I looked at each other and shook our heads.

After our moments of silence and reflection…Ian turned to me and said… "Alexandria, why don't you stay here with me this weekend?" I looked at him and said, "Are you really serious?" He said, "I know you, unlike me, did not come prepared with a change of clothes, so I'll drive you back to your place to get some things. What do you say?" Surprisingly, I agreed to do so. He admitted he needed to stop by the market while we were out to get some extra food. Ian said, "C'mon let's get out of here." We headed to the garage and upon arriving there…much to my surprise, I saw a beautiful snow white Mercedes with red interior, and to top it off, it was a convertible. Ian saw me admiring it, and I turned and said, "Your grandmother's?" He shook his head, smiled at the car, and proceeded to open the door of his Infiniti for me to get in.

Ian and I went to my place, two markets, and then he gave me a tour of the surrounding properties on my way back to the house. I must say that weekend was one of the best weekends I've shared with a man. We were so comfortable together. He even allowed me to fix one of the snacks during my stay. At Ian's insistence, I had brought my work clothes for Monday, so I could also spend the night on Sunday night. We watched movies, walked along the lake, and sat in silence. As before, I worked on my paperwork on one side of the room as Ian graded papers on the other side. It was such a wonderful coincidence that Taylor was in town hanging out with one of his Philly conquests, so I didn't have to worry about Joshua that weekend. Carmen called while Ian was busy with his paper grading and asked what I was up to…I walked outside to the deck and told her the whole story.

She was quiet. When she spoke…she said, "Ian sounds wonderful, Xandy. He seems to have a lot going for him; he's a teacher and a softball coach, and obviously, financially secure, and it doesn't really matter how he got the money and the stuff…it's his," BUT (oh my goodness, I knew there was a but in the middle of this speech somewhere), "what's missing is your usual carrying on about how fine he is, how good he smells, how physically skilled he is, how well he fits with you, yada, yada, yada." I said, "Carmen, please give it a rest…this relationship has substance." She responded with, "Does it have substance or are you really attracted to this guy?"

My two shoulders' tenants both said, "And vice versa." Carmen continued. "Has he made a move on you yet? Or better yet…why haven't you made a move on him? I know how aggressive you usually are. Something is amiss, and you are not telling me what it is." I quickly took back the lead on this conversation with, "Look, Miss Red Hot-and-Ready, nothing is amiss. I'm just taking my time for a change if I have your permission to do so." With that, I said goodbye and returned inside where Ian was finishing his work. He was gathering his softball clothes, headed to the laundry room, and stopped to ask me if I had anything I wanted to toss into the wash. I told him that I didn't, but then I became tuned into the chatter on my shoulder. Miss Jesus Sandals was asking me, "Xandy, did I miss your and Ian's wedding? If I didn't know better, I'd swear I was in the presence of an old married couple." Miss Red Pumps would not be left out, so she said, "Yeah I couldn't agree more."

This man just asked you about tossing your clothes in the wash with his, and he was willing to do the laundry. Once again, they were in sync with each other regarding Ian; I must admit I found it a little odd. After getting the laundry started, he poured us a glass of wine as we settled in the kitchen area, where he commenced to making his "world-famous lasagna." I said, "Ian you are just the total package, aren't you?" I asked. He stopped mid-movement and looked at me as if I were an alien. He finally said, "How so?"

"You are so nice, and you have a lot going for you, and most of all, you don't seem to have a problem with the domestic side of life. In fact, you seem to master chores better than the average woman." Ian reminded me that he had told me about having to be the primary caretaker for his two brothers, while his dad was working and out drinking and his mom was working, gambling, and carousing. He had such a tormented look when he said that. I left that alone and moved on to a topic we had managed to not talk about at all. I said, "Why are you not involved with someone, Ian?" He responded quickly with, "Who said I'm not?" Seeing me flinch as if I had been slapped, he said, "I'm just joking with you, girl. I am not involved with anyone and haven't been for some time now." I laughed on the outside, but inside, I did not find his remark to my question humorous.

I continued my probing efforts by asking him what happened with his last relationship. He said, "Okay Alexandria, I see you are determined to delve into my history, so let me make it easy for you. My last relationship lasted over a year and has been over for about 2 years. Her name is Dana, and she is also a teacher but, for the record, not at my same school. We had a pretty good start, but she was not satisfied with the amount of time or attention she got from me. She said that I spent too much time working, coaching, or with my friends." My response was, "That doesn't even sound like you, Ian."

Miss Jesus Sandals said, "Hush, Xandy and listen!" "Is there more?" I asked. He said, "There's not much to say about Dana and me. We had some good times, but as I said, it was pretty short lived. She was a bit more high-maintenance than suits my taste or lifestyle." I seized the opportunity to get some clarification here. "What's high-maintenance to you?" He hesitated, but went on to say... "Well, in Dana's case, she wanted a lot of attention and affection, and sometimes, at the most inopportune times, and when she didn't get it…she acted worse than the kids in her second grade class. As you can see, I can be quite attentive, but I don't like demands being made on me for it." Miss Red Pumps said, "Sounds like he wasn't really into this Dana chick. It would be interesting to know if this is a pattern, because you know us girls-we love attention!" I agreed. I asked him what he thought about affection overall and PDA (public displays of affection). His response was short and surprising. He said, "Although I enjoy it, I personally think sex and affection are overrated, and everything has its place and time." "I agree, I think!" was the response from under the halo on my right shoulder.

Ian and I spent the rest of the evening just hanging out, doing nothing really special. We had a few drinks and then agreed to call it a night. Ian showed me upstairs to my room and made sure I had everything I needed. He told me that this was the room his parents always slept in when they visited his grandmother, and I could see that it still contained many pictures of Ian's parents and his dad when he was growing up, as well as Ian and his brother. Ian had left me with a lingering hug and a soft kiss on the forehead. I had wandered around the room, looking at the pictures, and realized that Ian looked just like his mother, and his brother had a closer resemblance to their father.

I turned the radio on to the local jazz station and opened the door to the balcony and walked out to enjoy the view. As I looked down, I saw that Ian was also out on the deck below. He obviously felt my presence and looked up at me, and right then and there, something inside of me clicked for Ian Sommers. He looked like a sweet angel standing there in the moonlight. Miss Jesus Sandals should have tossed him her halo to complete the moment. He smiled and said, "My fair maiden, are you unable to sleep on this beautiful night?" I laughed and said, "No, I can't, and it's obvious that neither can you,

Sir Ian." He laughed along with me and asked would I like for him to come up and join me for a little while. I readily said, "Yes."

In a flash, Ian knocked at the door and awaited my invitation to come in. He then grasped my hand, and we returned to the balcony and just stood there, looking at the full moon and enjoying the night breeze. Kenny G's song silhouette playing on the radio didn't make matters any better. It was the perfect setting for romance. After what seemed like a long time, Ian said, "Xandy, I'd better go, so you can get some rest." As he turned and was walking toward the door, I caught his arm and said, "Stay with me, Ian." Without hesitation, he said, "okay" and pulled me down on the bed and held me in the spoon position, until the morning, without either of us saying another word.

I felt so "at home." During the night, I got as close to Ian as our bodies would allow, and I fought to control the feelings or shall I say the desire stirring inside of me.

(SIDE BAR: We all know that the spoon position gives a woman full court advantage to any previews she needs to have of what a man has to offer, because there is nothing between your lower body parts blocking access or exploration. But Ian was sound asleep with me wrapped inside of his arms, and no matter how much moving and re-adjusting I did...NOTHING changed.)

Oddly, I awoke before Ian and sneaked downstairs and managed to prepare him a light breakfast and coffee before he came down. So there we sat barefoot in our pjs, watching CNN on a beautiful Sunday morning, with the morning breeze from the lake accompanying our serenity. We spent the day out at the lake. Ian took me for a boat ride on his pontoon, and we shared a picnic on the other side of the lake near a field of wild flowers. I was completely caught up in this whole scenario. Being with Ian was like being with Prince Charming in his kingdom, called La-La land. We made our way back to the house. As we drove back across the lake, there was a slight chill from the wind, and Ian reached out and pulled me close saying, "Aw baby, you have goosebumps. I should have brought a jacket for you." He was so thoughtful and sweet, and I was lapping up every second of it like a dehydrated dog!

After a pretty uneventful day of continued R&R, I found out

that we both loved board games. We were playing a rousing game of Scrabble and listening to some wonderful classical music by Guiseppe Verdi, who just happens to be one of my mother's favorites. I had fixed a pitcher of pomegranate martinis, and while we were enjoying our cocktails, we were both startled by the doorbell. We looked at each other, and I shrugged my shoulders and laughed, "What are you looking at me for? I don't live here."

Ian disappeared into the foyer, and I soon heard voices-male voices. After about ten minutes, Ian reentered the room followed by one of the most gorgeous men I believe I have ever seen. Ian said, "Alex, I'd like to introduce you to my rude best friend, Nicholas." This man rushed over and grabbed my hand and said, "So you are Alexandria? The lady that's light on her feet." This guy had a limp handshake, but a smile that Carmen would sell her deceased grandmother's china to see again.

I laughed and said, "I guess so." Nicholas was not only handsome, but also dressed like a runway model with an unfamiliar cologne to die for. After releasing my hand, he went over and sat on the love seat next to Ian and continued to chatter about how wonderful it was finally to meet me, and he was glad I was up and around again. He then jumped up and flitted to the kitchen, shouting on the way, "My, my, dude what was on the menu...it smells wonderful in here... got any leftovers?" He turned to me and said, "I see you have been the benefactor of Ian's cooking skills." While Nicholas was busying himself in the kitchen, peeking in pots and rummaging through the refrigerator, Miss Red Pumps was standing on my shoulder with her mouth frozen open.

When she finally spoke she said, "Wait a minute! Something is not right with this picture, and I'm trying to figure out what it is. This drop dead hunk of a man is a little suspect if you ask me!" "Well nobody asked you," said Miss Jesus Sandals. She then added, "Xandy, what's up with this man, and most of all- this picture?" I tried to ignore them, as usual, but was finding it hard, because finally, both of them had made points worth exploring. While Nicholas was fixing himself a plate and a drink, Ian turned to me and said. "I'm sorry Alexandria. Nicky knows he's supposed to call before he comes barging over to my house, but I guess you know you can't always control your friends."

"Nicky?" I repeated to myself. Nicholas returned to the den with a plate and drink in hand and asked, "What were you guys doing?" We told him we had been playing Scrabble and listening to music, and he then suggested we watch this movie he had just purchased, which was one of the sequels to the blockbuster *Twilight*. We looked at each other and agreed to do it. It seems that Ian and I had both seen the movie *Twilight* and was kind of interested in what was going to happen next. Well, we spent the rest of the evening engrossed in the movie, with a large part of the conversation centering around who was the cutest, Edward or Jacob. Miss Jesus Sandals said, "Alexandria, don't you realize you are having a girl's night out?" Miss Red Pumps piped in to remind me that *The Twilight Saga* was definitely not a "manly man's" choice in movies. I shrugged them off by telling myself Ian is just secure enough to be in tune with his sensitive side and Nicholas.... Well, Nicholas was another story.

# CHAPTER 10
## ◆ IAN (PART 2) ◆

After the movie ended, Nicholas went back in the kitchen and fixed himself a to-go plate for tomorrow's lunch and came and gave me a farewell hug. As he was leaving, he turned and looked at me from head to toe and said, "Alexandria, you are really pretty with the bod to match. No wonder my guy here is all caught up at the moment. You give the competition a real run for their money, girlfriend." With that, he winked at me and jerked his head, while making his dramatic exit with Ian right behind him. "THAT DID IT!" I said to my shoulder mates (and I rarely talk to them) "NICHOLAS IS GAY!" I screamed. "No SHIT, Sherlock," yelled Miss Red Pumps. She immediately covered her mouth and apologized, because she knew I hated profanity- not to mention Miss Jesus Sandals over there about to hyperventilate.

I gathered my thoughts and calmly said to myself, "What's the big deal, Xandy? You have gay friends, co-workers, and even family members. Why are you carrying on about this guy?" Miss Red Pumps said, "Because this frigging man is too doggone handsome to waste himself and the goods on same sex escapades." Miss Jesus Sandals responded with, "Or Alexandria, is it because "Nicky" is obviously close to Ian?" I honestly couldn't say which one of these ladies' points was the right one to me at this moment. I sat there listening to music and finishing my drink, while Ian was obviously outside in the driveway, saying goodbye to Nicholas. It ended up being a long goodbye. When he came back inside, he was laughing to himself.

◆

I had cleaned up the kitchen, which wasn't hard, because Nicholas had been thoughtful enough to wash the dishes, since he took the last food out of them. He said, "Thanks Alexandria, for being so kind and patient with Nicky…as you can see, he is a nut and can be quite the handful. We went to college together and have been friends ever since. Some folks might find it strange that a straight guy and a gay guy can be so close…but it's worked for us." That settled it for me, "But certainly not for us," said the shoulder duo in unison.

After both of us got all of our work stuff together for the next day, we said good night at the stairs and went our separate ways. I turned on the radio, jumped in the shower, and hit the sack in less than twenty minutes. I was nestled in my pillow looking out at the moon from the bed, when I heard Ian through the door. "Alexandria, may I come in?" He was barely audible from the other side of the door. I said, "Sure Ian, come on in." He came in a sat down on the side of the bed and just looked at me. The radio jazz was playing in the background, and the room was lit only by the moonlight. I said, "Ian is there something wrong?" Without a word or warning…he pulled me to him and kissed me so intensely that I could hardly catch my breath. There were no words exchanged before he stretched out next to me and kissed me again and again. I pressed my hands again his chest to put some space between us, so I could attempt to look into his eyes. I asked, "Ian where is all of this coming from so suddenly?" He said, "I don't really know, Xandy. But what I do know is I just want to be close to you, right now. Can I?"

I removed my hand and nestled into his body; we slept that way until morning. He held me so tightly throughout the night, until I was stiff the next morning from the confinement. I eased out of bed to begin my routine. When I came back in the room to get my toiletry bag, Ian was gone. We didn't talk or see each other until we met outside in the driveway. I could tell his discomfort, so I walked over to him and kissed him on the cheek and told him I had a wonderful time. Ian said, "Alexandra, I enjoyed you so much that it scares me." With that, he kissed me on my forehead, and we drove off in separate directions.

Miss Jesus Sandals was up and ready to pester me all the way to work if I allowed her to. "Alexandria, I can't help liking this guy, but something bugs me about him. Where did all that passion come from last night? You guys have spent nights together, and except for the time he kissed you when he was emotional about his family, things have been pretty platonic. Then all of a sudden, he's acting like someone just released from prison." Miss Red Pumps, said, "Look, Xandy, I'll agree that's he's different, but at least, you've got a preview of his skills and what could come later. That's not such a bad thing. I guess his friend needs to come around more often. It seems to have turned his flicker to flame." I truly had not associated Nicholas's visit with the onset of Ian's physical approach with me. But it did kind of go hand in hand. Or, did it?

Well, Ian and I did not talk for the rest of that week. This was a good thing, because I ended up with Edmund and Olivia for bowling for Josh's sake, and Edmund was still asking me questions about Ian that I found disturbing. "You are forgetting something," said Miss Jesus Sandals. "Oh yeah, Julian did stop by the night after my stay at Ian's home for one of his late night connections." Miss Red Pumps yelled, "Girl, you are going to need a traffic light at your front door soon," and burst into laughter. Of course, Miss Jesus Sandals did not think it was a laughing matter.

I thought it was strange that after such a great weekend and what seemed to be us bonding on a deep emotional level...Ian hadn't called. Joshua told me, when he got in the car at the YMCA on Thursday, he had been sitting outside at the ball field watching Mr. Ian take his team through some baseball drills. Ian had also allowed Josh to catch the balls and exercise with the boys, although Josh was too young for his league. I called Ian on Friday night and to my surprise, Nicholas answered the phone. He said, "Hello Alexandria, how's it going girl?" After recouping from my shock, I said "Well, hello Nicholas, how are you this evening?" His response was, "I'm good, but I will be doing a whole lot better, once Ian gets back here and puts the finishing touches on these steaks he left me to watch on the grill." "Oh I see," I said, "well, please tell Ian I called and take care, Nicholas." I heard him say, "I sure will, girl," as he hung up the phone.

Before the echo of the disconnecting click cleared the air, my shoulder duo was singing a duet. "What in the tarnation is going on?" asked Miss Jesus sandals. I'm glad she drowned out Miss Red Pumps, because she definitely did not say "tarnation." I was a bit taken back, but I brushed it off. After all, what is wrong with two friends grilling out and having dinner together? Carmen and I have done it hundreds of times. Miss Jesus Sandals said, "Something tells me this is not quite the same."

I dismissed the chatter that followed and went about preparing a light meal for Joshua and myself. After dinner, Josh and I played video games and watched Spiderman until he fell asleep. After tucking him in, I poured myself a glass of merlot and settled in to catch up on all my TiVo shows. The phone rang, and to my initial shock, I discovered it was Ralph. I let it ring...refusing to listen to his whining about being unhappy and wanting us finally to get it right, one day. Miss Red Pumps said, "Xandy, you know the real reason you didn't answer that phone was because you couldn't say no to him." "With his married behind," interjected Miss Jesus Sandals. Both of them were correct, and I did the right thing (at least the one right thing that I was strong enough to do-not pick up the phone).

I spent the entire night watching TV and ended up sleeping in the living room on the sofa. I was awakened bright and early by Josh running from his room yelling, "Aunt Xandy, Olivia wants me to come with them today for her and her dad's hang out day and to sleep over to do the SpongeBob parade and carnival tomorrow. Can I? Can I?" "Whoa Josh, baby, let your poor aunt crank up her brain first, before you force me to start thinking. You know I'm old." He laughed. "You know you are not old...although you are older than my daddy." I said, "Thanks. I think." In the end, I gave him the green light to go with Olivia and Edmund. When they arrived to pick him up, Edmund sent the two of them off to play for a minute, so he could shock me with an unexpected question.

He asked me to come sit on the balcony with him for a moment, because he had something to say that he wanted me to consider. When we were seated, he took my hand and said, "Alexandria, I have been thinking, you and I have shared a lot, and we really do have a chemistry that neither of us can deny. We are great matches intellectually and definitely physically, and I feel that it's time for us to stop playing games and take this thing to another level." The lump in my throat felt like I was trying to swallow Mount Everest.

Taking advantage of my silence, he went on to say…. "Alex, I don't know where you are in your head and, most of all, your heart when it comes to me, but I do know we've had a good ride, and I feel like we should stop wasting time and get back together exclusively. I don't want it to stop there…I want us to get back together with a mutual end in mind, and that's eventual marriage." The look on my face propelled him to continue. "I'm not asking you to marry me right now. I just don't want this Ian guy to complicate your feelings for me and risk losing you completely.

I know you have options, and I also know you are uncomfortable with my jealousy over your friends, at times, but these are things we can work out." I could no longer remain silent. "Edmund, you know I did not expect this, and I don't know what to say. I know I care about you, and I admit we are good together, but I really feel like you are doing this to keep me from possibly moving on with someone else." I also confirmed his thoughts about his jealous behavior. "Yes, your insecurities bother me. The fact that you don't really trust me out of your sight, not even with Vince, bothers me, and you know that, and I don't know if it will get worse in the future." I ended this exchange with, "Edmund, let's not say anymore, right now…I just need time to think and so do you. Okay?" He moved toward me and said, "Alexandria," before he could continue, Joshua ran out on the balcony with the phone in his hand saying, "Aunt Xandy, your knight in shining "Army" is on the phone."

Time stood still. Edmund and I stood there, both of us staring at the phone and Joshua staring at both of us. Miss Jesus Sandals said, "Oh my goodness, what now, Xandy?" Miss Red Pumps had her say- "Alexandria, you are a single woman…no explanations for your choices are necessary." As I was raising my hand (that felt like a concrete block) to take the phone from Josh, Edmund did something that made my heart stop. He grabbed the telephone and yelled into it, "Look, I don't know who you are, but if you think for one minute you are the best thing this world has to offer Alexandria Morgan, you are wrong...I am!" "Don't worry about who I am," he responded, obviously to Ian questioning his identity. "I am the only man that's meant to be with this woman, and you can believe that, and I'm not going anywhere, dude!" I was making every effort to get the phone from him, but due to his height and stature, I was not successful.

"Hello, Hello." It was obvious Ian had hung up on Edmund. Edmund stood there staring at the phone, totally oblivious that he was being stared at by me, Joshua, and most of all- his daughter, Olivia. When this registered with him, he looked at each of us and calmly stated. "It's my job to protect all of you from the crazies of this world, and that's all I was doing." He ended his embarrassing explanation with, "Okay kids?" I gave Edmund the look from hell, but I managed to say, "Okay guys, you all better get going for your fun day." With that, the kids scrambled to get their things and Edmund whispered, "Xandy, I can't believe I did that. I am so sorry. Can we talk tonight, once the kids are down?" I said, "No, Edmund, just leave me alone, right now." Miss Jesus Sandals said, "Well there you have it- two more men bumping heads about you. Where and when will this end?" Miss Red Pumps was surprisingly quiet with a big grin on her face.

When all of them were out the door, I walked back out on the balcony and just sat there, staring into space. I wasn't sure how I felt about what just took place. I had mixed emotions about what Edmund did. I think a part of me was impressed and a little turned on by him staking a claim to me. I have never had a man willing to do that. Even in the fiasco between Julian and Danny...neither one of them took an intimidating stance about that clash. Danny should have been willing to kick Julian out of my house, based on the intense relationship that we were just coming down from having. Miss Red Pumps said, "Xandy, Edmund is willing to fight for you, girl." Miss Jesus sandals really gave me food for thought when she said, "Fighting is only necessary when it's in self-defense. Does this man have another side that could be a real hot-head or something?"

After about an hour, I realized that I needed to call Ian. When I dialed, he answered on the first ring. "Hey Ian, I am so sorry about what happened a little while ago. Please accept my apology. He is an ex of mine that's still around because of Josh's relationship with his daughter and..." Ian interrupted me by saying, "Alexandria, it's okay. After spending this short amount of time with you, I can truly understand how a man that has spent a great deal of time with you may feel when he senses a threat from another man." "Well," I said, "I am embarrassed, but I promise you it will not happen again."

Ian changed the conversation quickly to talk about the kids in his summer school class and how much he was going to miss them and his baseball team. We kept our conversation general until Ian said, "Would you like to get together to enjoy what's left of this day?" I readily agreed. He said, "Get ready and I'm coming to get you." I didn't bother to ask about our destination. In about an hour or so, Ian was at my door. "You look beautiful, as usual," he said as he reached in to kiss my forehead. "Thanks," I responded. "You are looking rather sexy yourself." He said, "You'd better grab a hat, cap or scarf; you are about to get some wind in those beautiful long tresses of yours." Although I grabbed a convenient scarf, I wasn't quite sure what he meant until we got downstairs to the parking lot, and I saw his grandmother's beautiful white convertible Mercedes parked glistening in the morning sun.

I felt like a kid. I actually got excited about my impending ride. And ride is what we did for most of the day. It felt like we did all of Philadelphia and outlying suburbia. We went along the lake, stopped at some quaint shops, had lunch, and eventually spent the afternoon strolling through Bartram's Garden. As we were both leaning in to sniff some of the most beautiful and fragrant roses in the world, Ian took my hand turned me around, and gave me the sweetest kiss imaginable. I felt like I could have stayed right in this moment forever. It is something about Ian that touches me in places that's never been touched before. It's as if our spirits connect in a place of serenity and comfort.

Miss Red Pumps snapped me out of la-la land with, "Girl, what's happening here? Are you considering buying a pair of shoes that you haven't even tried on?" "Oh, hush!" interrupted Miss Jesus Sandals, "You are obviously dissatisfied with anything decent." I came back to reality when I heard Ian say, "Alexandria, are you okay?" Boy, was I embarrassed. I said, "Sure, I guess I wasn't expecting that, especially after the way our morning started." Ian said, "It's really okay, Alex. I'm not the least bit concerned about your ex."

We spent the rest of the afternoon enjoying each other's company. Somewhere along the way, we agreed to stop by my place, grab my bag, and spend the rest of the night together at Ian's. As we were en route to his house with hot cheese steak sandwiches, a great bottle of wine, and two new DVD releases in tow, Ian's cell phone rang. When he looked at the number, I saw some hesitancy in answering it, but he decided to do so anyway. At the traffic light, I could hear the man's voice, and from bits and pieces, I made the assumption it was Nicholas. Ian removed all doubt when I heard him say, "No, It's not like that, Nicky. I truly forgot. I'm sorry."

Ian was silent after that, because it sounded like he couldn't get a word in edgewise, anyway. The conversation ended with Ian saying, "No, I will not do that." And I assumed Nicholas hung up on him after that, because there were no obvious goodbyes. He turned to me and said, "Well, I guess it's my turn now. Yours was this morning, and mine is tonight, but my mind is made up…now, shall we enjoy our night?" I said "sure." I tightened my scarf and away we sped into the night. When we entered the house through the garage…the house phone was ringing, and Ian never looked to see who was calling, nor did he answer it. While he was changing clothes, I peeked and saw that it was an unknown caller.

When I went into the bedroom and closed the door to change into comfy clothes, my shoulder duo jumped me simultaneously. Miss Red Pumps said, "What the hell?" Miss Jesus Sandals said, "Alexandria, have you lost your mind?" I said, "What are you two carrying on so about?" Miss Red Pumps said, "Did you not hear what he said about the telephone call he got in the car? Are you deaf or stupid?" "Yeah, Xandy, I'd like to know the answer to that question, myself. This man just compared Nicholas' obvious tirade on the phone in the car with Edmund being on the phone carrying on with him this morning. Edmund is your EX BOYFRIEND. Duh!" These two characters on my shoulder have a flair for the dramatic and have a tendency to see more than is there to see, so I dismissed both of them and went back to Ian downstairs.

After we ate and had settled in for the movie, Ian and I started to talk, instead of actually watching the movie. He confirmed the thoughts and feelings I was having in the gardens. He said, "Alex, when I'm with you I feel like all is right in the world, and I can't explain why." I admitted that I felt the same way. He pulled me to him, kissed me, and held me for what seemed like hours, and I didn't want to move, and obviously, he didn't either. We found ourselves waking up on the sofa after midnight and getting up heading to bed. As we got to the steps, Ian and I looked at each other and the answer was obvious. We headed up the stairs into my room, walked right past the bed into the dark bathroom, and amazingly disrobed and stepped into a warm shower TOGETHER. The only light in the whole area was from the windows, and we were mere silhouettes.

We both lathered and surprisingly turned for good back scrubs, while laughing and enjoying the scrub and the company. After getting mine, I turned and said, "My goodness, Ian, that felt so good. How much do I owe you?" And he said, "Just this." We then merged for a kiss directly under the showerhead, and I think we kissed until the water ran cold. As always, I felt Ian's lips tremble as we kissed. Although odd…I always welcomed his kisses. When we finally broke apart, we both hopped out and dried ourselves. I wrapped my hair in a towel, and we ran for the bed, giggling like kids. Once there, we finished what we started in the shower.

Our ultimate physical connection was definitely not at the top of my list when it came to either the size of the ship, or the motion of the ocean. It paled in comparison to other men, but everything else before that was five stars in every sense of the word. Afterwards, Ian kissed me on the forehead, and we cuddled up and went to sleep. When I woke up, Ian was gone, and I quickly threw on a jogging suit, pulled my hair in a ponytail, and went on a hunt for him. I found him sitting on the ground out at the lake's edge staring into space. He hadn't heard me calling him, nor did he hear my approach. I said, "Ian, you okay?" He looked up at me and to my shock, he had tears in his eyes.

I quickly joined him on the ground and said, "Ian, what's wrong? What happened?" He said, "Everything is okay, Xandy. I was just sitting here thinking, and I kind of got overwhelmed. Alexandria, I enjoy being with you sooo much, and although I'm not a devout churchgoer, I believe in God's divine will, and I believe God has sent you to be with me." I started to speak, and he stopped me by saying, "Xandy, just listen, please. I am a thirty-two-year-old man who's never been married and may or may not have a child, but that's neither here nor there. I don't have anyone to call my own. Yes, I have my parents and my brothers, but as you can see, we are not really close because of the position my grandmother put me in. Yet, it's that position that makes me quite capable of taking care of and providing well for someone special in my life.

I need to tell you that the questionable child I speak of is Dana's son. Not long after we broke up…I ran into Dana and saw that she was pregnant. She got defensive, just by my staring at her swollen belly, and said to me, "Don't even think about it. I got tired of waiting on you to show me the attention I needed and begged for, so I got it somewhere else and, fortunately and unfortunately, this is the result." Ian's tears started to flow then and he said, "Alexandria, something in my heart tells me that's my son. The timing is so perfect for it to be, and the look in Dana's eyes says that it's true, but she will die and go to Hell before she allows me to know the truth. She is with someone else now, who she says is her son's father and will not interact with me at all. They have left the state, and she and her son are happy as can be, so I will never know."

All I could muster up to say was, "Ian, I am so sorry." Ian went on to elaborate on how much he had to offer somebody and his large capacity to love and care for someone. He said, "I know you may be wondering why I've never actually seriously tried to take the physical part of our relationship any further before now, and I'll tell you. After that situation with Dana, I made a vow to myself that I would not put myself in that position again. Dana was sexually high strung, and I found myself attempting to do everything -however, wherever, and whenever she wanted, just to keep her mind off of the physical part of our relationship. My grandmother always taught me to build a relationship on a solid foundation, and sex would and should never be that foundation."

"It's okay, Ian. I understand, and I'm fine with the way things are with us, physically." "Liar, Liar pants on fire," sang Miss Red Pumps. For some reason, my shoulder duo had been quiet lately, but Miss Red Pumps couldn't pass up this opportunity. I went on to say, "Ian, I've made a lot of mistakes in my relationships, and moving too fast has been one of them." I scooted in closer and put my head on Ian's shoulder, and we sat like that for a while. He reached for my hand and said, "Alexandria, I'm falling in love with you, although I am trying so hard not to." Out of nowhere came, "Me too, Ian." We continued to sit there in the grass, watching the wind blow ripples across the lake, listening to the singing birds, and both of us feeling at home.

Ian broke the spell and said, "Hey girlfriend, want some breakfast or shall I say brunch?" I said, "Sure." We got up and headed into the house, and Ian into the kitchen. He quickly reappeared and said, "Sit tight. I'm going to run to the store and come back and whip us up a breakfast fit for royalty." He sprinted for the garage and was gone in a flash. I grabbed the newspaper and headed out to the hammock to relax, while he was gone. I was deeply engrossed in the world's current events when I was startled to the point of almost flipping out of the hammock. When I collected myself, I looked up in the direction of the voice and looked right into Nicholas' face. Nicholas, although still handsome, was not up to par-fashion and hygiene- wise this morning.

He said, "Well, good morning to you, Miss Morgan. I didn't expect you to be here on the deck. I didn't see any cars, so I did not know Ian had company. Otherwise, I would not have used my key to come in." I stood up and walked over to take a seat at the table and said, "No problem, Nicholas. How have you been?" "I've seen better days" he responded. "I got upset last night and tied one on and can't seem to shake it off this morning. Where's Ian? Gone to the store to pick up something special for breakfast, I'm sure." The big mouths on my shoulders were awake and in gear. Miss Red Pumps asked three questions, without pausing for any answers. "He got drunk because he got upset last night. Was it because Ian was with you? He has a key? How does he know exactly what Ian was away doing this morning?" Miss Jesus Sandals said, "Xandy, use your head. This is an opportunity to get some answers. Ask this man some questions." Miss Jess Sandals was right. So, I proceeded to apply my investigative skills I learned at the University of Carmen.

"Yes Nicholas, Ian is gone to the store to get some things to prepare for breakfast. How did you know that?" A smile came across Nicholas' unshaven face, and he turned to me and said, "I'm closer to Ian than anyone else in this world. I know his habits, his likes, his dislikes and, most times, what he's going to do before he even knows himself." "Now that was a mouth full right there," said Miss Red Pumps. I hid my recoil from his words really well, but pressed in for more. "Oh really?" I said. "Sounds like you two have quite a history. How did you guys meet?" "Well, I see Ian has never told you about me, so please allow me." I buckled my emotional seat belt, because something told me I was in for quite a ride.

Nicholas went on to say, "Ian and I met in our senior year in college. He was your typical college boy, trying to hang out with the locals and fit in. We hooked up one night at a club, and we've been friends ever since. We've seen each other through a lot of trials and weathered a lot of storms together. I was close with Ian before his inheritance, and I know the pain and distance from his family that has happened since his grandmother's death." "Wow" I said, "I hate it that he is not close to his family, and it's a shame that it's over choices his grandmother made about her own money and assets." "Oh no... Miss Morgan, Ian's pain goes farther and deeper than that with his family. Maybe I shouldn't be telling you all of this, but I think you need to know, and I doubt he will ever tell you," said Nicholas. Miss Jesus Sandals said, "Alexandria, listen closely, but don't fool yourself. This man is enjoying every bit of this."

Nicholas continued, "I know Ian has told you about his cousin who was raised with him as a brother, right?" I said, "Yes." "Well," he went on, "that cousin had an older brother who was killed in the car accident with Ian's Aunt. This is the cousin that I feel affected Ian's life more than anyone else ever has. You see, this boy molested Ian, and the family knows about it, but since he was killed with his mother, nothing else was ever said or done about it. I think everybody just pretended it never happened. Ian has tried to do the same thing all these years, but it still haunts him in a lot of ways. One of those ways is that he has never forgiven his parents for not protecting him and not acting like it was the big deal that it was."

Nicholas saw how pale I was, sitting there, almost gasping for air-trying to breathe through his story, but that didn't slow his pace. He continued, "Ian being the chosen one to receive his grandparent's inheritance goes deeper than his dad's drinking and his mother whoring around. I think his grandmother was trying to make up for the hurt and confusion this whole thing has caused Ian by making sure his adult life was comfortable and not lacking anything." At this point, I didn't know if I should take a running start and go jump head-first in the lake or slap the hell out of this man for having the unmitigated nerve to tell me these private things about Ian to shock and hurt me. Miss Red Pumps said, "Go ahead and punch him, Alex. He deserves a bloody nose. This rascal is trying to run you off. Can't you see that?"

I took the high road and made Miss Jesus Sandals proud of me. I said, "As you can tell, Nicholas, I had no idea about all of this, but my heart goes out to Ian and to anyone who has ever been victimized by someone." Nicholas was quiet for a while, but after what seemed like giving it some thought…he went on to say… "Ian shared his story with me not long after we met one night when we were drunk and just getting back from raising hell at one of our local hangouts. I'm not sure what prompted him, but I'm glad he did, because then I was free to share mine. You see, I too grew up being repeatedly molested by a friend of my dad's, and although I told my story…no one believed me and cared enough to do anything about it so…. Voila! Here I am, today, after attempted suicides and much therapy…a happy, successful gay man!" I jumped up and walked to the edge of the deck and Nicholas followed me.

"Alexandria, Ian understands me and accepts me, because he knows, like no one else knows, why I've made the choices I've made. I have been there with him through his ups and downs, especially with that Dana, and I will admit I am protective and possessive when it comes to him." My silence urged him on. "I will admit that I got angry at him and, most of all, at you last night. He and I had talked about going to a party and when I caught up with him, he wouldn't ditch you for me." It was at this point that he stopped and looked directly in my eyes for my response. I didn't give him the response he sought. Miss Jesus Sandals said, "This rascal has some nerve. I'll give him credit for that, but nothing else."

"Nicholas, Ian told me about Dana." I said with the sound of impatience in my voice. Not wanting to leave well-enough alone, he went on to say, "Did he tell you that Dana may have a child for him, but won't let him find out or come near the child? The child is a boy, and she is worried that Ian has child molestation in his blood or even better than that, she's completely convinced that Ian is gay?" That was the proverbial shot heard around the world! I bolted from the deck and up the stairs to the guest room and slammed the door. As I was ascending the stairs, I looked back and saw Nicholas standing in the doorway with an undeniable smirk on his face.

Once in the room, I started throwing my things in my bag and then realized that I was stranded. I came here with Ian. I started pacing, trying to get my thoughts together. My shoulder duo said nothing! I pondered how to get myself as far away from here as possible. If I called Vince, I would have too many questions and too much explaining to do, so I checked my cash and called a cab, which I knew was going to cost me a small fortune because of the distance, but at this point, I did not care.

I don't know what took Ian so long at the store. It was my guess that he was running to different stores, as he always does to round up all of his special ingredients. I was praying he did not show up as I was sitting upstairs waiting on my taxi. When I heard the taxi blow, I quickly came down the stairs and was met by Nicholas, obviously having seen the cab. He said, "Alexandria, I am so sorry. Please don't do this. I was wrong to tell you all of that stuff. That was Ian's place to tell you or not tell you. I was mad, and I wanted to hurt you, because you are different, and I see how Ian feels about you. Please, please, forgive me." I could clearly see as I was standing there facing Nicholas on the stairs that he meant every word he said. He was shaking and tears were rolling down his face. He reached for my arm saying, "Alexandria, please don't go. Ian is going to kill me. Let me fix this please?" He begged. "No, Nicholas." I responded, "Please get out of my way and leave me alone. You have done more than enough. My cab is waiting."

At that moment, the door opened, and there stood Ian in the door to the garage with his arms full of grocery bags saying, "Nicholas, what in the hell are you doing here and better yet…why is there a taxi sitting in my driveway?" Nicholas and I looked at each other, and the floodgates to my dam burst, and I began to sob and ran down the stairs and out of the door. Ian had obviously dropped all the groceries on the floor and was right on my heels, with Nicholas coming right behind him. "Alexandria, wait! What is wrong? What happened? Somebody please tell me what's going on!" I was in the taxi still sobbing, and Ian was refusing to let go of the door, and Nicholas was standing there looking like he was on the verge of fainting.

I managed to speak. I said, "Ian please close the door and let me go home. I'm sure Nicholas will explain everything after I'm gone. Please Ian, don't make this scene any worse than what it is. I don't want to talk to you, right now. I can't. I just want to go home." "Alexandria, please don't go. If you've just got to leave, let me take you." "No, Ian," I finally screamed and managed to jerk the door free from his hand. With that, he reached in his pocket and threw a hundred-dollar bill in the front seat at the driver and said give her the change. With that, he stood there looking at me with tears in his eyes and turned and hit Nicholas square in the face with his fist.

As the taxi made its way around the circular driveway, I saw Nicholas lying on the ground, and Ian go up the steps into his house and close the door. Miss Red Pumps started in as soon as we were on the road, but Miss Jesus Sandals cut her off by saying, "Shhh! None of us need to speak before giving this situation some great thought."

When I arrived at my home, I got out of the taxi and walked through the gate to my house, carrying my overnight bag in hand. I was in such a fog, I was oblivious to my appearance and how my walking into my neighborhood carrying luggage looked to anyone. When I got behind closed doors, I fell across my bed and stayed there, staring into space for about three hours. The only reason I finally moved was my urgent need to go to the bathroom. The whole time I had been home, my phone had been ringing in the house, as well as my cell phone going off in my purse. After ignoring all of this, I managed to eat a bowl of soup and get in bed for the night, although it was only 6 pm. I woke early and called in to work and arranged for someone else to handle one of our biggest job fair's coverage for me, and then I went back to bed. I was jarred out of my comatose state by the sound of my front door slamming and my name being bellowed from the living room. I immediately recognized it was Vince. I covered my head with the comforter and refused to answer and prayed he wouldn't discover that the big messy lump in the middle of the bed was me.

No such luck, Vince stomped into my room and jerked the cover off and said, "All right, Alexandria, what in the hell is going on? You passing up the opportunity to land the Phoenix account and missing our biggest job fair is proof that you have either won the lotto or lost your mind. And don't lie to me…. Ian called me this morning, so I've already heard what happened." I was shocked over that bit of news, and although I had mixed emotions about Vince knowing all of yesterday's details, I was somewhat relieved that the cat was out of the bag with someone I trusted to talk about the "cat" with. Vince pulled me up out of the bed and said "You look a mess, and I am not going anywhere until we talk, and we are not going to talk until after you take a shower and tame that dragon in your mouth." I followed orders without saying a word.

Once the two of us had settled down at the table with a cup of joe…I still did not speak. So Vince took the lead and relayed everything to me that Ian had shared with him. When he finished, he asked me if Ian's account of things was accurate. To my surprise, it was. I was shocked that Ian had even confirmed Nicholas's story about his molestation as a child. I managed to find my voice and said, "Vince, I am so confused. I don't know if I'm hurt or angry for myself or for Ian or if I'm feeling betrayed or what." Vince told me that Ian had called this morning about 5:30 am and asked if he could meet him at the jogging trail.

Vince agreed out of curiosity, and when Ian arrived, he regurgitated everything. Needless to say, they did not jog, but sat at one of the pavilions and talked until about 7:30 a.m. Vince went on to say... "Alex, let me be straight with you, and pardon the pun, but I believe this guy is the real thing. Yes, he has a horrible experience in his childhood, a dysfunctional family, and a gay fool for a friend, but I believe he is legit and that he loves you." That was the last thing I expected to come out of Vince's mouth, because I have heard his commentary about gay people in the past, especially those rumored to be in the closet by day and out at night.

When Vince was finally silent, Miss Jesus Sandals said, "Can I please comment here?" That was strange, because neither of my shoulder companions had ever asked my permission to throw in their two cents in the past. When I said, "Yeah, you might as well," she went on to say, "Xandy, even as a shock to myself, I agree with Vince. I like Ian, and I believe he is a good man and that he has not deceived you in any way. Yes, he did not tell you about the horrid thing that happened to him, but who would share that in the beginning stages of a relationship?"

Vince and Miss Jesus Sandals both made sense, but I guess the fact that all of this information hit me like a meteor out of the sky the next morning after I had slept with Ian the night before was almost unfathomable. I really didn't comment on Vince's opinion about the situation. I just told him I had a lot of thinking to do, and that I just wanted to go back to bed, so I would be rested when Edmund came that evening to drop off Josh.

Vince said, "Okay Alex, but before you go off and make all these decisions, please at least talk to Ian and hear what he's got to say. Remember, your last conversation with anyone was with Nicholas.

You never gave Ian an opportunity to be heard, and I think, at the very least, he deserves that. That guy is hurting, but he's more concerned about you than he is himself, and I can only imagine what Nicholas feels like and, most of all, looks like. Ian said that he fractured his nose and busted his lip pretty bad." While Vince was ending his speech, I was thinking, "When did Vince, the iceberg Casanova, turn into a compassionate Dr. Phil?" My friend gave me a hug at the door and left.

In the quiet of my room, I tried to come to terms with my feelings about Ian. There was something so different about him. Out of frustration, I rolled over and called Edmund and asked if Josh could spend one more night with them, because I felt under the weather, and he readily agreed and said he would run out and buy Josh a couple of outfits to tide him over, until I felt better. Although he tried to engage me in a conversation about his telephone escapade, I told him I was not up to it and that we would talk later. After hanging up, I called Ian. He answered the phone on the first ring, and all I could say was, "Come over here" and then hung up.

He must have caught the Red Eye to my house, because he was there in record time. When he rang my doorbell, I yelled that the door was open. He walked in, looking like he had just escaped from a refugee camp. We stood there looking at each other, and without a word, both of us started to cry and melted into each other's arms. Although my confusion and anger was still there, I put it on the back burner to be there for Ian. I could only imagine the magnitude of his embarrassment having had two painful experiences revealed to someone he cared about before he was ready. Miss Jesus Sandals whispered, "Enough of this emotional stuff, Alexandria; you need some answers and don't let him off the hook until you get them."

It was as if Ian heard her. He said, "Sit down and don't interrupt me, please. This is not easy for me, but it's necessary. First of all, I want to apologize for Nicholas' behavior-it was inexcusable. He's never acted like this before. He admitted seeing how much I care about you, and he felt threatened that he was going to lose my friendship. He actually said he could look down the road and see us married with a family and not having the desire or the room for him in our lives. You see, Nicholas's family disowned him because of the disbelief about his molestation and that he is a self-admitted gay man. He sees me as the only person who sincerely cares for him. Nicholas has been suicidal in the past, and each time when the dust settled, I was the only one standing *there* to care for him and about him. He saw you as a direct threat to him being loved and accepted by the only family he has, and that just happens to be me. Mind you, this does not excuse or justify his behavior, but maybe, it will shed some light on the choice he made to do this.

Now…about me…yes, my older cousin molested me for about two solid years, before he was killed in the car wreck with his mother. I told my parents and neither one of them wanted to do anything about it. They didn't want the public scandal or the family implosion. My cousin denied my allegations and beat me unmercifully for telling, and my family just chalked it up to boys just being boys! My father convinced my grandparents, who were in another state, that I was getting therapy for the situation and made me lie to them to confirm it. My father just drank more, and my mother ran the streets more, and when my cousin was killed, they felt that it was resolved. So I suppressed the hurt, pain, and anguish I was feeling for a lot of years.

Now, you see, it's not just my grandmother's inheritance that has driven a wedge between my parents and me. Nicholas was the first person I ever told about it, outside of my family, until I told Dana. Telling her was the biggest mistake I could have made, because Dana's and my sex drive were on two opposite ends of the spectrum, and all of a sudden, she had her answer for why it was that way. Although we were sexually active or so I thought…it was never enough for her. It definitely did not help matters, with me being as close to Nicky as I am. According to her mathematics, she put two and two together and came up with three- me, her, and Nicholas being involved in a closet triangle.

When I accidently found out that she was pregnant, her last words to me were, "I am having a boy, and he's not yours, and besides- you will never come near him, because I refuse to have a gay son." He dropped his head even lower and said in a whisper… "So there you have it." Miss Jesus Sandals quickly yelled in my ear, "Alexandria Rae

Morgan, interrogate this man about his real sexual desires and orientation before you allow your jury to reach a decision." Unbelievably, Miss Red Rumps shrugged her shoulders and simply said, "I don't know what to think or say, Xandy. I really don't."

I mustered up the courage to ask the million-dollar question. "Ian since your molestation ended, have you ever found yourself attracted to men or thought about becoming intimate with a male?" Ian took my hand and looked directly into my eyes and said, "At the risk of losing you for good, I will be honest with you. When I was a teenager and my early college years, I battled with being attracted to males. After that, I remained celibate until my senior year in college, and then I kind of got promiscuous- but only with females. I am not gay and have no confusion about that. I love Nicholas as if he was my own brother, and because of our shared traumatic experience, I can relate to the torture to which he has succumbed. The only reason I was trying to be reserved in becoming too physical with you is because I knew you were special, and you felt special, and I wanted nothing to ruin that, but now all of my efforts seemed to have been in vain. When we made love, I felt something beyond the physical, and I did not ever want to lose that with you, but I know that I have already lost you, and it's breaking my heart."

I managed to say… "Oh, Ian, I want to say you have not lost me, but I just don't know." Ian said, "I understand, Xandy. I really do, but just know that I love you." With that, I pulled him to me and hugged him so hard, until I think he coughed. I looked up at him and said… "Stay with me, Ian." We turned toward the room, climbed in bed, and I think both of us sunk into unconsciousness…lying tangled in each other's embrace. Miss Jesus Sandals was screeching in my ear. "Well, did he or did he not sleep with guys as a teenager and during his early college years, before he became celibate?" I turned a deaf ear to her question! Strangely, both of us woke, just as the sun came up, and Ian turned to me and said… "I could see us watching the sunrise forever, Xandy…if not in this lifetime…maybe the next one." With that, he kissed me on the forehead and got out of the bed and walked out of my door. I called into work again and just laid there. I had to call Carmen or my mother or somebody. Ian Sommers had had a major impact on my heart, and I'm not sure why or how or what I wanted to do about it.

All I knew was… When I was with him, I was totally just "Xandy." He made me feel like I had arrived at a spiritual destination of some kind. The comfort I felt with Ian was not sexual or physical, but it was something so intense, although it had no name. Out of nowhere, Miss Red Pumps, for the first time in her existence in my life, gently made everything so crystal clear to me about Ian. She said… "Alexandria, there's something about Ian that reminds you of your Daddy!" I burst into tears, because it finally made sense to me.

I have had more than my share of men I care deeply about and that have professed intense feelings for me. The way Ian took care of me and doted on me and made me feel warm and protected were all the endearing things I had only felt with my father. Miss Jesus Sandals put the icing on my cake of confusion when she asked me, "Alexandria, what is the one thing your father would always do when he was coming or going or comforting you?" I started to ball uncontrollably, because the answer was – kiss me on my forehead!

# CHAPTER 11
## ◆ TIME OUT (OR TRIED TO) ◆

### Ian, Danny, Julian

Needless to say…after my situation with Ian, I had to call *a* serious relationship "Time Out." I called my CEO and went in to talk with him and explained that I was burnt out and wanted to take a month off to get my mental and physical state back in sync. It was not a hard sell, because I rarely ever took a vacation, and everyone knew that I was a die-hard numbers-girl. Whenever I returned, I would make up for the time off, and my numbers would pass those who had been there the whole time. Plus, I have enough money in my savings to take some years off, counting my mother's investment return on my inheritance from my dad and my personal savings account. Once the groundwork was laid at the office for my absence… I knew I had to have a plan.

The first thing I did was call Taylor and told him that I would be bringing Joshua home, because I was on leave and just needed to be with my family for a while. Taylor said, "Sis, are you okay? Is there anything I should know about or that I can help you with?" I assured him that I was fine and that my favorite nephew, his violin, and I would be home by the end of the week. I just had a few loose ends to wrap up. After that, I called my mom and told her I needed the comfort of her presence and the familiarity of my childhood surroundings and that I would be home for a couple of weeks. She was elated. She said,

"Oh, Alexandria, this couldn't have happened at a better time. I'm going to need your help and support with something, but I will talk to you about it once you get here." "Hmmm what could that be?" I asked myself, but I was too fragmented in my own life to dwell on it at the time.

Joshua and I spent the rest of the week packing and preparing the house for my absence. I gathered all the keys, garage remote, and upcoming maintenance notices that were due to be paid, and called Vince and told him I would be stopping by in the AM at the office to give him his instructions. In the meantime, Mr. "bigmouth Joshua" had told Olivia about my plans, and of course, Edmund shows up unannounced to plead his case. I was not in the mental place to entertain Edmund's relationship gab at the moment- or so I thought. Edmund said, "Alex, if I promise not to question you as to why you are leaving town so suddenly, will you at least go for a walk with me across the street in the park?" I agreed to do so.

We walked along quietly, and to my surprise, when he reached to hold my hand I did not withdraw. We stopped under a beautiful old oak tree and somehow decided to sit on the ground and gaze at a couple across the grass, who were obviously involved in what looked like a disagreement, but what soon turned into a make-up session. Edmund said, "Boy, Alex, why do we all make life so complicated? It would be so simple if we could just all be in the same thought process and emotional place at the same time."

"Yeah, you're right Edmund. No matter how we try...we always seem to miss the target, because I'm convinced the target does move." I said. In response to that remark, Edmund shifted closer to me and looked straight into my eyes. He said, "Alex, I have never moved- not once since we have been together. I've been right here, caring for you and trying to make sure you are always okay. I love you, Alexandria, and I believe you know that. I know you have issues with my ex, and I even believe you are somewhat jealous of my relationship with my daughter. I want to assure you, here and now, that the capacity that I have to love you and take care of you is limitless. We both know our age difference, and we also know that I am high strung and jealous when I feel threatened, but I only get that way when I'm not made to feel secure in my relationship."

"Look Edmund," I began, "no one can make you feel insecure; that comes from some place within you. I believe that there could be times when you act before you think out of jealousy-induced anger, and I'm not so sure what you may be capable of doing during those times. You frightened me and the kids with your outburst on the phone the other week." Edmund admitted that he understood my concern, but emphatically professed to never allow himself to lose control to the point he could bring harm to anyone. Miss Jesus Sandals inserted, "Well, there's a first time for everything, and buddy, you have already had your first time when you pushed your ex-wife down and hurt her." "I believe him Alex," said Miss Red Pumps. "Everybody has made mistakes, but he's older now and learned his lesson."

Ignoring the shoulder chatter, I acknowledged Edmund's statement that I knew how he felt about me, and I confessed to caring a great deal about him. We have so much in common. I readily admit that he turns me on, not only physically, but intellectually as well. We sat there just enjoying the breeze until the chemistry between us began to ignite each other's thoughts. I quickly said, "Edmund I promise you, when I get back…we'll talk more about this." With that, we stood up. As he was helping me to my feet, he pulled me in his arms and kissed my very soul.

I think I would have eloped with Edmund at that moment if his cell phone had not rung, and as he lifted it up, I saw his ex-wife's name on the screen. I said, "Go ahead, you don't have to ignore her call because I'm standing here." "Come on, Alexandria," Edmund recanted, "don't do this. After all, I haven't said one word about that Ian character. I bet he or one of those other losers you think I don't know about is going away with you to some far off place, so you can play footsies under the covers." "He didn't just say that-did he?" snapped Miss Red Pumps. As soon as he saw the look on my face, he said, "Alex, forgive me, I'm sorry -but before you walk or run away from me, look at me and tell me that you can't see yourself making a life with me. Tell me you don't want me or even love me. Tell me!" I couldn't say no to either challenge. All I managed to say was, "Walk me home Edmund…we'll talk when I get back." We walked in silence, and I didn't bother to look back as he got in his car and drove off.

I managed to spend the rest of the day preparing for our departure in the next couple of days. Joshua could sense something was not quite right about his aunt and made every effort to do silly things to make me laugh and even committed to fixing dinner for us. So…my nephew and I enjoyed some ham sandwiches, chips, grape juice, and a microwave brownie, while we watched the cartoon network that evening. Once Kiddie Kab had picked up Josh that next morning, I got dressed to go into the office to see Vince and fill him in on my plans and give him all of his do's and don'ts, which included no females in my house during my absence. When I arrived at the office, I was told there was an impromptu Sr. recruiter's meeting going on.

◆

I tried to kill time by going into my office to set my outgoing voice messages and my email messages. The meeting ran longer than expected, so I decided to walk over to the coffee shop to get some juice, since it was after the coffee rush. I was sitting there enjoying a large cup of pomegranate juice and perusing the Philadelphia Examiner, when to my surprise, I heard a familiar voice. I hesitated for a moment to prepare myself for seeing him again, and when I finally turned around…there he was… Danny and one of the most beautiful young ladies I've ever seen. Her profile was facing me, but Danny could clearly see me, yet made it obvious that he was not interested in seeing me or interacting with me. Although our eyes locked momentarily…his facial expression did not change, nor did he skip a beat in his conversation with her.

Miss Jesus Sandals was the first to *speak*, because she knew Miss Red Pumps would encourage me to cause a scene of some kind. She said, "Alexandria, leave well enough alone…it's obvious Danny has moved on -so leave him be." She was right. So I quickly turned back around and continued, though pretending now, to read the paper and finish my juice. I could swear I felt Danny's eyes burning a hole in my back, but I refused to take a peek to see. I did hear her say, "Daniel, you are so silly, cut it out." Miss Red Pumps said, "She's messing with you, Xandy. Don't ever think for one minute that a current woman doesn't have an "ex–in–the-place" radar." I ignored her and gulped the rest of my juice and scurried out of the shop and ran across the intersection against the light. The meeting was over upon my return, and Vince and I went into the staff lounge and chatted for a while. I refused to answer or comment at all about Ian. I told him about Edmund and Danny at the coffee shop.

Vince said, "Gosh, Alex, you've got a plate full of men and can't seem to figure out what to do or not to do with any of them. That Edmund guy would definitely give you a wonderful life, and he is truly a family guy. I'm not sure if you will be able to have any friends in your life, other than females, and they won't be around long if he feels threatened by their relationship with you." He concluded, "As a man, I do believe that a man will change for the better to keep a woman that he truly loves happy. It's not every day you find someone with his family values and secure future. He's been super with Joshua, and Josh genuinely seems to like him." I hesitated, but responded with, "That is something for me to think about Vince, but I don't think I will have to worry about Danny being on my plate anymore, because I just saw him with a runway beauty that made him ignore me. She had a flawless complexion and the body to match." Vince responded with… "Don't be so quick to make that assumption, Alex. I bet you that guy is still crazy about you. And by the way…a few trips to the tanning bed would do you some justice right about now." I hit him, and we stood and embraced and said our goodbyes.

While greeting several peers as I was leaving and was walking to my car in the parking deck, I heard my name. "Miss Alex, hold up!" My heart was beating like a kettledrum in the Philadelphia Symphony. I turned around and there he was. "Hi Danny," I said, trying to sound causal and nonchalant. "Hey Alex, how are you? Just wanted to say I'm sorry about being rude and not speaking to you over at the shop; that's why I ran over here with hopes of catching up with you." I responded with, "Danny, its fine. You don't owe me an apology. You did the right thing to respect your girlfriend." Miss Red Pumps chimed in, "Well, well, look who's on a fishing expedition."

He quickly responded with, "Even though it's really none of your business, I will tell you that that young lady was not my girlfriend. She's not even a friend. She is the owner of the company's daughter. She is in marketing training and stops by to meet accounts and visit with distributors occasionally on our routes. And for the record...she is very much engaged and planning a lavish wedding in five months." For some reason...I exhaled! "Danny," I said, "you didn't have to tell me all of that, but it was truly good to see you. And for the record, with your skills, you could make any woman cancel her wedding plans." He blushed and Miss Jesus Sandals threw up her hands saying, "Now where did that come from, young lady?"

We stood there chatting, in general, until I asked about Joseph. He said, "Joseph and I have moved into our own apartment, and he is very much involved in a respite center day care that also provides evening and weekend care when needed. He loves it and has made lots of friends. It gives me more freedom now." "That's great," I responded. "Maybe I can see him one day." "How about this weekend?" he quickly asked me. I told him that I was leaving town for about a month, just to clear my head for a while. Danny walked closer to me and, in almost a whisper, he said, "Xandy, I don't mean to add anything else in your head to clear, but seeing you today is what I've wanted to do for a while now. I know our last encounter that day at your place was awful, but I take the responsibility for that. You wanted more from me and with me, and I couldn't see past my guilt to allow you to enter my life. Yes, I still have Joseph and will always have him, but I'm not willing to continue to shut you out if you are willing to give us another try."

Danny looked as if the last thing he wanted me to do was interrupt him, so I listened as he continued. "My mother, grandmother, and whole family misses you, and I think we can make it stick if we try again. I'm almost through with my Associates Degree, and I plan to continue for as long as I can. What do you think, Miss Alex?" I found myself saying, "But I want children, one day, and you don't, Danny. In fact, you have had a vasectomy." "You are right!" He replied. "Who knows what tomorrow holds? Maybe we could get it reversed or even adopt, but I will be honest, the chances of that happening are slim... my mind has not changed about kids. Joseph is my kid!"

Miss Red Pumps said, "Girl, what are you doing? Don't you think you have enough irons in the fire?" Danny took my silence as me considering his revelation and moved in to me. Before I knew what was happening, he was kissing me, while walking me backward to one of the concrete columns. Once there, with my back against the wall, we started to make out like high schoolers. "God, I missed this man, his smell, his athletic build, his everything!" I said to myself. I think we both realized where we were at the same time and broke apart, giggling. "Well, that's what's up, Miss Alex. I'm going to walk away while I can for now...but call me when you get back. I'll always be waiting for you." He walked off looking oh so sexy, and it took everything in my being not to run after him and tackle him like an NFL player, right there in the parking deck. Miss Jesus Sandals quietly said, "Child, you need some serious help!"

The next few days were uneventful, except for a visit from Julian the night before I left. My shoulder duo agreed that my condo was busier than a bus station in Los Angeles. I reminded them that I was young and well within my rights to explore and sow my wild oats. Miss Jesus Sandals said, "Alexandria, my dear, you are way over your oats-sowing limit."

Julian and I had never parted as far as our physical connection. I love Julian's looks, his devil-may-care attitude, and his musical skills, not to mention other skills. He was finally under contract with Sony, and his CD was climbing the charts. In fact, he made me promise that whenever he made his public debut at the Grammys or any other award shows...that I would be on his arm. Oddly, he attributes much of his music to the inspiration that I bring to him, physically and mentally. Julian says that I am "the force in his life that centers him." On that night, while Julian and I were enjoying a candlelight dinner of take out and enjoying the sound of his music as it filled the room, he said, "This is it, Xandy; we are good together. Let's do this." "What are you talking about Julian?" I asked. "Are you high or something?"

"No, I'm not high, unless you want to count you as my drug

of choice," he responded. Both of us laughed. I pressed in for more information, while we were on the subject. "Julian, I know that your deceased child's mom is still close to you. In fact, she has carte blanche at your place. Are you still sleeping with her?" Without a pause, he said, "Yes I am. But I don't have sex with her." "Yeah right," squealed both of my shoulder companions. I reminded them that I have slept with guys, lately Ian, without there being any sex involved. Miss Red Pumps reminded me quickly, "Ian doesn't count and we both know why." Rather than get into a long debate with her, I turned my attention back to Julian. "Explain that please," I asked.

"Alexandria," he began, "you know what happened between us. She has never come to terms with the death of our child, and in many ways, neither have I, and there are just times when we turn to each for comfort that only we can give each other." "But," I began, "what if we do decide to get together-under one roof? What then?" He went into a distant like trance as if he had not thought about this before, and from the looks of things, he had not. His response deepened my confusion. He said, "I honestly don't know Alex, but I will work something out, because you are important to me and for me, and even though I want to be with you...I can't totally turn my back on her. We can fix this somehow." He got up and walked out on the balcony and stood there. With his hair loose and blowing in the wind and under the natural light of the night...he looked like a "Greek God." I followed him out there, and the rest of the night was a pure beautiful melody.

At dawn, Julian and I said goodbye, and he rushed out into the morning air to avoid the possibility of bumping into Joshua, who was going to be dropped off at the curb by Edmund. I had allowed him to stay over with Olivia for his last night in town. Edmund kept his promise not to get out of the car and blew me a kiss as he pulled way with a look of sadness on his face. Joshua and I ate some cereal, threw our things in the car, and headed off to Virginia.

When Josh and I finally arrived at the house, everyone was there. One would have thought that Joshua and I had just come home from fighting a war in the Middle East, the way they greeted us and was carrying on. My mother had prepared a feast that included all of my favorite foods, and it was obvious that Jeff had been up to his grilling tricks that morning. The wonderful smell of mesquite filled the air. Aunt Sandra was there with a nice piece of eye candy, who wasn't much older than Joshua, but he appeared to be her number one fan throughout the gathering. His name was Logan, and he was one of Jeff's flight students. His parents owned their own plane and demanded that he become a licensed pilot as a backup to their hired one. So considering his looks and background, I could see why he caught my aunt's eye. Aunt Sandra was never the type to be concerned about public opinion. About an hour after my arrival... Jeff's kids showed up and really made this a complete family affair. I was actually happy to see them, because it had been a while, and they were really cool people to hang out with. I continued to love the way they obviously loved and respected my mom.

Surprisingly, Taylor did not have a member of one of his harem present. His whole focus was on Joshua and us. He wasn't doing his usual, which was texting, Face Timing, and checking the market rates. Something was amiss. Joshua said, "Man this is like Thanksgiving; everybody is here." Everybody was talking and munching on all the many appetizers my mom had readily available. One thing that Ms. Abigail knew how to do was entertain. She could put on a shindig from one end of the class spectrum to the other (Dom Perignon Champagne in a crystal flute to Corona in a cooler).

I finally caught up with my mom in the kitchen alone and asked her what was really going on. I knew that all of this hoopla was not just because Joshua and I had come home. Her response to me was, "Alexandria, we thought it would be good to come together as a whole family. We haven't ever really done that before. All of you kids come and go at different times and never really get a chance to see and visit with each other." With that, she kissed me on the cheek and flitted back out and into the conversations that were going on around us. Eventually, she picked up her little crystal bell and rang it, which all of us recognized as being time for us to gather, pray, and eat.

Jeff delivered a touching prayer that included blessings upon us, individually and collectively, and then we all dived in to graze on the feast that was so eloquently set before us. Aunt Sandra and Logan were making goo-goo eyes across the table and giggling like high school kids. Taylor, Jeff, and his two sons were involved in a hearty debate about the state of the world's economy. Joshua was busy asking Cecily, Jeff's daughter, about her involvement in the orchestra and got her committed to listening to him play his violin after dinner. Mother and I were maintaining a general conversation about current events and life in general, which I thought, was so odd.

She had not mentioned or questioned the reason for me so abruptly deciding to come home for a couple of weeks. Just as I was about to call her out for not having done so, Jeff stood up and commanded everyone's attention. He said, "Since we finally have all of you under one roof, Abby and I thought it would be a good time to fill you in on what's going on with us." You could hear the blades of grass moving with the wind outside. It was so quiet in the room. I looked at Aunt Sandra, and she smiled and looked the other way. Jeff pulled my mom up from her seat and said, "Miss Abigail Morgan has said "yes" to becoming my wife." With that being said, they embraced each other and shared a lingering kiss as if they were in the room alone. The silence was still there, until Aunt Sandra jumped up clapping her hands saying, "That is awesome!"

The rest of us followed suit and joined Aunt Sandra in standing and applauding the couple. Taylor was clapping as if he had just seen a performance by Lady Gaga or somebody. I looked at the faces of Jeff's kids, and they appeared to be genuinely happy and excited. In fact, Cecily had tears flowing as she raced around the table to hug her dad and my mom. I was smiling and clapping on the outside, but for some reason, I felt as if I had just been kicked in the gut on the inside. I managed to perform what was expected. I hugged my mom and Jeff and congratulated them. Miss Jesus Sandals was coaching me in my ear the whole time, "Xandy, do the right thing. Do not embarrass your mother. She is happy. Please don't ruin it." I listened to her and joined in the gaiety that surrounded me.

Joshua leaped into Jeff's arms saying, "I've got me a grand daddy now!" Taylor validated his announcement by saying, "You sure do son... a really good one." The rest of the afternoon was spent laughing and talking and sharing old times and planning the future. Cecily pulled me to the side and asked if we could walk outside in the backyard. I agreed. We hooked our elbows and walked outside and strolled around the entire grounds. She looked at me and said, "Okay, my little sister to-be, what gives? Ray Charles can see that you are wrestling with this bit of news." I smiled sheepishly and responded, "Is it that obvious? I know if you see it, I am assured that my mom sees it, and I don't want her to think that I am against her marrying Jeff, because that is not the case. I guess it's one thing to say you want something to happen and a whole different thing when it becomes a reality." Cecily said, "Let me help you with this, Alexandria. You want your mom to be happy and you feel as though my dad is the best man to do it, but the idea of your mom actually being another man's wife, other than your dad, is lying on your heart, right now, like a ton of bricks." I looked at her and the tears fell. "I couldn't have explained it better myself," I said. "How in the world did…" She cut me off by saying, "You and I are at the same place emotionally. Imagining my dad with another wife that's not my mom is almost unimaginable, but I love him, and I see the love your mom has for him, so I'm able to get past myself." "Well said, Cecily." I responded, "I'm on board with this 100 percent and thanks for our first sister talk."

We hugged and headed back up the walk into the house. The evening ended with everyone forming an assembly line to clean up the kitchen and dining area and then Jeff and his kids going to his house. Taylor, mother, and I settled in on the patio with a glass of wine and Beethoven's piano concerto number 5 playing softly in the background. Joshua was sleeping off his overindulgence in food and dessert, and Aunt Sandra and Logan flew out of the door like two EMTs on a call. We all sat there in silence, enjoying the music we were raised listening to. Mother sat forward, put her glass down, and motioned for me to come and sit next to her. I did.

As soon as I sat down, she put her arms around me, and that's all it took…my damn broke. She softly said, "It's okay, baby. I know. I know." Amazingly, Taylor came over knelt beside us and joined in on the hug. His doing this made me sob harder. Taylor pushed back from us and said, "Xandy, please don't cry." His saying this took all three of us back in time to my daddy's death. The three of us were crying, and I believe this was the first time since my father was killed that my mom openly wept in front of us.

After the floods subsided, she said, "I love Jeff, and he truly loves me, and I want to spend what's left of my life with him." She then pushed back from us, looked into our eyes and said, "My two sweet babies... yes, I am marrying Jeff, but please rest assured I am not burying your father again. He will always be the greatest and the most powerful love of my life, and his love has never left my side and never will. I know I've always said I didn't want to be married, but life has ceased to be fun alone for me.

You two have your active lives, and the both of you are successful. Now, *Stella* is finally ready to get her groove back- the right way." With this last remark, the three of us laughed, hugged each other, and went to the kitchen to refill our glasses. I think, at this point, we all could use a drink. On the way out of the kitchen, Taylor stopped me and asked me, "Are you okay, Xandy, please be honest." I said, "Yes Taylor, I'm really okay, especially with mother marrying Jeff. I've just got a lot of things going on, personally in my life, right now, that I need to sort out...but I'm fine. You can believe me, little brother." I hugged him and kissed him on his cheek, and we walked hand in hand back out on to the patio, which put a big smile on our mother's face when she saw us.

I must say I don't ever recall us being as emotionally open and close as we were that night on my mother's patio. My mom's pending marriage and the outpouring of love and closeness I had just shared with my family was all a part of the emotional treatment I needed at this crossroad in my life. We chatted about old times, until the wee hours, and then we said our good nights and went to bed. As I snuggled into my bed, the comfort of the familiarity of my room, my home, and my family lulled me to sleep at the end of a long, exhausting, but good, day.

# CHAPTER 12
## ◆ RALPH AND BRENT ◆

Well, needless to say, my needing and seeking refuge at my childhood home with my mother was quickly upstaged by my mom's impending nuptials. Taylor rose early and took off for the golf course and other parts unknown, which I'm sure involved female companionship. I was awakened by the aroma of breakfast that drifted up the long staircase right into my nose -that was buried under the covers. I quickly jumped up, washed my face, and brushed my teeth, and crashed right in to Josh as I entered the hallway outside my door. He was headed to the kitchen as well.

We gathered at the island and ate like three Somalians. Miss Red Pumps whispered in my ear and said, "Girl, if you keep scarfing down homemade biscuits and the amount of food that you ate last night… you won't have to worry about deciding on which man to choose!" Miss Jesus Sandals came to my rescue by saying, "Leave the girl alone. She deserves to indulge for a change. Besides, those guys in her life want her for her inner beauty, and her weight does not matter." Miss Red Pumps quickly put her hand to her mouth as if she was holding a mic and said, "Ladies and Gentlemen, allow me to introduce to you Miss I-Know Nothing-About-Men" better known as Miss Jesus Sandals!" The three of us laughed out loud at that point.

Mother and I spent the day planning her wedding, which included looking at dresses, cakes, and venues online. She informed me that they haven't set a formal date yet, but it would be taking place at some point between Thanksgiving and Christmas. Being that it was the first of August, we had about 3 solid months to plan. She quickly stated that she was hiring a wedding planner to handle all the details. She said that she just wanted to pick out her dress and show up for the wedding and leave for the honeymoon and leave the rest to the planner. She told me she was considering securing Gertie Anderson as her planner. I was speechless, because everyone knows that Gertie Anderson is the Crème de la Crème when it comes to weddings and special events in the state of Virginia. My mother noticed my look at the mention of her name and said, "Oh don't fret, my love, Jeff has given me his permission to plan the wedding of my dreams at his expense. When I questioned him about the budget, he told me that he sets no limit to providing whatever it takes to make me happy." Miss Red Pumps yelled, "Damn, that's my kind of man!" Miss Jesus Sandals dropped her head, while shaking it, and covered her ears.

Aunt Sandra joined us later in the day with a glow that put the sun to shame. We scurried Josh off to a movie and Chuck E Cheese play date and settled in for a girls' afternoon of wedding talk and prying into Aunt Sandra's escapades with Logan. Just as she was getting to the good part…the house phone rang. We all looked annoyed, and being that the ringing would not stop…I was elected to answer it. Mother and Aunt Sandra changed the conversation to dresses as I was going to the phone. I picked it up and, lo and behold, it was Ralph. I said, "Hi Ralph, why are you calling the house phone, instead of Taylor's cell phone?" He responded with, "Well, hello to you, too. For your information, pretty woman, I am trying to reach you, not your brother. Since you didn't answer your cell phone, I tried the house." "Pretty woman? Uh oh, here we go," said Miss Jesus Sandals.

"Okay Ralph, What's up? I don't have to ask how you know that I'm here. Let's get one thing straight (I whispered as I walked out to the sun room), I do not want my family knowing that I'm still connected to you in any way, because they are well aware that you are married." "Whoa, Alexandria! Slow down. I'm just calling to say hey and to check on how you are feeling about your mother's wedding announcement. I know what a Daddy's girl you are, and I felt like you could use a friendly ear. That's all." While he was talking, I was asking myself how in the world Ralph knew this bit of news so fast.

He then answered my silent question. "I'm in town this week, and I played golf with Taylor this morning, and he shared the good news over a couple of Bloody Marys after our game." All I could say was "Oh," while silently making a mental note to stuff a sock in Taylor's mouth on sight. Ralph went on to say, "Let's get together for drinks later this week, so we can catch up. I'm sure, by then, you will be in need of a sounding board." I told him I would let him know. When I returned to the den, Mother and Aunt Sandra were rolling around on the floor laughing, and Aunt Sandra had just thrown a pillow and hit my mom with it saying, "Abby, that is not funny." I asked, "What did I miss?" My mom responded with, "Xandy, ask your aunt, the cougar, to pull up her shirt and show you her lower back." Before I could ask her to do so…Aunt Sandra rolled over on her stomach and raised her shirt. There, right in the middle of her lower back, was a Ben Gay pain pad.

I too began to laugh hysterically. After catching my breath, I said, "What's wrong Aunt Sandra? Suffering from an overdose of Logan?" My mom quickly yelled through her laughter, "Alexandria, leave the cougar alone. Can't you see she's in recovery mode?" I laughed and responded with, "Well, it looks to me like this cougar needs to retire or get older cubs that don't leave her in pain and smelling like a nursing home." All of us roared with laughter.

The rest of the week included more time with Taylor, who was in and out, Aunt Sandra, Joshua, and yes…Logan. I was so caught up with enjoying my family that I had not focused on the state of my romantic life. I had chosen to ignore calls from each of the men who played a role in my being here. Vince called me and shocked me by telling me that he had also received calls from Ian and Julian, inquiring about my well-being. Despite my efforts to talk myself out of it…I did meet Ralph for drinks at week's end.

I was sitting in a little out of the way (of course) pub, waiting for his arrival when I saw him park and head toward the entrance. I sat there, totally immersed in a complete assessment of his appearance and image. Over the years, Ralph had gotten even more handsome, and he had the walk and demeanor of a man who was self-confident and no stranger to navigating the world to get his desired outcome. As he approached the table, his smile lit up the room, and his outstretched arms summoned me. I could feel the tremors on my right shoulder from Miss Jesus Sandals, stomping her feet and shaking her finger at me, without saying a word. Of course, I ignored her.

Ralph and I sat there talking until the pub closed. He had matured so much and appeared to be all I ever wanted him to be. Miss Jesus Sandals interrupted my thoughts by saying, "Oh yeah? Did you want him to be married to someone else, while seeing you?" That should have snapped me back to reality, but it didn't. Ralph talked about his farce of a marriage, but the conversation always ended with, "I love her too, and I just can't hurt her." This time, he went so far as to say, "Alexandria, you have no idea how bad I feel when I see you and leave you. I wish that I could just walk away from you completely, but you are such a part of me that I can't make myself let go." Hearing this made me cry almost inconsolably.

We were standing in the parking lot at 2 am and under the street lights; he looked down at me and said, "Some of those tears don't belong to me, do they?" At that moment, the proverbial flood gates opened and suddenly, I realized that Ralph's holding me had turned into a kissing frenzy, right there in the parking lot. The next thing I knew...we were in Ralph's car headed for parts unknown. Miss Red Pumps interjected, "Oh! You know where you are going, and you can't wait to get there." I said, "So what? We are two grown consenting adults who love each other." Her response was, "If you say so, but I suggest leaving love out of this and just enjoy the ride –literally!" Miss Jesus Sandals was not having it. She yelled in my ear, "If he loved YOU... he would not be putting you in this situation, and he would come clean with his wife and get a divorce!" Ralph had no idea of the debate that was going on in the seat next to him as he sped down the interstate.

The rest of the story (for that night) shocked me and my shoulder sitters. Upon entering Ralph's suite... he poured us a glass of wine, and we sat on the bed and talked about my feelings about my mom getting married and the current state of our lives. At the end of our conversation, he took our wine glasses, sat them on the table, and proceeded to kick off his shoes, and I followed suit. Just as I stood to attempt to disrobe, he caught hold of my hands and pulled me down on the bed next to him, and said, "School girl, just be close to me tonight." With that, he wrapped me in his arms and held me in the spoon position all night. No sound from my shoulder. "Hmmmm."

Upon waking, he ordered room service, we ate breakfast while keeping the conversation general and light, and then he took me to the pub to get my car. When we arrived, he looked at me and said, "I could say I'm sorry, but I'm not." "Neither am I," I responded. He then asked me, "How are you going to explain your overnight absence to your mother?" I said, "I don't know. I'll probably tell her I ran into a couple of my old high school party pals and after over-indulging… we all just decided it was better to do a sleep over. She is much too distracted to be concerned about my whereabouts, right now, anyway." He agreed. We hugged and he drove off.

When I got home, the house was empty. It didn't look as though anyone had been there at all during the night. As I was finishing my walk-through, I heard my mother coming in from the garage. We met in the kitchen, and she looked and said, "Good morning sweetie, you are up early!" She went on to tell me that she and Jeff had stayed up so late compiling their guest list that she had crashed at his house. "Whew! You dodged that bullet! You and your mother were definitely on the same frequency last night," said Miss Red Pumps. I then remembered that mother was not at home when I left to meet Ralph, so she had no idea what I was wearing. Gosh, the relief I felt was like that of a teenager.

❖

The following week was filled with non-stop wedding stuff. Mother, Aunt Sandra, and I met with the infamous Miss Gertie Anderson and were totally in love with her personality and her ideas. At the end of our meeting, her services were secured. When Ms. Abigail Morgan chooses a vendor without the slightest consideration of talking to someone else…you must be good! That "goodness" came with a hefty price tag, but mother did not blink as she presented Gertie with Jeff's credit card. Miss Red Pumps was grinning like a Cheshire cat over the fact that mother already had Jeff's trust with his credit card and didn't require a phone call before making a decision.

The only things Mother had to do was pick out her dress, give Gertie the final guest list, sit through an in-home tasting to make her selection of the wedding cake and reception menu. Gertie also took care of the honeymoon arrangements as well... which was going to be a trip to the French Riviera. Miss Jesus Sandals said, "Your mother is truly a blessed woman; if only her daughter would do things the right way." Miss Red Pumps would not let the opportunity pass to whisper in my ear, "I guess old sandals over there is going to just choose to ignore that Ms. Morgan has been fornicating with Jeff all these years." She snickered, but quickly stopped it when I said, "You shut your mouth... that's my mother you are talking about and don't forget it!" Miss Jesus Sandals mumbled, "Boy, that is something that is long overdue... if you ask me!" You know who, responded with... "Nobody asked you anything!"

During one of our pit stops, when mother and I were out and about with Aunt Sandra, my giddy aunt extended an invitation to us that surprised the both of us. She invited us to go with her to a spiritual seminar at the convention center on the next Saturday night in the neighboring city. Upon further exploration, we discovered that Logan wanted her to be there to support one of his fraternity brothers and his dad, known as the "Purposeful Pair," who were the seminar headliners. Logan had asked her to invite us and other friends to hear their powerful message entitled, "Better Choices, Better Life." My mother and I both said that it sounded like something all of us could benefit from and that we would go to support her and "Better our lives" at the same time.

Well, Saturday evening arrived, and my mother, Jeff, and I met Aunt Sandra and Logan at Penelope's for dinner, prior to attending the seminar. We enjoyed some really great steaks with an array of delicious sides, but we all agreed to forego the wine, because we were en route to a spiritual seminar. Being at the table with Aunt Sandra and Logan gave me an opportunity to scrutinize their presence together. Logan was very attractive, and so is Aunt Sandra. It's obvious that there is quite an age difference, but they really **DO** look good together. Aunt Sandra is in her mid-forties and Logan is twenty-nine (four years younger than me), but somehow, when the two of them are together...they seem to be a fit. Both of them are so funny and seem to have great chemistry and genuinely enjoy each other's company. And in my book, that's what a good relationship is all about. At that statement, Miss Jesus Sandals piped in with, "What would you know about what a good relationship is all about?" I ignored her, of course.

Taylor called my mother's cell as we were wrapping up our meal, inquiring about our plans for the weekend. He informed my mom that Joshua was spending time with his mother, and that he was en route to a weekender with one of his many girlfriends-camping and white water rafting. Mother told him that we were on our way to be spiritually enlightened and jokingly (I think) ended with the announcement that all of us would be praying for his safety as he enjoyed his "Daniel Boone" weekend. We left the restaurant, climbed in Jeff's Suburban, and made our way to the Benson Convention Center. The traffic was heavy, and we girls were busy chattering away about wedding details as Jeff and Logan focused on getting a good parking space. All of us agreed that after that filling meal we had just finished, a good walk would be in order.

As we entered the venue and approached the will-call line, my cell phone rang, and seeing it was Carmen, I stepped to the side to chat a moment, while Logan retrieved our tickets. I was caught up filling Carmen in on the wedding plans and discussing whether she was going to fly into Philly to come with me or come directly to Virginia. Right in the middle of my conversation with Carmen, Logan walked over to me and handed me my ticket. I looked down at the ticket and accompanying handbill and became totally paralyzed in mid-sentence and mid-stride. On the two items in my hand was a gorgeous picture of Aaron Brent Girard and his father! Carmen was repeatedly saying hello and calling my name in my ear, and Logan was beside me saying, "Carmen, are you okay?" I managed to find my voice and get the blood circulating in my legs again. I murmured,

"Carmen, I'll call you later." I spun toward Logan and asked, "Logan, you know these people? How?"

He looked at me questioningly, but said, "Brent, his father, and I are in the same fraternity, and Brent and I played Rugby with and against each other for years. My grandfather was one of Dr. Girard's professors and mentors in Seminary." I was still trying to regain my bearings. While in the process of doing so…Logan went on to say, "In fact, we are invited to join the Girards after the seminar for coffee. You will just fall in love with them. They are some awesome folks you will definitely enjoy meeting…especially Brent. That guy has so much going for him. He has a patent pending device that's going to impact the real estate industry and on top of that, he's destined to follow in his dad's footsteps in the ministry." As I stood there silent, Miss Red Pumps said, "Uh oh, time for the big girl panties!"

As my mother, Jeff, and Aunt Sandra returned from the product tables to join me, Logan excused himself for a quick trip to the men's room before the program started. Aunt Sandra looked at me and said, "What's wrong, Alex?" I responded with a gesture to the handbill and ticket. As Jeff and Aunt Sandra were looking at it, I heard my mother say, "Well, well, well, who do we have here?" she asked rhetorically with a grin. "What are you two grinning and smirking about?" asked Aunt Sandra, while looking from one to the other then at the handbill. It was Jeff who broke the ice with, "Alexandria, isn't this one of your old boyfriends?" The panic in my eyes made my mother nudge Jeff with her elbow and shake her head. Aunt Sandra, holding the picture up to face height, said, "It sure is that handsome young man you use to be so caught up with." My mother, my champion, said, "Hush Sandra, that's obviously not for everyone here in the convention center to know, especially Logan, at the moment." "Oh ok. Sorry Alex!" as she winked at me.

Logan returned, and all of us entered the auditorium. I was asking myself, how did I not know this was Brent and his father's program? After taking our seats, I sat there in reflection and realized the marquee and PR materials only indicated the title of tonight's show and referred to them as the "Purposeful Pair." The lights dimmed, and the MC for the evening entered the stage and executed a rousing repertoire of inspirational and motivational quotes and stories leading up to the introduction of our speakers for the evening. Prior to their introduction, Brent's mother, who was sitting in the front row right in front of the podium, was introduced. As the spotlight found her, she stood, turned to the audience and waved. She was a pretty woman, with all her glam and social graces on point. As she took her seat, the introduction took place, and then Dr. Girard and his son Brent entered the stage. The crowd rose to their feet with a warm and welcoming applause. Everyone in my party stood as well, but me. I was too busy looking at Brent.

The evening proceeded with two amazing speeches given by Brent and his father. They gave a wonderful tag team performance, touting the importance of change and choices. As I looked around, many of the audience members were busy taking notes on their smartphones, tablets, or random paper. While Brent had the mic...you could see the pride in his dad's eyes for him. Brent's delivery was nothing short of awesome. I thought back to our time. It had been about three years since I had seen Brent. We had spoken a few times on the phone, and I knew about his realtor robot system that he was creating, but he never shared anything about taking to the stage or pulpit with his dad. Seeing him in action made me wonder if he was really happy doing this or was it just his effort to please Daddy. Either way...the guy had skills! Miss Jesus Sandals couldn't possibly miss this opportunity to remind me that she thought Brent was a good catch, despite our age difference.

At the end of the show, the crowd returned to their feet, and this time gave a thunderous applause, indicating their satisfaction with the information shared. Jeff turned to me and said, "Gosh Alexandria! You know how to pick them. That guy is really good and is definitely going places." All I chose to do was respond with, "Yeah, he is!" Logan ushered us out of the auditorium, while telling us that we were to go to the Hilton hotel across the street to meet the Girards for coffee. I tried to get out of going by saying I had a slight headache and didn't want to put a damper on the evening, but Logan was not having any of my excuse. "Alexandria, you've got to come. I told them I wanted them to meet my girlfriend and her family, so you've got to come. Plus, all of us are riding together, so you are trapped, my friend." At that point, Logan went to get the car, and while we waited, all eyes were on me. I said, "All right, all right, I'm going to do this, but neither of you had better say one word about me having dated Brent in the past or that you've met him before, because his parents are not aware of our relationship." Miss Red Pumps said, "My goodness, aren't you being the nervous type?"

We arrived at the hotel and waited in the lobby until one of the Girard family's entourage came to summon us. I found my heart fluttering as we entered the elevator. They were located in the penthouse suite, of course, and as we entered… Logan took the lead and was met with a big hug from the man of the hour and his wife. Brent was not in the room, thank God. Inside, I was saying to myself, "Whew, I dodged that bullet." Logan then proceeded to introduce Aunt Sandra to the Dr. and Mrs. Girard, followed by my mother, Jeff, and then me. To my surprise, all of us received hugs from the both of them. As we were seated and refreshment service began, I could have sworn that Mrs. Girard was looking at me strangely. Miss Red Pumps reassured me by saying, "Girl, you are just being guilty and paranoid…that's all." Logan was beaming with pride to show his long-time family friends his new girlfriend who was old enough to be his mother. The strange thing is that, if the Girards had an issue with their age difference, it didn't show.

The subject of my mother and Jeff's pending nuptials came up, and everyone became engrossed in the excitement. We were having a great time with them. Mrs. Girard had a warm personality, and his dad had a wonderful sense of humor. In the midst of his staff refreshing our drinks…the elevator doors opened and in walked Brent. Our eyes locked immediately and to my utter shock, he called my name rather loudly and approached me with open arms. I stood, and we embraced. Needless to say, the rest of the party was staring. Logan broke the silence by saying, "Hey guy, how's it going? You walked past me and the rest of us like we didn't even exist." "I noticed that too, Logan," said Dr. Girard. Mrs. Girard stood, walked over to Brent and I, and locked elbows with him and said, "Well, these two are obviously not strangers. What gives, Aaron?"

"Mother, this is Alexandria," he said, as if she should have remembered something that she had forgotten. He went on to say... "Remember, I told you about the wonderful recruiter that I met when I first started looking for a job in my field in Philadelphia? She was so helpful to me by critiquing my resumes and giving me pointers that helped me land my ideal job." Miss Red Pumps and Miss Jesus Sandals both looked at me and said, "Huh?" I was still standing there smiling when Mrs. Girard said, "Oh yes, I remember now. You told me all about Alexandria when I questioned you about so many calls to her number on your cell phone bill." She went on to say, "Thank you Alexandria, for helping our boy get on his feet." She was about to say more when my mother interrupted by clearing her throat. As we all turned toward her, Brent said, "So this must be your lovely family?" I can't repeat what Miss Red Pumps said in response to that comment. Before my mother or Aunt Sandra could get close enough to slap him, I said, "Yes, this is my family."

As I introduced them to Brent, Dr. Girard stepped in saying, "So it is you, young lady, that I have to blame for getting my son sidetracked with this engineering business, instead of giving this ministry his undivided attention, huh?" It was again silent, until he burst into a hearty laugh and everyone else joined him with the last person being Brent. The mood lightened, and everyone was engaging in light chit chat as the elevator doors opened again and a group of people came in that appeared to all know each other. After they expressed their congrats to Brent and his dad, they went about their way mingling around the room. In the midst of this soirée, Brent and I managed to steal away for a sidebar conversation. "Alexandria, you have no idea how excited I am to see you. You are even more beautiful than the last time I saw you, and I never thought that was possible." "It's good to see you too, Brent." I responded. "I must say that I was literally shocked by two things tonight. One, seeing you on the stage with your dad and two, the story you concocted about me for your mom and then pretending you've never met my family, after having shared Thanksgiving with them a few years ago."

He stepped closer to me and said, "Come on, Alex, don't be upset. Spend the day with me tomorrow, and we'll talk, and I'll explain." I just turned and walked away from him, while smiling to keep up the pretenses. I walked over to Logan and told him that my headache was getting worse and wondered how soon we would be leaving. Mrs. Girard overheard what I said to Logan and interrupted me by gently putting her arm around my waist and steering me in her direction, while saying, "Oh no, there's no need for you guys to rush off. Come with me, Alexandria. I have just what you need for that headache of yours in my room." I reluctantly walked down the corridor with her and entered what I discovered was her room and dressing area. She closed the door behind us and said, "Ok Alexandria, I have some Aleve or a cold glass of Chardonnay. Which would you prefer?" Miss Red Pumps said, "Oh my!"

While waiting for me to answer…she poured herself a glass of wine from her personal stash in her private refrigerator. As she was doing so, she went on to say, "My husband is very much against drinking and forbids me to do so in front of others, but you seem to be a gal I can trust." With that being said, I responded with, "I'd love a glass of wine." After our glasses were filled, she pulled me down next to her on the sofa. "Now Miss Alexandria, please allow me to cut to the chase. I know exactly who you are and all about your affair with my boy, Aaron. You see, all of Aaron's expenses come through our business and when reviewed for accuracy, as well as an attempt to satisfy my maternal curiosity, your number appeared more than any number on any bill for the entire company during that time. So I did what any protective mother would do. I found out who you were and what you were to my boy." All I could say was, "Wow, Mrs. Girard. I don't know what to say." Miss Jesus Sandals said, "Hush and listen, I think you will learn a lot from this woman."

"That whole farce in the next room about you helping him with his job was a story he and I concocted for his crazy ass Daddy's sake." I nearly fainted when I heard her say that. She went on to say, "Alexandria, I know that Aaron was with you and sleeping with you every chance he could get. I also knew that my boy had fallen in love with you. He looked different, acted different, and appeared to be the happiest I had ever seen him as an adult." She went on talking as if I was not even in the room. "You see, my husband is an accomplished man, a brilliant man, and a strategic-minded man when it comes to everything and everybody, including his wife and child. He has an anointing upon him to motivate and inspire others into greatness. He refuses to allow his wife and son to fail at anything- so he has our lives planned to the letter and won't accept any detours along the way."

"This is way too deep for me," responded, Miss Red Pumps. When I found my voice, I said, "Gee, Mrs. Girard, I really don't know what to say or what you are expecting me to say. Yes, Brent and I were very much involved for well over a year, but he was uncomfortable with it when it came to you and your husband because of our age difference. He had made a vow to you guys that he would remain celibate and on the straight and narrow after disappointing you by losing his virginity at a young age." She was silent for a moment, and when she spoke, she literally floored me. "Well, all doubt has been removed about how my boy really felt or feels about you. He has never shared that story with anyone, because that whole thing hurt my husband immensely because the young lady that my boy slept with became pregnant and my husband did the unthinkable in his eyes--He encouraged and paid for an abortion. The young lady and her parents were then coerced into moving to another city under the guise of starting a new ministry there.

Since that time, Aaron has messed around, and I know that, but his father does not. Aaron only publicly dates the women that his father is convinced are saved, devoted to the church by their actions, and have sworn a vow of virginity or celibacy- until marriage. Aaron knew that, if his father had met and knew you, his cover would be blown, and my husband would also think you are much too old to be involved with his son." "What about Logan? He's young enough to be my aunt's child and your husband appears to be okay with that." "Alexandria, Logan, although dear to us, is not my husband's son or heir to this dynasty that my husband is working so hard to build."

Then a look of sadness crept across her face, and she then began to speak in an even quieter tone. "I love my husband dearly. We have been married for twenty-eight years. I live a life that millions of women would kill for, but it's not my life that I'm living for me...

it's my life that I'm living for him. One that he feels is best for me. Underneath all of this pomp and circumstance, I'm just a plain old country girl who's happy with the simple things in life, like dirt roads, fishing holes, and swatting flies, while sitting under an old tree. My name is Lillie Rose, but my husband asked me to use just Rose years ago. In fact, honey, call me Rose when we are alone." At that point, we actually hugged and while doing so, there came a knock on the door. After we gulped our last wine and tucked the glasses away, "Rose" answered, and it was Brent who came bursting in telling us we were being anti-social, and that his father had food brought up for everyone.

When I re-entered the room, everyone in my party's eyes were on me, except for Logan, with questioning looks to ascertain if all was well. I nodded and smiled and joined the group for a bite to eat. The rest of the night was pretty uneventful. After leaving the suite, while Logan retrieved the car, I told my folks that I didn't want to talk about Brent nor his parents and what happened tonight. I assured them that everything was fine, and that if we ever talked about it, it would be much later.

# CHAPTER 13
## ◆ EDMUND, RALPH, BRENT ◆

S o much for rest and retrospect that I was seeking in the refuge of my childhood home-it didn't happen. It was truly my intention to get my thoughts and head together. I showed up here reeling from the chaos of my relationship choices, and seemingly, I am still almost just as much in the throes of my chaotic love life, right here in Virginia. First, there was my rendezvous with Ralph, followed by my ending up almost paying to see Brent Girard, live on stage. After having that heart-to-heart with Brent's mother, I had decided I would see Brent if he called me after that night. Yes, as you would suspect…he called the next day. He asked me if I would agree to drive down to Virginia Beach for the day. I agreed.

It was just over an hour's drive, and it had been far too long since I had been there. I told my mother my intended destination, and she said, "Alexandria, are you sure? There seems to be a serious disconnect with you and Brent when it comes to his parents. Jeff was up early this morning on the phone with me with his concerns about the odd dialogue that took place after Brent entered the room last night." I then discovered that Brent had taken a moment, while Rose and I were out of the room, to reassure Jeff that everything was fine and that he would talk to Jeff later over drinks one evening. Well, I had no idea how long Brent was planning to be in Virginia, but today, we would do something we hadn't done in a long time-be together. He picked me up around 7:30am, looking like a GQ model. He went out on the patio to say good morning to my mother and tell her that he was genuinely sorry for the way things appeared last night, but that it was somewhat complex and the outcome would be fine. Before my mother could speak, Miss Jesus Sandals said, "Yeah, so you say, but in the words of the infamous Ricky Ricardo… "you got some 'splaining to do!" My mother simply said, "Ok Brent, I'm going to keep out of this and let you and Alex mind your own business."

We left right after that. He was driving a beautiful black

Convertible 750li BMW, and it was awesome, and if I must say so myself…we looked awesome riding in it. We stopped for breakfast at a little mom and pop diner and ended up talking less about us and more about his pending patent, as well as both of our future career plans. I discovered that he is still not seriously seeing anyone, but has recently bought a beautiful home in Camden, NJ, which is only about 200 miles or so from his parents in Norfolk. At a lull in the conversation, he suddenly said, "Alex, let's go ahead a deal with this neon elephant in the room. I do apologize for that performance last night in front of my father. My mother told me that you and she talked and that she made you aware that she knew about our relationship years ago." He went on talking as if I wasn't sitting there or expecting a response from me.

I had to stop him, just to get one question off my mind and chest which was, "Brent, why are you still carrying on this façade for your father? You are twenty-four years old, successful in your own right, and now partnering with him in his ministry? I don't understand it." Miss Red Pumps and Miss Jesus Sandal's ears were on pause, waiting to hear the answer to this question. He said, "Alex, please hear my heart when I tell you this. My father means the world to me. It is nothing that man wouldn't do for his family, and my choice to act grown long before my time caused him a great deal of hurt, embarrassment, and eventually money. He has worked hard to get where he is. His membership is rapidly approaching 30,000 people, and he has so much riding on the line. I feel like I'm obligated to walk a straight and narrow path before him and the public. Me being seen gallivanting around with unsaved women, having the appearance of fornicating, drinking, and partying would break his heart and negatively affect his plans for his future."

I quickly responded with, "You forgot something when you were reciting your list of things you can't do on the straight and narrow path." He looked at me inquisitively, and I quickly responded with, "Let's not forget dating older women." A look of sincere hurt came on his face. He said, "Alexandria, if he had met you or heard of us dating, he would have known that I was not being celibate. You are older, more experienced, and drop dead gorgeous. My father is no fool." I told him about the details of my conversation with his mother, and he told me that he knew, and that his mother was far more accepting and supportive of his choices, and that the two of them frequently conspire to have a life outside of the microscope of his father's eye.

It was obvious we needed a change of subject for a while, and I attempted to do that, but Brent was not having it. He went on to say, "Alexandria, there is something I want to say to you, and I need to say it now. When I saw you in the audience last night and then later shocked with finding you in my parents' suite...I knew then that I want to be with you. I believe that I have always been in love with you, Alex! I couldn't sleep last night anticipating spending time with you this morning. If you will have me or give us another chance- I'm willing to bring our relationship out in the open with my dad."

I was stunned. Miss Jesus Sandals was the first to speak. "Well, well, well, looks like we've finally got a real man on our hands after all." I managed to say, "Come on, Brent, let's go enjoy this beautiful day at the beach and let life happen, Okay?" He responded with, "That's a great idea...let's go!" As always, Brent opened my car door for me, and as I walked around him to get in... he pulled me to him for one of the most passionate kisses I have had in a long time. Both of us were trembling as we pulled away from each other. Without saying another word, we took off down the highway for a day of fun, frolicking in the water, and an amazing horseback ride at the water's edge at sunset. At dinner on the pier, Brent ordered a bottle of the best champagne, and when the waiter asked what the occasion was, Brent responded with, "New beginnings." When I inquired about his possibly being seen with me and especially drinking, his response was, "New beginnings, Alex." Miss Red Pumps said a quiet, "Yeah right."

It was getting late, so Brent suggested we stay over and drive back the next morning, especially since we had been drinking. I agreed and was secretly thankful I had brought enough clothing and toiletries to handle an overnight stay. We left the pier and drove to a breathtaking home, right on the beach. We parked in the garage, and as we were entering, Brent informed me that this place belongs to his parents. I was pleasantly surprised and impressed. He showed me around and then we both agreed we'd like to freshen up a bit before having a nightcap glass of wine on the deck. Once we finished and met downstairs, Brent grabbed the bottle, two glasses and opened the door to one of the most magnificent Atlantic Ocean views I've ever seen.

This time, I initiated the toast. "To new beginnings… Mr. Aaron Brent Girard." Like magnets, we drew to each other, right there under the moonlight. Brent was absolutely amazing. When we came up for air, he propped on his elbows and listened to me talk non-stop about my mother's pending marriage and how I was trying to be a big girl about the whole thing. As I continued talking…I started to cry, and he cuddled me up and rocked me like a baby until we both fell asleep, right there on the chaise. What I've always loved about Brent is that he listens to me with the intent to understand. Despite the length or frequency of our talks or my venting sessions, he never seemed to get frustrated and rush to try to find a solution for me. When he did respond, it was usually clear that he was very much in tune with my thoughts and feelings. That is a rare trait to find in a man-one that I find invaluable. It goes without saying that, after spending that time with Brent, I was ready to take on "Dr. Daddy" because his son was definitely worth the fight.

Brent had informed me that he was leaving that next evening because he had to be back at work, but we committed to talking or texting every day. After returning to my mother's house, I returned to the subject at hand-the wedding! When I came down from cloud nine with Brent…my mother informed me that she and Jeff had set their wedding date for April twentieth. They had decided against having a winter wedding and preferred a spring ceremony, instead. The wedding was going to take place at the Benson Oaks Golf Course and Country Club on the Veranda overlooking the lake and the eighteenth hole. There are big beautiful magnolia trees and azaleas gardens leading down from the huge veranda on to the edge of the golf course. Just the thought of that place in the springtime brought tears to my eyes.

I hugged her and told her how much I loved the date and venue they had chosen. Mrs. Gertie was definitely going to make this wedding an affair to remember. I spent the rest of the week running a few errands for Aunt Sandra's florist shop when she needed me and reading and relaxing. I was also feeling like my head was much clearer. I could always tell when I was functioning at my best, because my two shoulder-tenants were very quiet. I spent a lot of time on the phone with Carmen and Vince. Carmen was actually getting to be kind of boring these days. She had not mentioned a new beau in quite some time or being in love with some new church-going, tall, handsome man with good teeth, lately. In fact, she talked more about her seemingly increased activities at church. She told me she was giving the dating and party-girl persona a rest for a while. I said to her, "If you're happy, I'm Happy."

I brought her up to date on all my issues, including the last amazing moments with Brent. Her words to me were, "Okay, Xandy, tread lightly and slowly with Brent. You know how he really is when it comes to that father of his...the Pope." We both laughed, but I knew she was serious. Vince kept me up to date on all the office stuff and on the men in my life (at least the ones that he ran into or that contacted him). He told me that Ian had called him every week since I've been gone, asking about me. Vince said, "You know, Alex, I don't like to intrude in your business, but that guy is the real deal. He misses you so much, but yet respects your wishes to cease contact while getting your thoughts together. Most guys would ignore your request, solely seeking to get their needs met in more ways than one."

Miss Jesus Sandals said, "Listen to your friend. Men know about other men." "Is that so?" came from my other shoulder. "I'm a woman and that doesn't qualify me as an expert on other or all women. I only know what I would do." Well, I told Vince, I was always open to his thoughts, because I knew that he is a genuine friend and truly cared about me. As If my conversation with Vince had summoned it…my cell phone rang a couple of hours after I had hung up with Vince. I saw that it was Edmund. Against my better judgment, I answered it. He then said, "Hold on, Alexandria, someone is dying to speak to you." In a moment, I heard the voice of Olivia on the other end. Though surprised, I was actually glad to hear her voice. She said, "Hello, Miss Alex, I have been asking my Dad about you. I miss hanging out with you. Where is Josh?" I told her that I was at my mother's house in Virginia and that I was taking a vacation to get some rest, and Josh was here with his parents. As I was about to tell her that I missed her as well, she interrupted with, "Miss Alex, my daddy is sad since you have not been here with us. He misses you too." I was caught off guard with that coming from Olivia and to top it off…she sounded so sincere.

I responded with, "I miss you guys too, Olivia. I will be back soon, and maybe the two of us can go to the movies and do some girly things together." "But I want my Daddy to come with us too. Okay?" she countered. "Ahhhh, okay Olivia, I think we can make that happen. It was so good to hear from you. Be sweet, okay? May I talk with your Dad now?" She handed her father the phone, and I heard her footsteps on the hardwood floor as she walked away. When Edmund returned on the line, he immediately started asking me about my time spent at home, including requesting details of my past and future itinerary. I said, "Whoa Edmund, it would be nice to ask me about how I'm doing or even inquire about my family before beginning your interrogation." "I'm sorry, Alexandria," he said, "It's just that I haven't talked to you in a while, and I was just excited about hearing your voice and catching up with the details of your life, right now. Will you forgive me?"

"Sure Edmund, but I must confess that I truly believe you coerced and scripted Olivia's conversation with me." There was complete silence on the phone. I finally had to call out to him to make sure he was there. When he did answer, he said, "Alexandria, why must you be so negative when it comes to me and my feelings for you. I did not plan nor plot with my daughter to call you. She asks about you all the time and like she said- we really do miss you. Whether you know it or not, she really looks up to you and enjoys the time she spends with you. Her mother is far too self and relationship involved to give Olivia what she really needs. You have become a light in her life and her Daddy's life too." Miss Jesus Sandals said, "Wow, Xandy, he really is sincere; cherish this and be kind." Miss Red Pumps began shaking her head back and forth and grimaced. When I asked her what was wrong, her response shocked the two of us. She said, "I'm in total agreement with Old Miss Sandals over there about this one."

◆

After hearing that, I immediately softened my tone and conversation with Edmund. We stayed on the phone for hours and somewhere during our conversation, I realized that I did miss him. I even found myself wishing he was here with me at the moment, because I know that he would comfort me and be so supportive as I told him about the upcoming wedding plans and some new ideas I needed to pitch regarding my career. Edmund brought a sense of wellness to my life. He had a way of making me feel that everything would always be all right, because if it didn't happen on its own...he would do whatever it took to make it happen. Miss Red Pumps simply said, "Alexandria, that's priceless." My mom came in as Edmund and I were hanging up, and he asked to speak with her to congratulate her, and even they stayed on the phone for quite some time chatting about the arts and philanthropic events on the horizon. I took note of the ease that seems to come along with Edmund when it came to my family and our personalities. When I went to bed that night...surprisingly enough, it was Edmund that I yearned for- Not Ralph, nor Brent. But as I began to doze off, my text message alert went off, and when I looked- just like clockwork, it was Brent saying, "Good night baby, I love you, and I miss you already."

The rest of my time at home was pretty uneventful. We managed to get a lot of the preliminary wedding stuff done. One of the biggies we were able to check off the list was my mother finding a wedding dress. When I say that this woman found a fabulous dress…it is a gross understatement. She chose a Jenny Packham original! The lady in the bridal boutique literally had to catch her breath when Ms. Abigail Morgan asked her for the best dress she had access to, and after looking at several samples, chose one and said… "I'll take it!" She made an appointment for the fitting, and we walked out feeling the woman staring at our backs as we left. My mother said, "Alexandria, there comes a time in your life when you've got to just GO FOR IT, and this is my time. Your father and I didn't start with much, and we had a very intimate quiet family wedding ceremony. I've done well in life, and I am marrying a man who is successful so –if not now-WHEN?"

My mother had no idea of the enormous impact those words actually had on me. I spent the next two weeks, volleying between Ralph and Brent with text messaging, phone calls, and seeing both of them again on two separate occasions. Once again, Ralph and I met at an out of the way place, and although the chemistry was high and the pheromones were swirling about our heads…he kept it purely non-physical. It felt like he was so into getting to know me as a person, finally, with no emphasis on himself. To say that Ralph Harris was not focusing on himself is like trying to convince someone the Pope is not Catholic. "You can say that again," said Miss Red Pumps, of course!

Brent and I went to dinner and back to my mom's house for an evening with Logan and Aunt Sandra. During our conversation, while gathered around the fire pit, Logan said, "Hey Brent, we should drive down to Norfolk to see your folks tomorrow and check out "jazz on the green" which is part of the Shrimp festival that's going on this weekend." I immediately said, "Wow, Logan that sounds like a great idea, because you are looking at two people who love to eat shrimp any way that they come-My aunt and me." Just as I finished talking…Brent interjected, "Are you kidding me, Logan? Do you think that I want to spend the precious little time I have with this sexy woman in the company of others? The answer is no!" Aunt Sandra and I exchanged looks, but I forced myself to maintain my chipper disposition with the intention of talking about it as soon as we were alone. When the last wine bottle was emptied, Aunt Sandra and Logan bid us farewell. As they were heading out of the door, Aunt Sandra stopped mid-stride and said, "Alex, let us know if you change your mind about the Shrimp Festival, because I can taste them now," and slyly winked at me. I responded with, "Okay, I sure will. I am in the mood, as always, for lots of shrimp." Brent did not make eye contact at all when I said that. My mother and Jeff had gone to visit his daughter for the weekend, so we were alone for the evening. As we were cleaning up, I said to Brent. "Brent, you still have a problem with your Dad knowing about us don't you?"

He said, "Somehow, Alexandria, I knew you were going to think that when I said that I didn't want us to go to Norfolk. The answer to your question is no. Have I talked to my father about us? The answer to that is no, as well, but I have every intention of doing so. With my father, timing is everything." I stood there looking at him without saying anything. Of course, Miss Jesus Sandals had to throw in her two sanctified cents. "I know you are not dumb enough to fall for that nonsense!" "Trust me Alex!" was the last comment Brent made before he took the dish towel out of my hand and gently pulled me down on the kitchen floor. Miss Jesus Sandals covered her eyes and dropped her head and said, "I see I was wrong. Don't you have any shame? Your mother is going to kill you."

I did not meet Brent's Dad again, while I was at home with my mother. The rest of my weeks there were spent between wedding details, girl talks between my mom, Aunt Sandra, and I, and clandestine meetings with Ralph. There were also long phone conversations with Brent and Edmund. Two days before I was scheduled to head back to Philadelphia, I decided to touch base with Vince to get up to speed with the mountains of things to do at the office when I returned. When I finally got him to answer his phone, I heard a lot of background noise as he told me to hold on until he could find a place to talk.

As he was en route to that quiet place, I actually honed in on the background noise, and I immediately recognized the sound. When he came back on the phone, my first question was, "Why are you at the club this time of day?" Vince response was… "Silly woman, what makes you think I'm at the club?" Before he could continue, I countered with, "Okay Vince, I know Julian's music when I hear it, and from the other sounds, I don't think you are listening to one of his demos in your office." "Gee Sherlock! You are right about one thing and that is that it is definitely Julian's music you hear, but you are not going to believe where I am." "Vince, just tell me what's going on," I said impatiently. "Okay Alex, get your panties out of a wad. I'm actually on location with Julian at a penthouse apt in The District. A lot has happened since you left. This guy's career has taken off. One of his tracks has been chosen for the background in M. Brenae's latest video, promoting her new hit single. Can you believe that?"

"WHAT? That's something serious, Alexandria!" screeched Miss Red Pumps. I must admit I was quite taken back by this news. M. Brenae was not only the newest hot artist on the charts. She was a homegrown girl from Philly who was commanding the attention of music lovers across varied genres on the charts. Last but not least.... she was as beautiful as she is talented. Vince interrupted my thoughts, because I had grown silent on the phone. "Alex, I know you are wondering how in the world did I get on a video shoot with Julian, right?" All I could say was, "Ummm Hmmm." Vince went on to explain that, in my absence, he had gone out one night to catch one of Julian's performances, and they had met for drinks afterwards and inevitably become good friends. "Well that's good Vince." I said, "I haven't talked to Julian in quite some time, so I had no idea what he was up to these days."

All of a sudden, Vince lowered his voice to just above a whisper and said, "Alexandria Morgan, never think for one moment that Julian's silence means he's done with you or that you are not on his mind. In fact, he has disconnected from you to prove his worthiness to re-connect with you." Before I could get a word in.... Vince kept right on talking. "This guy speaks of you daily and has told me that when he makes it to the top of the charts...you will be the woman by his side, which brings me to a question I've been dying to ask you, girlfriend." My response was, "What is it Vince? (Wrapped in a sigh). Without the slightest hesitation, Vince responded with, "What in the hell is it that you have or can do to a man that would make him willing and able to ignore the advances of M. Brenae? Whatever it is that you have or do…you should patent it and sell it so both of us can retire!"

Miss Red Pumps answered before I could, "I'm with him! Whatever you are packing must be powerful-I've seen that singing vixen." "Yeah right, Vince," was all I could manage to say, although internally, I was quite taken back by this bit of ego-boosting news. We talked at great length about my work and house updates, until Julian surfaced out of the background and took the phone. "How's my favorite girl in the whole world? I knew it was you on the phone. Vince never gives his women this much phone time." "Hi Julian, I'm good." I was only able to say that before I heard the voice of a woman say, "There you are …hang up that phone and come take care of me." It was without a doubt Miss M. Brenae, herself. Julian abruptly said to me, "I'm sorry Alex, duty calls. I'll see you when you get back!" "Well, well," murmured Miss Jesus Sandals. "Looks like he has his hands full, and so will you if you chose this guy." Miss Red Pumps shook her head and whispered, "We are leaving "old Sandals" at home when we go to the Grammys!" I actually laughed out loud, despite being perturbed by Julian's behavior.

Vince and I talked again at the end of that week prior to my leaving Virginia. I saw Ralph and Brent again that week. Ralph was still on his best behavior, although things got pretty heated during our efforts at bidding each other farewell. His parting words were, "Alexandria, I know my situation is not ideal, but I know you know how much you mean to me and just trust that I'm doing my best to make things right for us, without hurting my wife and embarrassing my family any more than necessary." "Sure you are," -came from under the halo on my right shoulder!

My mother, Jeff, and Aunt Sandra wanted to have a little cookout that evening, prior to my departure on that Saturday. Taylor and Joshua came over and, to my amazement, Brent also joined us. The evening was a lot of fun, and Brent was actually a lot of fun. He, Jeff, and Taylor had become totally submerged in a game of basketball in the backyard, while the three of us sipped mimosas on the deck! Aunt Sandra looked at me and said, "Xandy, there's something about that guy that I really like." Before she could complete her statement...my mother chimed in while laughing- "yeah, his youth." We all laughed, but Aunt Sandra went on to say, "If you can get him to take you out of the closet where his daddy, the Pope, is concerned...I think you'd have yourself an awesome husband." I didn't respond, and neither did my mother.

The guys finished their game, and we had a wonderful steak meal and drinks under the stars. As if my Aunt had set the Cosmos in motion...Brent's cell phone rang while we were sitting in the swing, and I could clearly see it was his father and to my shock... he answered it, without excusing himself. More shocking was that he said, "Hello, father, how are you? I'm great, because I'm sitting here under the moonlight with a beautiful woman enjoying a great meal and her family." My eyes were glued on the side of his face. My shoulder mates were both staring, while holding their breath. His father obviously asked him whom he was with, and he responded with, "Alexandra, the very pretty friend of mine you met in your suite after our seminar. Remember, I told you about her, Father?" He was silent after saying that for a while, listening to his dad. When he did speak, he said, "Okay, Father, sounds good. I can do that. See you then." He turned, looked at me, and then surprisingly gave me a big hug and said... "let's not talk now...I have other things in mind."

I reminded him of us not being alone, and he just held me closer in the swing, while we laughed the night away over drinks with my family. As I walked him to his car in the wee hours, he said, "Alexandria, I have really enjoyed you this summer and being with your family tonight has been so awesome for me. As you heard, I am working on my dad. He wants to meet with me about doing a few more seminars with him to include one in Hawaii. So we are going to be spending some time together and I'll keep you posted." Before I could speak...he put his finger to my lips and replaced it with his lips and something shifted.

I left the next day with a lot to think about as I drove home. My head felt near explosion with thoughts of my time in Virginia and thoughts of what my near future had awaiting me in Philadelphia.

# CHAPTER 14
## ◆ JULIAN ◆

My return home was bittersweet. I found my home to be in great order, and I owed that to my buddy, Vince. There was no visible evidence that he had used my place for any of his after hour shenanigans. I quickly unpacked and began preparing for my workday. I had such mixed emotions about returning to my office or just the rat race, in general. I realized I was missing my family. On the drive home, I spent a lot of it talking to Carmen, who had been missing in action a lot lately. Every time I questioned her about her activities or whereabouts, she would respond with something to the tune of, "Oh Alexandria, why bore yourself with my mundane life. I'm not the one with the harem that includes: a blue-blood boy toy, a soon to be Grammy recording artist, a life-long spoiled first love that's still in hot pursuit, and not to mention a rich CEO of a pharmaceutical company, a wealthy trust-fund grandson, and a poor but steaming hot/great in the sack water boy!" After a moment of thought, all I could say was, "Wow Carmen, when you put all of them in one descriptive line-up…I have had quite a few balls to try to juggle over the past twelve years." "Pardon the pun huh!" said Miss Red Pumps as she burst into laughter.

I knew Carmen far too well not to miss all the cues that something or someone has her time and attention these days, but I also knew that sooner or later she would fess up. I'm sure she's caught up with her latest conquest with perfect pearly whites that sings in the choir on Sunday and uses handcuffs and whips during the week. Our hour-long chat ended with her committing to coming to the wedding and adding in some extra days, so that we could make up for the lost time between us. She didn't hang up before telling me, "Sooner or later, Miss Morgan, you are going to have to decide who you are going to focus on for the future –if any of these guys. All this juggling is going to get confusing and tiresome, so you might better start trying to narrow your field of choices." "Yes Ma'am, old wise one," I responded, and we both laughed, exchanged our sentiments, and hung up.

Now that I'm back in my home, which suddenly feels like a tomb, I'm like a lost soul looking for a body to occupy. I ate a bowl of frosted flakes (my comfort food), took a shower, and hopped in the bed. Just as I was dropping off to sleep…my phone rang, and I grabbed it like an NFL wide receiver. I saw that it was Edmund. As soon as I answered, he started a monologue that could not be interrupted. "Hi Alexandria, welcome home, sweetheart. I tried to not call you tonight to allow you to get settled in, but as you can see, I couldn't help myself. I've missed you so much and the mere thought of you being here in the same city with me and so far away was more than I could bear tonight. Please let me come over. I'll even sleep in the guest room or on the sofa. I just want to be near you. Please?" Surprisingly, I didn't argue at all. I merely said, "Sure Edmund, I've missed you too. Come on over. Buzz me at the gate, because I've changed the code because of my absence and not totally trusting my buddy, Vince." We both laughed, and he said he'd see me within the hour.

He kept his word. He was at the gate and in my house within the hour. I must admit that I was really happy to see him. Miss Jesus Sandals managed to say, "Oh boy, here we go again!" just before the embrace of the century. I must say that Edmund was a man of his word in spite of the initial fireworks between us. He climbed in bed with me with his jogging suit on and held me all night, and I will admit…being in his arms felt soooo good! Edmund and I talked briefly during our morning rituals preparing for work and promised to continue to stay close, but also to allow things to progress slowly.

Returning to work was not as difficult as I had predicted it would be. My workload was normal, with no unexpected turn of events. My life returned to normalcy. I threw myself into my work and managed to squeeze in a happy hour with the girls in the office on the Thursday evening during my first week back. I agreed to do Thursday, because I felt that things would be slow, and that would give all of us as opportunity to catch up on each other's lives. They suggested we meet at Ashton's Cigar Bar over on Walnut Street, which was a swanky lounge that was popular with the preppy professional crowd. When seated, we had a wonderful time, and the ambiance was awesome.

The truth about the bar choice finally came out, that my younger sorority sister was dating the owner, which explained all the special attention –not to mention the special discounts on our drinks. When the "lady of the hour" finally decided to return to the table to engage with us, she came bearing exciting news. She said, "You guys are not going to believe who's in here, downstairs at the cigar store in disguise." Every one of us tried to guess, but we were wrong. Finally, she said "M. Brenae! I'd know that face and bod anywhere, in spite of her dress down appearance and no makeup." At hearing that, I had a sinking feeling in my stomach that I could not explain. Just as I was trying to challenge that sinking feeling, I looked toward the end of the bar in the mirror and saw Julian with a woman with a baseball cap on and sunglasses take a seat. "You see, Xandy, your gut is rarely wrong," said Miss Jesus Sandals.

I pretended to enjoy the balance of the evening with the small talk, while also trying to ignore the call of my bladder. I knew that to go to the ladies' room, I was going to have to pass Julian and his sidekick. Well my bladder won, and I had to head that way. To my surprise, before I could get close to where he was sitting, he spotted me and met me in the walkway with his arms wide open. He picked me up off the floor and swung me around in front of everybody, including M. Brenae, herself. "Surprise, Surprise!" said Miss Red Pumps. Surprised was an understatement, and Julian appeared to be genuinely happy to see me. In fact, he said it for the whole bar to hear. "Alexandria, it's so good to see your beautiful self. I have missed you!" I returned his hug and his sentiment, and then we both started laughing when we realized he was still holding me up in the air. When he put me down, I realized that M. Brenae had turned around completely on her bar stool and removed her sunglasses and the hood she was wearing over the cap. She exposed her identity to all those present. That move totally shifted all the attention to her (Including Julian). Miss Red Pumps said, "Now that was a smooth move. She used her celebrity to trump the attention you were getting from the people present."

Julian interrupted the chatter between me and the folks on my shoulder when he said, "Well it's no secret who my companion for the evening is. Come on, Alex, allow me formally to introduce you two." Although his intentions appeared to be pure...Miss Brenae was definitely not interested in getting to know me. When she finished addressing those who wanted to speak to her and ask for autographs... She nodded my way, refused my extended hand, and looked at Julian and said, "Can we leave now Ju Ju?" "Ju Ju? Who in the heck is that?" Miss Jesus Sandals smelled a major attitude and confrontation coming on, so once again, she said, "Xandy, ignore this young lady and be the professional, classy lady that you are. That way, you will show her why Julian is so taken with you, in spite of her presence." I agreed and so did Miss Red Pumps (ODD).

Julian responded to her with, "I'll be ready in a few. I want to talk to Alex for a second. Come on Alex, come sit with me." She obviously pouted, but turned her attention to a couple of admirers who had quickly parked themselves on the bar stools next to her. Julian and I sat at an empty table and proceeded to talk. "Alexandria, please don't make tonight into any more than what you see. M. and I had been working on a set, and we decided to grab a drink at the close of a day. She and I are collaborating well. In fact, she has agreed to sing on one of my tracks, and that is major for me. The only thing left to do is for our agents to come to an agreement on the terms involved. Please be happy for me, Alex." I responded with, "I am happy for you Julian, and I do understand that when artists collaborate...it increases their audience and exposure." We brought each other up to date and agreed to get together for dinner soon. He walked me back to my party, hugged me, and asked if it was okay if he could call me later. I agreed. As he walked away, the girls were filled with questions about him, M. Brenae, and of course, a couple of them were lusting after Julian because of his looks.

As I was hoping…Julian called the next day, we met for dinner on that Friday, and we didn't part until that Sunday. I was totally shocked that he was able to spend that kind of time with me, but he explained that, since he had been signed by Sony and working on bigger projects…he was not playing the club circuit like he used to do. During that weekend, I realized just how much I was so physically connected with him. When I say that, I don't mean just sexually. His looks, his smell, his presence makes me happy and awakens all of my senses. He's the one man that, just the thought of him or locking glances with him, gives me mini emotionally climatic feelings. "It's that hair and natural smell of him laced with weed," said Miss Red Pumps as she chuckled. That weekend was uninterrupted by Edmund, due to a pharmaceutical conference he was attending in Oregon, Brent was on an engagement with his dad, and I guess Ralph was playing devoted husband.

On that Sunday morning, while having breakfast on the balcony, I asked Julian to be patient with me as I try to digest his life as an artist and all the women and liaisons that come along with the program. He stated he understood how trying his lifestyle could be, and he went on to warn me that it could get worse if he becomes the success that he's striving to be. I took advantage of this one-on-one time with him to address the elephant in our potential relationship. "Julian, you do know that M. Brenae wants more than a business relationship, right?" "Sure I do, Alex. But that means nothing to me." He responded to me so quickly that I was at a loss for words for a moment. When I gathered my thoughts, I said, "Julian, do you really expect me to believe that you are not turned on at all with this woman's looks and celebrity status and the big obvious fact that she wants you?" He sat there quietly before speaking, and when he did, I was not expecting to hear what he said. "Look Alexandria, I am always going to be honest with you. Yes, I have been turned on by her and her status. What man in his right mind wouldn't be? I got that out of my system early on. I've moved on and want nothing but a business/friendship with her."

Miss Red Pumps quickly asked me, "What in the heck did he mean he got that out of his system?" That was the same question I was going to ask and managed to do so. Julian responded with, "Come on, Alex, we are adults. I've slept with her before." I gasped so loud that it caught him off guard. He held up his hand to signal that he was not finished. He went on, "Before you go getting all bent out of shape…it's obvious that you and I do not have an exclusive relationship. Not now or never have. But we are two people who sincerely care a great deal for each other, and we are trying to figure our relationship out in the midst of all of this." Miss Jesus Sandals said, "Well, well, the guy has made some valid points. After all, he was the one who came face to face with one of your suitors right here in your kitchen. So keep your mouth shut, Xandy! You have no room to complain." I was not listening to Miss Jesus Sandals as usual. I stood and said, "You slept with her, Julian? And now you just expect this woman, who is used to having her way, to just forget about that?" Julian quickly stood up from the table and said, "Look Fran, I'm not going to keep going over and over this." Just as he got to the period in that statement, he and I were locked in a frozen stare that could melt steel.

He realized he had called me "Fran" and so had I –at the same time. He said, "Alexandria, I'm sorry. I didn't mean that. It's just that Fran is still somewhat possessive of me, but not in an intrusive way. I'm honest with her, too. She knows about you, and she even knows that if you will have me…I'll take our relationship to another level." He came around the table and pulled me to my feet in an embrace and my knees became putty. He picked me up, carried me inside to the bed, sat me on the side of it, and sat down beside me, and looked into my eyes and said… "Alexandria Morgan, do you want me? Do you want to be with me exclusively? If so, all you've got to do is say so!"

I responded with, "Julian…I just need to figure all of this out. Okay? You are a budding celebrity, sleeping with other celebrities, and still maintaining an obligation to Fran, your deceased child's mother. It's a lot for me to ingest all at one time." "I understand, Alex. Take your time…there is no competition for you to feel that you are racing against. Please believe that." With that, he left me sitting there, showered, dressed, and kissed me goodbye and left. Miss Red Pumps slowly raised her hand and said, "If you ask me, this guy has been nothing but honest with you. He seems to have no hidden issues and has refused to disconnect from you since the two of you got together. There's a lot to be said about an HONEST, consistent man." Miss Jesus Sandals said, "Old Red over there does have a point, but nobody asked her." I sat there in a trance for a while. I reached for the phone and called Carmen and got no answer —as usual.

# CHAPTER 15
## ◆ IAN ◆

A s soon as Edmund got back, he was in hot pursuit again. I allowed him to wine and dine me to the max. A couple of those times were a threesome with Olivia, but much to my surprise...I realize I had missed her a lot. The conversation eventually surfaced about the impending cruise that Edmund, Olivia, and his ex-wife were planning. I was terribly upset about the whole thing, because I felt that it was totally inappropriate and unnecessary. Miss Jesus Sandals could not pass on the opportunity to remind me that I was in no position to pass moral judgment on any one of the men I had been dating!

Their ship was set to sail in a week, and I think Edmund was doing everything within his power to make sure his spot in my life was secure prior to his departure. I told Edmund that if the shoe were on the other foot...he would have to be resuscitated in the ER. Miss Red Pumps whispered in my ear and said... "Honey if he only knew a third of the stuff you've been up to, he'd need more than resuscitation." I giggled and kept my high moral stance on Edmund's cruise choice. As it turns out...during Edmund's absence, Brent's speaking engagements were still keeping him occupied, and Julian was literally in the throes of music/video production, so I had some "exhale" time.

Thoughts of Ian crossed my mind, but I refrained from calling him, because for some reason, interacting with Ian was a slippery slope. He did things to me emotionally that were still a mystery to me. When Carmen called me back…she, in her effort always to be my female version of Dr. Phil, said that Ian was also baffling to her as well. One thing she did bring to mind was that, if I was really turned on by Ian physically and sexually…I would have attempted to bridge the gap by now. But she also added that the non-physical/sexual hook that Ian seemed to have in me had a lot of credence that warranted some exploration. So against my better judgment and the advice of the dynamic-duo on my shoulders…I called Ian's home phone and left a message on his voicemail, telling him I would love to have dinner with him one day soon. That was my chicken way of making the first move, without seeming to be so forward.

Well, a couple of days passed before he called me, which was a bit rude-so I thought. Anyway…he did ask me to dinner, and we agreed to meet at Vetri for an exquisite Italian meal. Miss Red Pumps was the first to ask, "Alex, don't you think it's odd that Ian didn't offer to cook a meal for you or, at least, pick you up?" Miss Jesus Sandals seconded that question. When I drove up and gave the valet my keys, Ian was waiting for me outside the entrance. He literally ran towards me and engulfed me in the biggest, yet sweetest, hug imaginable and my traditional kiss on my forehead. He said, "Just let me look at you, Alex. Wow, you are sooo pretty this evening. That dress, a different hairdo and a nice tan!" I said to myself, "Hmmm he noticed that I was darker-it came from my beach time with Brent, but that's my secret." We spent the evening catching up on his YMCA adventures, his summer school class ending, and some new landscaping additions he was having done at the house. I told him about my mom's wedding plans in the spring, and he really honed in on my wishy-washy feelings about the whole marriage thing.

Well, we talked and drank wine until the place closed. When we decided to leave, I discovered that the owner was a colleague of his and agreed to allow us to leave our cars in the parking garage and drive us home in his personal vehicle due to what may have been our exceeding the wine limit. We laughed en route to my house. When we got there, I told Ian to come hangout with me for the rest of the night, and I would get Vince to pick us up to retrieve our cars. He agreed. Well, the evening consisted of more wine and lots of cuddling. We took our showers. I gave Ian a pair of Vince's old sweat pants that were clean in the laundry room, and we jumped in bed together to watch National Lampoon's Vacation. As I was drifting off, I heard Ian's cell phone buzzing, and he answered it in a whisper, assuming I was asleep.

The conversation went something like this, "No, I won't be back home tonight. You know where it is. I'm not dealing with this right now. Make sure the alarm is on and the pier lights are on at the lake." As he hung up, I threw the covers back and startled him. I said, "Ian Sommers, who was that and what's going on?" He said, "Alexandria, calm down; everything is fine. Let's just finish the movie and enjoy the rest of our night. It's been too long." With that...he tried to kiss me, and I wasn't having it. I said, "Ian, I want the truth. You are lying here in my bed and not being honest with me. In my book, the two don't go hand in hand." "First of all, he shouldn't be in your bed for more reasons than one," interjected Miss Jesus Sandals. "Okay Alexandria, if you must know...Nicky is staying with me at the house for a while. He has been under the weather and he has no one else to take care of him. You know the story." I countered with, "Ian are you the only person in this world that Nicholas knows?" "No, I'm not," he responded, "but he's like family to me."

Before I could filter myself, I said, "Ian has it ever occurred to you that this man may be in love with you?" "Yes it has, Alex. In fact, I know he's in love with me." I heard screams on both of my shoulders, and I believe mine was the loudest.

He recoiled from my outburst and said... "Come on Alexandria, can't you understand our closeness, considering our backgrounds. I am not having a sexual relationship with Nicky or anyone else for that matter. You are the only person I want to have sex with." Silence in the room. "No, I take that back...I want to make love to you and you only, but only when it's right!" With that, he pulled me from standing on my knees in the bed towards him and planted a gentle kiss on my forehead and cradled me in his arms. I had no more fight or opposition left. The silence continued on my shoulders. The next morning, I called Vince to pick us up, and at Ian's insistence, I packed an overnight bag for the rest of the week at his place after I left work. He wanted me to get to know Nicholas and give him another chance. Against my common sense…I agreed.

Well, when I arrived at the Sommers Manor…I was blown away at the changes Ian was making to the grounds. He had a beautiful gazebo erected at the water's edge that had a small outdoor kitchen in it. He had also added several palms and more shrubbery and a fire pit seating area. This whole place was breathtaking. When he saw me admiring it …he came up behind me in the yard and whispered in my ear. "I'm glad you like it, Xandy, because something tells me that, one day, this will be your home." My heart leaped, and I turned and inhaled him deep into my soul. Miss Jesus Sandals said… "My God, My God…somebody get this girl some help!" Miss Red Pumps was still too busy gazing at the magnificence of the house, grounds, and the total package.

I went upstairs and put my things down, and there was no sign of Nicholas. As we were preparing some shrimp kabobs and pouring glasses of merlot, Nicholas entered the house through the garage, carrying two pharmacy bags. He stopped and waited to see what was going to happen next before coming towards me. I said, "Hey Nicholas, I hear you aren't feeling well." He responded with, "Hey Girlfriend, it's good to see you again. This bronchitis has gotten the best of me, but I'm going to whip its butt!" With that, he opened his medication, sashayed by me, and poured himself a glass of orange juice. He went on to say, "Well I'm not dead yet, so throw a couple of those kabobs on the grill for me too, and by the way…what are we watching on TV tonight? I'm going upstairs and finish my recorded "*Say Yes to The Dress*" and I'll be back when the dinner bell rings." Ian looked at me and shook his head. As Nicholas was midway up the staircase, he turned and yelled, "Alexandria, the only reason I didn't hug you tonight was because I didn't want to give you the cooties. I'm really glad you are here." Then he made is final ascent to the second floor, like the starlet that he is.

Those days at Ian's were a lot of fun with Nicholas being the belle of the ball, per se! My shoulder pals were extremely quiet, which was unusual. As if having heard me think that, Miss Red Pumps spoke and said, "I think both of us are quiet, because we've got this situation under close surveillance." After my second day there, I noticed that Nicholas appeared to be doing just fine. I mentioned that to Ian, and it was then that he told me that Nicholas was going to go back to his place tomorrow, which was Friday. All of us had been staying in separate rooms, which was a bit concerning to me. But when I brought it up to Ian, he said… "Alex, I just like to keep my private life private." I just sat there staring at the water with no response.

Ian was correct. Nicholas busied himself the next day preparing to make his exit. I realized that since Nicholas had been brought to the hose by Ian, he was going to have to be driven home. So we helped him to load his stuff in the car, which included several containers of food and soup that Ian had fixed for him to tied him over until he felt like returning to the kitchen. Miss Jesus Sandals couldn't pass up commenting…

"It is nothing wrong with Nicholas that is preventing him from cooking or fending for himself." I totally agreed. When we got to Nicholas' house, I was impressed. He has a beautiful, though modest, ranch style home that is decorated to the nines -including pics of him and Ian as finishing touches. His place was immaculate inside and out. He is a buyer for a national retailer and a successful real estate agent, and his earnings are definitely reflected in his décor and lifestyle. We stayed and had some coffee and watched CNN for a while, and then Ian and I headed to the car. Nicholas walked with us -thanking Ian the whole way. He said, "Alexandria, I honestly enjoyed spending time with you and getting to know you. We must do it again soon." He reached and pulled me in for what felt like a sincere hug, and as he was embracing me, he whispered, "Thank you for giving me a second chance to start over with you." I then tightened my embrace and said, "You are welcome, Nicky." He quickly withdrew and said, "No offense Alex, but no one calls me Nicky, but Ian, and I like it that way. Okay?" I recoiled somewhat, but said, "All right, Nicholas."

Ian was standing there shaking his head as he reached to open the door for me, but Nicholas beat him to it, giggling and being carefree the whole time. As Ian turned to walk around the car to the driver's side…Nicholas reached out and slapped him on the butt and said,

"See you, dude." He then turned to me saying, "Take good care of my guy, you hear?" He did all of this seemingly in one swift movement and breath before moving quickly up the sidewalk to his front door. Ian stood there at a loss for words and just shook his head and got in the car saying, "What am I going to do with that nut…he's as crazy as hell?" I tried to find words to say and looked to my shoulders for help, but all I could see was the soles of their shoes…both of them had fainted! That slap on the butt sent all of us into the twilight zone!

The rest of the weekend went so well. I put the issue with Nicholas out of my mind and soaked up all the attention I was getting from Ian. We went out to eat several times, to the movies, and an art gallery opening. Ian taxied me back and forth to get the appropriate attire for the art gala, and we had a ball. It was the first time I had been to an opening that had a jazz ensemble for guests either to dance or listen as they enjoyed the art. There was one particular abstract piece that I fell head over heels for, called "*The Soul.*" It was amazing, but the five-figure price tag caused me to quicken my steps to the lesser priced displays. We left the affair really early because both of us had been drinking quite a bit of wine. Once home…we both raced each other upstairs, disrobed, jumped in the shower together, and spent the rest of the night in one of the sweetest states of closeness, without actual sex, that I have ever experienced. Ian was definitely not the best skilled, but there was something so "soul-stirring" about the way he touched me, held me, and just simply connected with me.

Miss Red Pumps and Miss Jesus Sandals were very much awake, and both of them were burning holes in the side of my head with their laser stares. Miss Red Pumps was the first to speak. "Alexandria, this Ian is really a great guy, but even I can't say that I'm totally on board with him. The only things I can give him an "A" on is his kindness and his money." "Of course, you would say money," said Miss Jesus Sandals. "Ian Sommers has got some skeletons in his closet that I believe he resurrects from time to time, but it's just a feeling with no supportive facts. At the end of the day, all of us are wrestling with demons of some kind." "Soooooo," interrupted Miss Red Pumps, is there anyone willing to talk about the pink elephant in the room…

that being our dear friend Nicholas' addiction to Ian?" There was complete silence.

Ian dropped me off at home that Sunday evening. He watered my plants, while I got ready for the workweek. We shared a cup of tea on the balcony to close out our days together. As we sat there at sunset… he reached for my hand and said quietly… "Alexandria, you complete me. I know that sounds corny, but it's true. I have never said this to anyone nor felt this complete since my grandmother passed. It scares me beyond words, but I didn't want another day to pass without me telling you how much you mean to me." I sat there looking at him, and as I was about to speak, he said, "Shhh sweetheart. You don't have to say a word. Your spirit speaks to me, and that's more than enough." He then rose from his chair, pulled me to him, hugged me, gave me a kiss on my forehead, and quietly walked out of the door.

I sat there experiencing feelings that I could not describe in words if someone put a gun to my head. With Ian, there is stillness in my spirit that surpasses everyone else. How can I ignore these feelings? Yet, I don't really know what to do with them. Miss Jesus Sandals offered her analysis. "Your problem is you have spread yourself so thin with all these guys that your thoughts and feelings are becoming inner-twined." I sat there touching my forehead, replaying moments and times with each of the men that have come to mean so much to me in similar, yet different, ways.

I went inside, grabbed my phone, and dialed Carmen. After a couple of rings, a male voice answered. "Hello. Hello?" he said. As he was about to repeat himself, I said, "Oh, I'm so sorry, but I've misdialed." His response was, "No you haven't, Xandy. This is Carmen's phone. She's downstairs at the door with the Chinese delivery guy, and I saw it was you, so I picked up- knowing she would not want to miss your call." I was speechless! "Are you there, Xandy?" he asked. "Ah yes, I'm here. I was just a bit thrown off. May I ask your name, being that you already know mine?" "Of course," he responded. "I'm Kevin. I've heard so much about you, and I do look forward to meeting you one day." "Well, Hi Kevin, it's nice accidentally meeting you by phone as well." (I'm sure he picked up on the bit of sarcasm in my voice. In spite of the closeness that Carmen and

I share…I had never heard of this man before and I was quite miffed about it).

I then heard Carmen in the background, "Hey Baby, who are you talking to?" He quickly responded with, "It's Alexandria, honey." I heard, "Oh gosh!" from Carmen as she came closer to the phone. As he was handing off the phone he said, "Here's Carmen. Come see us soon." There was a rustling noise then Carmen came on saying, "Hey Alex." "Oh no, don't you hey Alex me!" I snapped! "Hold on," she said. "Hey sweetheart, I already plated your food; it's on the counter in the kitchen. Go ahead and eat. I'm going to talk to Alex for a minute." He obviously followed orders and disappeared. When Carmen returned to me, she quickly said, "All right, Miss Morgan, don't you start with me. I know you've got a lot to say, but now is not the time. I'll give you all the details you are dying to hear later, okay?" "No it's not okay," I snapped again. "At least give me something- you sneaky wench!"

She laughed and said, "Okay, Okay. Yes, I have a boyfriend. His name is Kevin. I've been seeing him about two years, and he's moved in with me. I'm bringing him to Mrs. A's wedding, and you two can get to know each other then. Okay?" "TWO YEARS, CARMEN?" I screamed in the phone. "I know, Alex. I didn't tell you, because I was blindsided with this whole commitment thing I found myself in, and most of all, liking it, and I seriously wanted to test-drive this for a while under the radar before I debuted it to you and the rest of the world. I know it's strange and really unexpected for me, but please work with me. Okay Alex?" Hearing the sincerity in her voice, calmed me temporarily, but I was still in a state of shock. She interrupted my internal conversation by saying…

"Now, tell me, which one is it that you are calling me about? I know you were initially calling me to vent about one of your beaus. Right?" "Wow, was it true that I only called her to be a sounding board for my relationship chaos?" I asked myself. I said, "Okay, you got me. I was calling you about Ian." Before I could go on, she said, "Are you still seeing Mr. Boring? I can't believe it!" I quickly brought her up to speed on Ian, and as I was about to close, Miss Jesus Sandals piped in with, "Hmmmm I see you mentioned nothing about Nicholas, and why is that?" I totally ignored her. Carmen interrupted my spill and said something that really surprised me. "Alexandria, it's obvious that you have not been going to church, nor praying like you were raised to do, because if you were, you wouldn't be in such dilemmas with these different guys. Some things can only be made clear through prayer. Each one of the men you've been seeing for the last twelve years have wonderful qualities, along with some issues, but at the rate you are going and with the method you are using...you will never settle down." "Well, well," I interjected, "I see I've got Mother Theresa on the phone." We both laughed. "Look sweetie, I've got to go for now. My dinner is getting cold, and so is my man," she said laughing. "Go to church girl and use that brilliant brain of yours and put those hormones on ice for a change. I love you Alex. Bye now." With that...there was silence.

# CHAPTER 16
## ◆ JULIAN, EDMUND, DANNY ◆

C armen did have a few good points after I spent some time thinking about it. I took her advice; from that following Sunday forward…I was in church. And to my surprise…each one of my love interests accompanied me on Sundays at different churches, including Julian. The Sunday we went together, we had chosen one of the new up and coming non-denominational churches that had been getting lots of publicity lately. It was reported to have a charismatic pastor and dynamic male chorus. Julian and I were there sitting near the front, and of course, we did attract some attention, because Julian had become quite the household name with his rising CD and his appearances with M. Brenae.

In fact, the choir director acknowledged Julian in the audience and invited him up to the choir loft and asked him to play. I froze. Miss Red Pumps said, "Oh my goodness, is he about to play his jazz in church?" I had no idea, but to my amazement…Julian took the stage, seated himself at the keyboard, and played the most beautiful rendition of "*How Great Thou Art*" that I have ever heard. The congregation gave him a rousing standing ovation, and Julian was moved to tears as he descended the stage. I couldn't have loved him any more than I did at that moment. When I saw those beautiful hazel eyes filled with tears, I took him in my arms, right there in the pew, and never wanted to let him go. On another note, my church visits with

Edmund led me to discover that he has an amazing singing voice, and that he really did know a lot about the Bible, as did Olivia. She went to church with us a couple of times, and to be honest, sitting there with them felt so right and to the strange eye...we were the perfect family (and a good-looking one at that). Edmund sat between Olivia and I each time and kept his arm around me and held Olivia's hand off and on during service. Everything about worshipping with Edmund was great, with the exception that he suggested that we change the church we were visiting, because he thought it would be so easy for me to get a crush on the "good-looking young pastor" who kept looking my way." Gosh, I was really seeking spiritual guidance, as well as trying to bring balance to my life, and this collection of men that I had somehow allowed to run in and out of my life was mindboggling.

In my efforts to quiet my head and slow down the relational traffic, I was asking each of them to just give me some space, because the demands of my job had increased due to losing one of my senior recruiters, and my load was feeling almost unbearable. One evening, I was having a conversation with Taylor on the phone when Hannah, Danny's sister, beeped in. When I answered, she said, "Hi Alexandria, I know it's been a long time since we've seen each other, but I wanted to invite you personally to a celebration dinner for Danny at my grandmother's house next Saturday afternoon. Everyone would love to see you." I was stunned, but asked her if she thought Danny would be okay with my being there. Her response was, "I told him I was going to invite you, and he smiled and said, "Yeah, that's what's up." That's definitely Danny. Before hanging up, I realized that I didn't know what we were going to be celebrating. Hannah proudly said, "Danny's graduating. He's finished his AA and is already accepted into the Bachelor's program in special education."

My heart swelled with pride for Danny. I told her that I would be there. I googled and found out the actual graduation ceremony date and time and planned to surprise Danny and the family by attending that as well. I planned to sneak into the back somewhere inconspicuous to see him receive his degree. As Saturday was approaching...I shopped and decided to purchase Danny a set of personalized business/school supplies, including a Floto Italian leather book bag. When Saturday came, I took great pains in selecting my outfit and ensuring that every hair was in place before heading to the auditorium. I arrived early and found a good seat with a great view of the stage. I saw Danny's whole family enter the auditorium, including Joseph. Collectively, they made a beautiful family. Mrs. Edna walked so proudly as she entered the seating area. Soon, the commencement began, and the graduates entered. Although Danny's entire family had not seen me…Danny's eyes connected with mine as he entered his row of seats, and he gave me a big smile and winked. Miss Red Pumps whispered, "My God, that is a good looking hunk of a man." "And a good one too," added Miss Jesus Sandals.

When Danny crossed the stage to receive his degree, there was no doubt that he had a big support team present. I was so proud of Danny and equally enthralled with the harmony of his big, beautiful family. After the program ended, Danny catapulted right to Joseph first and then to his mom, grandmother, and siblings. He then proceeded to place his mortarboard on Joseph's head, and everyone gathered around his wheelchair to take a family pic with him as if he were the graduate. When I made my presence known, I was greeted warmly by his entire family, with Joseph bringing up the rear. His hug was so crushing…it nearly took my breath away. We all walked together to our cars, and as always, Danny had Joseph in the van, and I followed them to Mrs. Edna's house. Upon arrival, I was blown away by the effort that had gone into this celebration. The front yard, house, and back yard looked as though a professional decorator had put great effort into this event.

Everyone was there, including extended family that I had not met before, but surprisingly, they knew my name. After a soul stirring prayer by Ms. Eva, with Ms. Edna as background, the festivities began. The food had been catered and was delicious. Danny was glued to my side, with the exception of a few times he had to attend to Joseph's needs, which Hannah described as an upset stomach due to the excitement and over indulgence. As things were about to come to a close, Danny took the floor and poured his heart out in a speech he had obviously prepared prior to tonight, thanking everyone for their love and support, including me. I was so shocked to hear him acknowledge me as the motivating source for him moving into his own house and entering college. He then lifted me off the floor in one of his bear hugs, right in front of his entire family.

They were giving us a rousing round of applause. Miss Jesus Sandals had a big smile on her face as she said, "There's something really special about this guy. Even I can't deny that." "Yeah, from the sound coming from the back room, it sounds like he's needed for diaper-duty again," interjected Miss Red Pumps, while laughing. While Danny was gone taking care of Joseph, Ms. Eva approached me and said, "Alexandria, I want to warn you that as soon as Danny finishes with Joseph, this time, I am going to put him out of this house to go out to celebrate with you. He's going to go, and none of us are taking no for an answer." Sure enough, everything went as planned, and Danny shockingly agreed to go out on the town and to pick up Joseph tomorrow. Danny and I went out dancing and had a wonderful time. At the end of the night, we went back to his place, which was a first for me.

I was so impressed with his house. It was immaculate, of course, and much nicer than I expected. Danny poured us a glass of wine and put on some music, and we sipped, laughed, and danced into the wee hours of the morning. "I have really missed you, Miss Alex. There have been so many times that I wanted to call you, but I had vowed that when or if we connected again-I wanted to be in a different head space." "What do you mean –a different head space, Danny?" I asked. "Yeah, we want to know that too," said in unison from the two on my shoulder. Danny went on to say, "Alexandria, you are a beautiful woman with everything going for you, and I had little to offer, other than a sincere heart. So I created a life plan for myself that includes getting my master's degree and forging a career in the field of special education. I haven't told my family yet, but I'm being promoted on my job, and things are really looking up for me." I had a lot of internal debate going on in my head, regarding his revelation, that did not include my shoulder pals. Danny and I talked a great deal that night. He shared with me that I was the only woman he had been serious with in a long time, and he was rethinking his decision to push me away.

Listening to him caused me to venture off into "what-if" land, because I truly cared about Danny and enjoyed being with him to the max. That evening was perfect for us, because I had never seen Danny so relaxed and willing to be transparent with me. We fell right into sync, physically, as if we had never spent time apart. When I awoke during the night…I heard Danny up vacuuming and cleaning, which was a habit he could not seem to break. Even when he stayed over at my place, he could not rest until everything was in order in the house, according to him. Breaking out of my flashback moment…I ran over to him, after standing there drooling over watching his muscular physique as he pushed the vacuum. He turned and looked at me, and I could tell immediately that something different was on his mind. "What's wrong, Danny?"

All of a sudden, Danny jerked the vacuum cord from the wall and threw it, while looking at me with tears in his eyes before beginning to yell. "What's wrong, Alex? What's wrong?" he repeated. "I'm in love with you! That's what's wrong." I was more caught off guard by the manner in which he spoke as opposed to what he said. From the looks of things…my shoulder mates were equally surprised and baffled. I was finally able to say… "Danny, what's going on? Why do you seem so angry about saying this to me, instead of being okay with it? I am truly surprised and confused." Before I could continue what I had planned to say, Danny butted in with, "Alexandria, this thing with you is driving me crazy, because I know that I cannot be with you, regardless of how I feel about you. I will not place the load that I have to carry with Joseph upon your shoulders too. You know first-hand how difficult that can be, and I just can't do that to you."

I cut him off before he could say any more by walking up to him and wrapping my arms around him and covering his mouth with mine. I felt him tremble, and the tears flowed. "Oh Danny, it's Okay," I said, "I love you too, and I love Joseph. Please stop trying to make choices for me. Please?" "Alex, you have no idea what my life is really like. There isn't a day that goes by that I'm not stressing and worrying about Joseph. And…it's going to get worse." "Uh oh," said

Miss Red Pumps. "Hush, so I can hear what he's saying," Miss Jesus Sandals quietly said. Danny pulled me down to the sofa and shared with me that since our hiatus…Joseph has been suffering from renal problems. He went on to say that the prognosis is not good. Joseph will need dialysis and an eventual kidney transplant to sustain his life. My silence confirmed Danny's belief that his burden was far too great for me to attempt to share it with him. He said, "Alex, I don't blame you at all, but it just hurts so bad knowing how much I want to have a life with you."

When I looked to both shoulders for some sort of feedback and support…there was none. I encircled Danny in my arms as he cried, and I softly recited 1 Corinthians 13:7- *"Love bears all things, believes all things, hopes all things, endures all things."* Danny's tears turned into sobs, and we sat there for a long time, holding on to each other. Miss Red Pumps, much to my surprise, had tears flowing as well. Miss Jesus Sandals said, "Xandy, you have given this man what he has needed for a long time-the freedom to cry," as she too wiped her eyes. I believe that was the closest I've ever felt to any man in my life, other than my father. "Could this be the man for me?" I asked myself. Danny was not a man of means and credentials and blue blood background, but what he did offer me was priceless. Miss Jesus Sandals was quick on the draw with, "Xandy, slow down and stay logical. Danny is a really good guy, but the package that he is bringing to the table is a bit too much for any woman. Don't let your emotions rule your brain. You are too smart for that." "Let us not forget the part that her hormones are playing in this too," said you know who, dressed in red.

The time I spent with Danny did nothing but complicate an already complicated situation. The morning that we parted, he told me that both of us needed to take some time to think about the possibility of us having a future together. I was so ready just to tell him that I had nothing to think about until he said the following, "Alexandria, if we stand a chance, I have to be totally upfront with you. I've told you about Joseph's health, and I want you to know that the doctors are 99.9 percent sure that I will be a match for him, and you know that means that I will be giving him a kidney. I just want to put it all out there." I responded with, "Danny, I had no doubt that you would automatically be the donor for Joseph. I would expect nothing less. The only thing that concerns me is if, God forbid, our future child needed an organ from you…there would be no possibility." Danny looked at me incredulously and said, "Child? Oh my God, Xandy, have you forgotten, or are you refusing to accept that I am unable to have children?" "No!" I said quickly. "I have not forgotten. You had a vasectomy, and that's reversible." Before I could say anything else, he shut down the whole conversation by saying, "Alexandria, mine is not going to be reversed. Our only child will be Joseph." And then there was silence.

# CHAPTER 17
## ◆ BRENT ◆

significantly changed gears in the relationship department after that. I was honest with each of the men I have been seeing. The winter was about to settle in, and usually, I always made it a point to have a serious relationship going on in cold weather. It was just something special about have someone to cuddle with on a consistent basis. Against the advice of my shoulder companions, I continue to see each one of them, but not nearly as often. For the life of me, I can't quite say which one of them means the most to me. Brent shocked me in the midst of all of this chaos by announcing that he and his father would be doing a one-day leadership seminar in the city, and he wanted me to join the two of them for dinner that evening.

I was shocked, although Brent and I had stayed connected throughout this whole period, by talking and texting daily. I was so nervous about the evening. I called Carmen, and she asked a question that caused me to think. She said, "Alex, Brent is obviously very much a "Daddy's boy" but is that such a bad thing, being that his daddy is a successful goal-oriented man? You constantly brag that Brent stimulates you more than anyone when it comes to communicating and with how much he seems to be in tune with your emotional self and makes you laugh. That's rare, my friend," "Hey, communication is not the only thing this dude stimulates with, Miss Xandy. His rebellion toward the ministry really brings out his kinky side, and old

Miss Xandy here loves that," interjected Miss big mouth Red Pumps. Carmen went on to finish with, "So what if Dad has the potential to call all the shots in your relationship with his son?"

Given that food for thought, I met the two Mr. Girards for dinner, and I must say I was pleasantly surprised. As I entered the restaurant, Brent met me with open arms and escorted me to their table. Dr. Girard rose and said, "Alexandria, I'm so happy finally to get a chance to spend some time with you, since you are all my son here finds to talk about. Tonight, I can certainly understand why. You are stunning!" "Wow, what is going on?" I thought to myself. The evening consisted of small talk, but eventually, turned to what felt like an interrogation. Brent kept his knee against mine under the table the whole time, and he took on a spectator's position in the conversation

"Well, Alexandria, I'm a man that does not mix words, so let's cut to the chase. Shall we? It is obvious that Brent is quite enthralled with you, and unbeknownst to him, I am aware of the extent of the relationship you two have maintained. And…I have no problem with it at all." Brent, Miss Red Pumps, Miss Jesus Sandals, and I looked at each other in silence. Dr. Girard continued, "I know and see the age difference between the two of you, but I respect you, Alexandria, because you have helped to keep Brent on the straight and narrow, and for that, I am truly thankful. My son has a bright future ahead of him, and involvement with the wrong woman could definitely derail it. You two have managed to enjoy yourself, while keeping a low profile, and that's important to my ministry, and my brand, as well as my son's. When this invention of his hits the market, along with his vey public work with me, discretion is of the utmost importance. So thank you, Alexandria."

Brent said, "Father I don't know what to say. You knew about Alex all this time, and you were okay with it? ALL of it?" "Of course, I knew, son." Dr. Girard responded… "I make it my business to know about everything and everybody that has any potential of affecting my livelihood and my future. You have continued to date reputable girls and keep yourself publicly intact while with Alexandria, so I had no complaints. Your mother doesn't know that I am aware. I wish she could have been here with us tonight, but she had a prior engagement." Brent reached for my hand, and we smiled at each other and appeared to be slipping off into a mutual la-la land with each other, when Dr. Girard broke the spell by saying, "I want the two of you to be mindful that there is much more work to be done with the network and empire that my son and I are building, and although I have made concessions with accepting his engineering job and pending patent, we must maintain status quo in his relationship arena for quite some time, and that's where the difference in your age may cause a problem. You see, Brent has no room in his life for a wife and family until the stage is set for such."

Miss Red Pumps spoke up before either of us could with, "So what you are saying is… Brent has your permission to date Alexandria as long as it's under the radar?" My mind was trying to process the whole thing, but Brent quickly confronted the unexpected issue at hand. "Father, you cannot be serious. You have just sat there and revealed a plan and timeline for my life that I was not a part of, and I can't believe you said this to Alex before talking to me!" It was obvious that Brent was upset, but his father was unmoved by his son's displeasure with his revelation. Dr. Girard said, "Aaron Brent Girard, trust me…I know what I am doing, and one day, you will thank me. What we are creating is a legacy for the Girards for generations to come. You and I will become household names in the field of spiritual leadership and motivational seminars with books, videos, and curriculum on top of multi-thousand member congregations around the country. All of this requires focus and impeccable moral standing."

Brent and I were sitting there looking at him as he spoke, as if we were seminar attendees. Dr. Girard went on to say, "Brent, you will be the face and poster child for professional success, while maintaining purity and incomparable moral character." Sensing our silent disagreement, he went on, "We dodged a bullet at great cost in the past, and we are never going down that road again. Alexandria, you must understand that Brent will continue to make appearances with approved young ladies for the good of our cause and what the two of you continue to do discreetly is fine with me. It's worked this far. Am I right?" Brent quietly asked, "Does Mother have any idea what you are proposing?" Dr. Girard responded with, "Brent, your mother supports the rise of our empire and fully submits to my leadership as any good wife would, except for her drinking, which I've decided is a battle that I choose not to fight as long as long as she keeps it under wraps."

I was wavering between wanting to throw up and wanting to slap sparks from Dr. Girard's face. Brent was obviously embarrassed and livid. He stood and reached for my hand saying, "Come on, Alex, it's time for us to leave. I'm assuming that I have your permission, my dear father, since I'm obviously not an adult in your eyes." To my utter amazement, Dr. Girard spoke in a hushed tone, "Brent, take your seat. You will not give the impression of discord in this restaurant. We came here for dinner, and that's what we are going to do." Brent sat down. His father went on, "I am only guilty of looking out for your best interest and planning a wonderful future for you and your eventual family. That could very well be Alexandria if her biological clock will allow her to be patient." He smiled at me. Miss Jesus Sandals said, "This man has some nerve, but I truly believe his intentions are good."

I politely said, "Dr. Girard, I seem to have lost my appetite, so if you will, excuse me…I'm leaving." Brent reached for my hand, but I avoided it saying, "Brent, I will talk with you later-much later." With that being said, I walked away from the table with a smile. Miss Red Pumps was in my ear the entire time that I was waiting for the valet to bring my car. "Alex, think long and hard before you reach any rash decisions about Brent. Is it so wrong for a father to protect the legacy he's trying to build for his family? Remember, Brent breached the trust between him and his dad in the past, so there are some trust issues. That Daddy has a lot riding on the future, and he doesn't want Brent's hormones to mess it up." "You have got to be kidding me," said Miss Jesus Sandals. "Both of you -SHUT UP!" I screamed as I jumped in my car and peeled off.

Brent was beside himself as the result of that dinner fiasco and called me incessantly until I answered. He had a toe-to-toe with his father, and then his mother entered the ring as Brent's advocate. How do I know this? "Rose" called me and we talked for about two hours.

She gave me so much insight about Brent's father and their marriage. She said, "Alexandria, you won't have any more problems from that husband of mine." She went on to say, "Aaron Brent Girard went after his father's jugular vein that night. In fact, I had my driver bring me to Pennsylvanian to support Brent the next day." Miss Red Pumps commented, "My goodness Alexandria, it's obvious to me now that Brent is so serious about you that he stood up to that dictator father of his, without fear of the consequences." Miss Jesus Sandals responded with, "I never thought I'd see this day come, but my whole mind just shifted in Brent's favor, because he is truly a great guy."

I quickly told them, "Will the two of you be quiet, so I can listen to the person who is the real expert on Brent?" Rose revealed that when she and Dr. Girard met…she was the girl from across the tracks. Her husband's family never thought that she was worthy of their son's interest and certainly not their last name. Her husband listened to his parents, dated, and later married someone else. That marriage ended in an ugly divorce. Dr. Girard came looking for Rose and the rest is history. She told me that she came to Philly to remind him of how miserable he felt trying to live someone else's life and asked him if he was willing to do that to his son for the sake of "the people's opinion." Rose ended her intentional plea for leniency for Brent by saying, "Alexandria, my son did something I have never seen him do, and that was walk right up to his father almost nose-to-nose and say, "Father, I love Alexandria Morgan, and if she'll have me after that stunt you pulled…that's exactly who I'm going to be with, whether you like it or not."

She said that the last statement Brent made to his father was the one that put the icing on the cake. "Father, if you don't like my choice…then get yourself another son." Rose said that Dr. Girard stood there in silence, as if cemented to the floor, then left the room without speaking to either of them. She is convinced that his mindset regarding me will change-if given a just a wee bit of time for him to get over the sting of being affronted by his wife and son. I thanked her so much for calling me and told her that I would be in touch. As I hung up the phone, Miss Red Pumps was looking puzzled and Miss

Jesus Sandals was cheering, "Yay Brent!" As for me, I realized that my heart was smiling.

# CHAPTER 18
## ◆ THIS IS IT ◆

Well, to make a long, confusing story shorter…I made a vow to myself, after talking to Brent and his mother, that I was bringing all of my relationship madness to a screeching halt. As I said at the beginning, any one of the men that I had been involved with during the past twelve years would be a catch that most women for kill for. The confusing part is that I care deeply for each of them, and I know that the feeling is mutual. Since that night, Brent has done what he does best, other than call me, which is shower me with flowers and emotionally revealing cards and letters. On one occasion, I did speak with him and ask him how he ever expected to have a life and make his own decisions if he did not have the courage to stand up to his father and say no to his control. Brent was adamant about asking me to be patient and, in the meantime, continue to enjoy each other. I told him I wanted a break. He responded with, "Alexandria…I have always been here for you to support you, and I'm not going to stop now. If giving you space from me is what you want, then so be it. Just know that there is no one I'd rather be with than you, and not my father nor anyone else can or will stop that." "Okay Brent…we'll talk soon," I responded and then we hung up.

With an attempt to place all of my men on ice, I was able to focus on my job again and made Vince my consistent sidekick. It was the middle of the fall, and time was rapidly moving toward Christmas.

Julian was a rising celebrity and continuing to make his occasional late night visits to my place when he could not sleep. Most of those nights were just to be close to me- confessing his feelings for me.

On one occasion, I had been out with Vince and my sorority sisters and called Julian to see if I could come over for a sleep over in lieu of going home alone. His answer was one far from what I anticipated. He said, "Alex, I've got to be honest with you. Fran is here, and I can't ask her to leave. She is having one of her nights, and I can't have the both of you here at the same time -that's disrespectful to both of you. Please understand, Alex." Tears began to flow, and I went home with Vince instead. Miss Jesus Sandals made an effort to get me to see how compassionate and supportive Julian was being to a woman still grieving her dead child. Miss Red Pumps was not having it. "This man is not a psychiatrist, and he is not running a shelter for emotional women. He is confessing love for you, which means no other woman comes first."

Well, the days and weeks went by fast. Christmas was upon me, and I made it clear to each of them that I was not spending my holiday with any of them. One morning in December, I was busy getting ready for work when the entrance gate buzzer sounded. When I answered, I was told it was a courier with a delivery for me. When he arrived with a large box with no sender information visible, I was beyond myself with curiosity. When I managed to open it, I was speechless. Before me was the painting- "The Soul." Ian had paid five figures for this gift and sent it to me for Christmas. The note attached said, "For the one in my soul." I picked up the phone with tears in my voice to call Ian to thank him. Nicholas answered the phone, and I hung up. Miss Jesus Sandals said, "Xandy, you are batting a thousand, aren't you, my darling?"

As if the plot needed to be thickened, Edmund began to make non-stop efforts to get me out on the town for holiday events with him and Olivia. I refused most of them, but reconsidered Olivia's feelings and agreed to go to the Ice Spectacular and attend her holiday recital. This time, it was uneventful, other than Claire making it obvious that she, Olivia, and Edmund had gone on a cruise and had a marvelous time. She bragged that they had taken some family pictures for

Olivia's sake that were beautiful. Edmund's parents looked directly at me for a response. Edmund spoke up and said, "Claire, we are no longer a family; we share a child whom we both love, and you need to grow up before you make a mess of things as usual." Claire was so obviously embarrassed, but held her peace.

After his speech, Edmund moved to my side and didn't leave it for the rest of the evening. However, the unthinkable happened. Olivia appeared to have forgotten her recital piece and made a huge blunder while playing that caused her to rise from the piano and run off the stage. She was quickly followed by her mother and father, who was also holding tight to my hand as we entered backstage. Claire was trying to console Olivia, but it was Edmund's arms that did the trick. The shock of the evening was that Olivia reached out and called my name, requesting a hug and attention from me as well. Claire could have killed me on the spot, as she shunned her boyfriend's attempt to be close with her for the moment. I left the venue alone, telling Edmund that his place was with Olivia, and that he needed to corral Claire. His response was, "I will, Alex. I will. Just don't let one of your young suitors steal you from me while we are in this process." All I could manage to say was, "Oh Edmund please!"

Christmas drew near. I made plans to spend time in Virginia with my family. I fielded calls intermittently from each of them until I left Philadelphia. Once I got home, I became immersed in the holiday prep, wedding prep, and Joshua's agenda for me. In the midst of it all, Ralph showed up with Taylor, demanding that we talk. Although we had been maintaining contact, including a few visits since the summer…he was still maintained the position as a contender for my heart. "How can this be, Alex? This man has hurt you more than once, and confessed to you that you are not the only woman that he has used to cheat on his wife," said Miss Jesus Sandals. Miss Red Pumps countered with, "Give the guy a break. You know how long they have loved each other, and he's growing up. We all make mistakes."

I agreed to squeeze him in and met him at our usual spot. Wouldn't you know it? The pub had mistletoe hanging everywhere, and Ralph took advantage of the opportunity. When he released me from the lip-lock of all time, he whispered in my ear, "I did it, Alex. I've asked my wife for a divorce." I didn't know what to say. I had such mixed emotions. I responded with, "Ralph, are you sure?" He answered, "Yes I am sure." I was in such internal turmoil that my head was spinning. I rose from the table saying, "I can't do this, right now, and please don't force the issue by using my brother to get to me." With that being said, I exited the pub and drove home. During the drive, Miss Jesus Sandals asked, "Why didn't you tell Ralph that you haven't just been sitting and crocheting while waiting on him to decide what he wants? Little does he know that there are at least five other applicants for the position of "the only man" in your life." I ignored her.

When I arrived home, Taylor managed to say quietly, in passing, "I can tell, dear sister, that you've been informed of Ralph's new status. I don't know where your head is, but I do know that he drives me nuts about you." "Not now little brother, Please," I said quietly as I side-stepped him and walked off.

I made it through the holidays by keeping my focus solely on my family. I returned home and to work and managed to help my mom as the wedding drew near and talked to Carmen when the time she spent with her love interest allowed. Carmen repeated over and over, I needed to stay in church and cut all interactions with these six men if I was going to make a sound and rational decision about one of them. Collectively… my talks with her, Vince, and the Lord were so helpful. My two shoulder companions were not offering any guidance at this time. I took a couple of weeks of leave leading up to my mom's wedding in April. I told everyone that I was going to be in Virginia for my mom's nuptials for a couple of weeks. Each one of them, except for Danny, asked me if they could be my wedding date, and I knew why. He could not leave or would not leave Joseph.

A week before the wedding, everything was complete. Gertie Anderson made sure of that. Carmen kept her promise and flew in to spend time with me and my mom and family. We talked into the wee hours every night. Carmen looked wonderful, and I figured out what it was-she was happy. She told me how she met Kevin and that he was not like her usual conquests by no stretch of the imagination. She said she enjoyed living with him, and to my shock…my best friend Carmen confessed that she was head over heels in love and considering marriage. I almost fainted, but instead, I burst into tears and cried uncontrollably. I was happy for her, but her news increased my feelings of confusion with all the male irons I had in the fire.

Carmen and I analyzed each one of the men in my life, and she readily admitted that each one of them had a lot to offer me, but came with quite a set of baggage. We decided that we would put all of those on hold and focus on my mother and Jeff. Well, the day before the wedding came. Everything was going off without a glitch. Ms. Gertie cracked a pretty mean, though classy whip, when it came to her team and events. The entire wedding party, which consisted of our immediate family members, were able to relax and enjoy the festivities. The ladies spent the day at the spa. The guys played a round of golf and actually got some personal services at the country club as well.

The rehearsal dinner was a spectacular fare of food, with an ambiance to die for. All of Jeff's colleagues and fellow officers and professors were there. Surprisingly, my Aunt Sandra ignored all of them, because she only had eyes for Logan. After the dinner, the men disappeared, and the women retired early to get their beauty rest. As all of us parted ways in the hallways, my mother asked me to come to her room. Once there, she said, "Alexandria, are you okay sweetheart? I see the distance in your eyes, even though you are very much here and actively involved in my special day." I responded with, "Sure mother, I'm fine. I've just got a lot going on personally in the relationship department. I'm at a crossroads and not sure which road to take." My mother said, "If by saying crossroads you are meaning choosing between men, then listen to your head first, Xandy, then your heart. Alexandria, you already know the answer. I think it's a matter of having the courage to make the choice to settle down/ commit to one man and taking the risk of failure or being hurt."

After hearing her say that, something clicked on the inside of me. Was it true that I was afraid of losing the man I love and who loves me in some way? Was I trying to prevent that from happening by keeping a horde of men to try to sidestep the reality of risk? It was if a weight lifted as my mother engulfed me in her arms. I looked for feedback from my shoulders and to my surprise, neither of them was there. It was like they never existed and I was so sure they did exist and had been there ever since I had left home for college. My mother obviously observed my actions, because she said, "Alexandria, is there something wrong? Why do you seemingly keep looking over each shoulder?" My mother and I talked for a long time that night about her future with Jeff and my options.

When we were about to part…she reached for me again and said, "Well, baby, this is it. I will be a wife tomorrow, but please know that I love you and Taylor with all my heart, and I always will. I trust you Xandy, and I know you will make the right choice. You've just got to trust yourself." With that, we stood there holding each other and cried softly for a while. She then openly prayed for me and for her, and she ended the prayer with "Thank you God for allowing Billy to watch over us all these years, and Lord please don't let him stop… because we will always need the presence of our Angel, Amen." Billy is my father! She kissed me on my forehead and said good night.

When I climbed in bed, sleep would not come. I tossed and turned, and for the first time, I quietly called out to my daddy, and it seemed as though I felt a peace enter the room and my heart. I said, "I'm ready Daddy. I know that now. I love Jeff, but he will never take your place in my heart or my life. I'm ready to trust love, and I know you've got my back, right?" I got out of my bed, got down on my knees, and asked God to forgive me for all of my sins and to help me as I walk the path that I was raised to walk. I called my sins by name and, particularly, talked to God about my long years of fornication and repented for it, vowing never to turn away from him again. I knew better than to spread myself so thin sexually and emotionally and to allow fear to lower my morals and standards. I wanted to walk the path that I was raised to walk.

I said, "Lord, I have several guys that I believe truly care about me or even love me and want to build a life with me. Please make it clear to me who I should choose. I know each one of them have faults and flaws, but ALL of us do and yet, you love us anyway. Please help me God, because I've created a mess, but I want to love and be loved, just the way my daddy loved my mother-eternally. Amen." The longer I prayed, the clearer I became about my life and my choices. I arose from my knees, climbed back into bed, and slept like a baby.

Everyone awoke to a beautiful spring day. The weather was as if it was special ordered. We all had a light breakfast on the deck. As we were finishing, Joshua ran out and said. "Auntie Carmen, there's a man outside looking for you. He said his name is Kevin." Carmen ran for the door like an Olympic sprinter. I followed close behind, eagerly awaiting my first face-to-face with the love of Carmen's life. When she opened the door- standing before us was a guy just an inch or so taller than Carmen, a little thick around the mid-section, and a smile that included a gap. I looked at her and she looked at me and laughed and wrapped her entire body around Kevin. Seeing this, I then knew, without a doubt, what loving someone meant.

Introductions were made, just as the limos arrived to transport all of us to our prep suites at the country club. As we approached the club from the long driveway…all of us were mesmerized by the enormous span of pure breathtaking scenery. Hours later…the guests were starting to arrive. After the traditional hustle and bustle, hugs and tears…the ceremony began. My mother was so beautiful standing there on Taylor's arm that she literally took my breath away. Jeff was just as handsome and debonair. Everyone was aligned for his or her place in the ceremony. As the orchestra ensemble and harpist began their second song, which was "Ave Maria," the procession started, and we all seemed to float with the melody as we entered. As my mother proceeded down the aisle, my heart overflowed with love for her. Suddenly, there was an undeniable certainty of the new spirit of freedom I was feeling. I knew, without a doubt, that I am ready to give myself completely to one man and allow him to love me and to develop the type of relationship with me -befitting a lifetime of marriage. The question still remains, to some degree-WHO? As I watched Ms. Abigail Morgan walk down the aisle toward her new love and life…my heart felt as if it was going to explode with my love for her and finally for ME. I looked up towards the heavens, smiled and quietly said, "Thank you."

# EXERCISES

To assist you in the task before you...I am giving you a table which allows you find each of Xandy's potential choices in the chapters in which they are included.

This will possibly make it easier for you to refer back to their times with Xandy as you attempt to choose or discuss your choices and formulate your answers to the discussion questions.

| Choices | Chapters |
|---------|----------|
| Ralph | 1, 4, 12, 13 |
| Brent | 4, 12, 13, 17 |
| Edmund | 5, 8, 13, 16 |
| Julian | 6, 8, 11, 14 |
| Danny | 7, 8, 11, 16 |
| Ian | 9, 10, 11, 15 |

The *Moment* has arrived…

♂ ♀ **Who** do **you** choose for Alexandria to possibly spend her life with?  Which **one** of her 6 suitors will be **THE ONE**?

**Drum Roll Please…….**  NAME: " _____ "

**Why is HE your choice? (Please be detailed)**

_____

_____

_____

_____

**Please state or list all of his PROS (positives)**

_____    _____

_____    _____

_____    _____

_____    _____

**Please state or list all of his CONS (negatives)**

_____    _____

_____    _____

_____    _____

_____    _____

**After identifying or listening to his pros and cons...do you still choose him?   YES     NO**

**If you answered "NO" please indicate your reason for changing your mind and complete another 1st choice sheet!**

_____

_____

_____

_____

_____

_____

_____

# Now let's take an analytical look at the ones you DID NOT choose:

♂ **1. Why I did <u>NOT</u> choose**_____ **(list name)**

_____

_____

_____

_____

**Please state or list all of his PROS. (positives)**

_____    _____

_____    _____

_____    _____

_____    _____

**Please state or list all of his CONS. (negatives)**

_____    _____

_____    _____

_____    _____

_____    _____

After identifying his pros and cons and possibly having the opportunity to think about and discuss them… do you still <u>NOT</u> choose him?   YES       NO

If you changed your mind…what made you do so?

_____

_____

_____

_____

If you didn't change your mind, <u>is there anything HE could do</u> that would make you choose him?   YES   NO

If yes, please be specific:

_____

_____

_____

_____

♂2. Why I did <u>NOT</u> choose_____ (list name)

_____

_____

_____

_____

**Please state or list all of his PROS. (positives)**

_____     _____

_____     _____

_____     _____

_____     _____

**Please state or list all of his CONS. (negatives)**

_____     _____

_____     _____

_____     _____

_____     _____

**After identifying his pros and cons and possibly having the opportunity to think about and discuss them... do you still <u>NOT</u> choose him?   YES     NO**

**If you changed your mind...what made you do so?**

_____

_____

_____

_____

If you didn't change your mind, <u>is there anything HE could do</u> that would make you choose him?  YES  NO

If yes, please be specific:

_____

_____

_____

_____

♂3. Why I did <u>NOT</u> choose_____ (list name)

_____

_____

_____

_____

Please state or list all of his PROS. (positives)

_____    _____

_____    _____

_____    _____

_____    _____

**Please state or list all of his CONS. (negatives)**

_____ _____

_____ _____

_____ _____

_____ _____

**After identifying his pros and cons and possibly having the opportunity to think about and discuss them… do you still <u>NOT</u> choose him?   YES      NO**

**If you changed your mind…what made you do so?**

_____

_____

_____

_____

**If you didn't change your mind, <u>is there anything HE could do</u> that would make you choose him?   YES   NO**

**If yes, please be specific:**

_____

_____

_____

_____

♂ 4. Why I did <u>NOT</u> choose_____ (list name)

_____

_____

_____

_____

**Please state or list all of his PROS. (positives)**

_____     _____

_____     _____

_____     _____

_____     _____

**Please state or list all of his CONS (negatives)**

_____     _____

_____     _____

_____     _____

_____     _____

After identifying his pros and cons and possibly having the opportunity to think about and discuss them... do you still NOT choose him?   YES      NO

If you changed your mind...what made you do so?

_____

_____

_____

_____

If you didn't change your mind, <u>is there anything HE could do</u> that would make you choose him? YES   NO

If yes, please be specific:

_____

_____

_____

_____

♂5. Why I did NOT choose_____ (list name)

_____

_____

_____

_____

**Please state or list all of his PROS (positives)**

_____  _____

_____  _____

_____  _____

_____  _____

**Please state or list all of his CONS (negatives)**

_____  _____

_____  _____

_____  _____

_____  _____

**After identifying his pros and cons and possibly having the opportunity to think about and discuss them... do you still NOT choose him?   YES      NO**

**If you changed your mind...what made you do so?**

_____

_____

_____

_____

**If you didn't change your mind, <u>is there anything HE could do</u> that would make you choose him?  YES NO**

**If yes, please be specific:**

_____

_____

_____

_____

# GENERAL QUESTIONS FOR
# THOUGHT & DISCUSSION

♀ How **would you describe Alexandria Rae Morgan – " Xandy"**

_____

_____

_____

_____

♀ **Please state or list all of her PROS (positives)**

_____          _____

_____          _____

_____          _____

_____          _____

♀ **Please state or list all of her CONS (negatives)**

_____          _____

_____          _____

_____          _____

_____          _____

♀ **What race is Xandy?** _____

♀ **What information did you use to determine her race?**

_____

_____

_____

_____

♀ **Were any of the men she dated a different race than she?**
**YES   NO**

**If so, Who?** _____

♀ **What information did you use to determine your answer?**

_____

_____

_____

_____

♀ If all of the men she dated were the same race as Xandy…what information did you use about <u>each</u> of them to determine your answer?

1. _____

2. _____

3. _____

4. _____

5. _____

6. _____

♀ Would you describe Xandy as being PROMISCOUS?
____Yes    ___No    ____Not Sure

Please explain your answer.

_____

_____

_____

_____

## ♀ How would you describe Xandy's family?

➤ **Her mother, Abigail Morgan:**

_____

_____

_____

_____

➤ **Her brother, Taylor:**

_____

_____

_____

_____

➤ **Her Aunt, Aunt Sandra:**

_____

_____

_____

_____

➤ **Her best friend, Carmen:**

_____

_____

_____

_____

♀ **What are your thoughts about Xandy's "shoulder companions"?**

> **Miss Jesus Sandals:**

_____

_____

_____

_____

> **Miss Red Pumps:**

_____

_____

_____

_____

♀ <u>**WHY**</u> **do you think they existed in Xandy's world?**

_____

_____

_____

_____

♀ __WHY__ do you think they finally disappeared?

_____

_____

_____

_____


♀ Describe Xandy's relationship with God.

_____

_____

_____

_____


(Optional question for thought or possible discussion)

♀ In YOUR opinion, is Xandy a Christian?  _____Yes  _____
No _____Unsure

Please elaborate on your answer:

_____

_____

_____

_____

**Now that you have delved into the world of** *Xandy*
and made some choices and observations, let us switch channels
and take a look at *YOU!*

So....... Here we go!

♂♀ Now that you have chosen a potential life mate for Xandy...
please rank all of her suitors in the order that you, personally,
would choose them-FOR YOU!! (1 being your top choice, of
course)

1. _____

2. _____

3. _____

4. _____

5. _____

6. _____

**Are your personal choices different from the choices you made for
Xandy?** _____YES _____NO

**Please comment on your answer:**

_____

_____

_____

_____

## Additional comments:

_____

_____

_____

_____

# Introspective Exercises

## Exercise A.

List #1: Take a sheet of notebook paper and make a vertical list of all the qualities and traits that you want or require your mate/spouse to have. (Please be as inclusive as possible)

## Exercise B.

List # 2: Take a sheet of notebook paper and make a vertical list of the "DEAL-BREAKER" traits/habits/ behaviors that will cause you _not_ to choose a person as a mate. (Please be as inclusive as possible)

For example: smoke, drink, overweight, refuse to go to church, more than _____ children, jealous, stingy, boring, etc.)

# Exercise C.

Let's play...
## "BUILD A BEAU"

On a scale from 1 to 10 with 1 being (not important or valued at all) and 10 being a (MUST HAVE)...please rate the following EXTENSIVE list of traits and attributes in regards to mate selection for _YOU_.

Handsome/Pretty _____

Tall____

Slender build_____

Muscular/fit_____

Coke bottle ...36-24-36 (for the men) _____

The bodybuilder type_____

Nice smile____

High School graduate____

College graduate____

Very intelligent_____

Good manners_____

Good Job_____

Makes lots of money_____

Good credit____

Significant savings account____

Goal oriented____

Health benefits for himself and can provide them for you_____

Retirement plan____

Nice car_____

Great dresser_____

Close to his/her mother_____

Close relationship with his /her family_____

No children_____

Only _____children (indicate maximum number_____

Attends church_____

Obvious relationship with God_____

Good sense of humor_____

Does not drink_____

Does not smoke_____

Has lots of friends_____

Has a small social circle_____

Likes to go out to parties and clubs_____

Fun to be around (makes you laugh) _____

Likes animals_____

Good kisser_____

Generous with money and other resources_____

Involved in the community_____

Faithful_____

Likes children_____

Wants children_____

Great in bed_____

Good communication skills_____

Self-confident_____

Affectionate_____

Honest_____

Can cook and willing to do so_____

Maintains neat/clean appearance and environment_____

Home owner_____

Likes to travel_____

Spontaneous_____

Quiet/laid-back personality_____

Healthy_____

Loves children_____

Emotionally stable_____

High sex drive_____

Exercises and stays fit_____

Eats right (most of the time) _____

NO prior marriages_____

Loves to_____ (you fill in the blank and rate it) _____

Just in case I left some things off...

_____(_____)

_____(_____)


Once you have finished... the things that you rated (*3 and below*) appear to be traits and attributes that do not matter to you or that you value the least.

The things that you rated (*8 and above*) appear to be the ones that you place the most value in and your "10 ratings" appear to be the items that you value at the absolute highest and they, will therefore comprise your "MUST HAVE" list.

The (*4-7 ratings*) appear to be those things that fall in the negotiable range. They may be those things that you would like to have- but you are possibly willing to pass on, considering the number of "must haves" on your list

NOW.....compare this exercise and your ratings with your List #1. Were all of things that you rated 8-10 (especially your 10s) on List #1- initially? _____ YES _____NO

If not... Hmmmm! BUT, it's ok to add them.

# Here's the "FUN" part!

## Exercise D.

First...

**List #3:** Take a sheet of notebook paper and make a vertical list of all of your 8-10 rated traits, from the previous exercise (C), in descending order (10s at the top, followed by 9s, with the 8s at the bottom)

Next...

On a separate piece of paper, write the names of ALL of the significant others in your life (past and present) including ex-spouses.

*Some will have many.*

*Some will have few.*

*Even if it's just one,*

*It's a reflection of YOU!*

Then...

Next to each trait on List #3, place the name of each significant other next to <u>every</u> trait that person possessed or possesses (doing one name at a time).

When you finish...what you will have created will resemble a chart and you just may have made some surprising discoveries ☺

If so....What did you notice or discover?

_____

_____

_____

_____

_NOTE_: For those of you with the time or interest, you can complete this exercise using the computer for a clearer, easier-to-see and analyze version.

## Example:

(List of my
8-10 ratings)                              (significant others)

| Cute | Timmy | Scooter | |
|---|---|---|---|
| Sweet | Scooter | | Bill |
| Funny | Bill | Scooter | |
| Expensive car | | Scooter | |
| Good cook | Timmy | | Bill |
| Nice hair | Bill | Scooter | |
| Pretty smile | Bill | Timmy | |
| Likes animals | Bill | | Timmy |

## FINAL one!

## Exercise E.

Take **List #2** which is the list you compiled of the things that are "DEAL BREAKERS" for YOU. These are traits and behaviors that you will NOT accept in a mate, therefore choosing not to have a relationship with them.

NOW…Same as before, using the separate list you made of ALL of your present and past significant others (including ex-spouses) create the same kind of chart. (Next to each trait on **List #2**, place the name of each significant other next to every trait on the list that person possessed or possesses (doing one name at a time).

# Example

| (List of my "Deal Breakers") | | (significant others) | |
|---|---|---|---|
| Drinks | Timmy | Scooter | |
| Boring | Scooter | | Bill |
| Stingy | Bill | Scooter | |
| Overweight | | Scooter | |
| Non- spiritual | Timmy | | Bill |
| Married before | Bill | Scooter | |
| Dishonest | Scooter | Timmy | Bill |

**What did you notice or discover?**

_____

_____

_____

_____

In this particular exercise (E), If you were able to place the names of your significant others in the chart (especially spouses)...you are or have been in relationships with people who possess the very things that you indicate that you <u>DO NOT WANT</u> in a mate.

In Exercise (D), if you were NOT able to place the names of your significant others in the chart (especially spouses)... you are or have been in relationships with people that DO NOT POSSESS the very things that you indicate that YOU WANT in a mate.

You have now created a visual snapshot of the relationship choices you have made.

If what you see before you is not a pretty (healthy) picture … your task now is to determine your WHY?

Could it be…?

Poor self-esteem

Unrealistic expectations.

Fear of being alone.

The attainment of money & tangible things.

You have a "rescuer" personality, etc.

The answer(s) can be extremely varied.  If you recognize that you have established a pattern of choosing the same kinds of mates that, in the end, prove to be unhealthy for you…you now have a starting point from which you can begin to work toward learning to make BETTER choices.

When you make the conscious decision to break or intercept unhealthy relationship patterns, you will have taken the FIRST STEP!

# OPEN UP YOUR MIND, HEART, AND MOUTH AND SAY.....

## AHA!!!

**Don't fret…ALL of us have room for improvement!**

*THANK YOU* for participating in helping "Xandy" make her choice. In doing so, I hope you have gained some personal insight into the criteria/standards that you adhere to or consider when making personal relational choices.

Also, you may have discovered personal areas of cultural biases, stereotypical thinking and unwarranted judgment of others that may be affecting the overall state of all relationships in your world.

This book is designed to cause you to self-examine your thought processes when it comes to mate selection and establishing healthy relationships. I hope you have had the opportunity to not only evaluate yourself privately but to also share, discuss, and maybe even compare your thoughts with others during what I call a "*Xandy Party*"

A "*Xandy Party*" is a wonderful way to have a "Girls' Night IN" to discuss *Xandy's Choice* in a FUN, yet personally enlightening manner. Sooo call your friends, tell them to get this book, READ IT, do the *WORK*, and schedule your party. Then…**WATCH THE FUN & ENLIGHTENMENT UNFOLD**!!

Please send me an email about your experience with Xandy and the choices you made. I'd love to hear from you and I will respond to EVERY email.

Email Address: XandysChoice@gmail.com

ALSO…if you host a "Xandy Party" and email me a video clip of the discussion and "carrying on" ☺ that took place, I will make every effort to eventually feature your video on the up and coming interactive website for "*Xandy's Choice*" as well as YouTube and Facebook.

Thank you so much for joining me on this journey and May God Bless You ALWAYS & FOREVER!

"Still believing in Happily Ever After!"

*Belinda*